POLITICAL
PARTICIPATION

POLITICAL PARTICIPATION

How and Why Do People Get Involved in Politics?
Second Edition

Lester W. Milbrath
State University of New York at Buffalo

M.L. Goel
University of West Florida

UNIVERSITY
PRESS OF
AMERICA

LANHAM • NEW YORK • LONDON

University Press of America,™ Inc.

4720 Boston Way
Lanham, MD 20706

3 Henrietta Street
London WC2E 8LU England

Library of Congress Cataloging in Publication Data

Milbrath, Lester W.
   Political participation.

   Bibliography: p.
   Includes index.
1. Political participation. 2. Political psychology. I. Goel,
Maden Lal, 1936–   . II. Title.
JF2051.M48   1982   306'.2   82–13391
ISBN 0–8191–2647–0

To

Erik, Shully, and Anu

Preface

The first edition of *Political Participation* was published in 1965 by Lester Milbrath. Incorporating literature up until 1964 on the study of political behavior, it served as a compilation of propositions on political participation with supporting discussion.

Since then, research findings on political behavior based on empirical field studies have been fast accumulating. Evidence for certain relationships has formed patterns and is cumulative in that one finds the same relationship, in study after study, even in several different cultures. To synthesize the findings that have appeared since 1964 and to up-date and expand our own conceptualizations on the topic, we felt it necessary and useful to revise the first edition to incorporate some of the changes reflected in the literature.

What are some of these changes? First, the literature is now more cross-nationally oriented than in past years. Whereas most empirical studies of political behavior in the 1950s were focused on the United States, and some on Europe, those in the past two decades focus more even-handedly on Asian and African countries as well. India and Japan have received a great deal of recent scholarly attention; studies also have been conducted in Bangladesh, the Phillippines, Malaysia, and Korea, in addition to scattered studies from a number of other countries. In the Middle East and Africa, Israel and Nigeria, respectively, have received more attention than other countries in those parts of the world. Latin America, with the exceptions of Chile, Argentina, and Mexico, has also received relatively less attention. In general, however, it is fair to say that there is substantial cross-national validity for the propositions reported in this book. The incorporation of cross-national research will be somewhat uneven, having been drawn to a greater extent from those regions of the world that are more familiar to the authors. While the coverage is broad, it was not possible to be comprehensive.

The second important change has been in the conceptualization of political participation. In the early years of behavioral political science, political participation was defined in most studies as simply voting turnout. As studies became more sophisticated, the operational definition of political participation was broadened to include other electoral activities such as campaigning, attending political meetings, giving money to a candidate or a party, running for an office, and so forth. Several studies conducted in the late 1960s cast a much broader net in the attempt to understand the variety of ways people participate in the governance of their society. For example, the cross-national research teams led by Verba and Nie disclosed "modes" of democratic participation: voting, campaign activity, community participation, and particularized contacting. Milbrath worked with colleagues in a study of Buffalo which cast a similarly broad net and found similar "modes of participation." Several studies have more broadly defined political participation to incorporate unconventional participation (protests, demonstrations, political violence) into their inquiry.

A third and important change has occurred in the methods of analysis. Earlier studies seldom went beyond simple bivariate or "control table" interpretations of the data. While many studies continue to use these simple methods, many others have begun to use more sophisticated analytic techniques, such as multiple and partial correlations and regressions, path analysis, and causal modeling. These more sophisticated techniques make it possible to sort out in greater detail the causal influences on a dependent variable.

Despite twelve years of research findings between this publication and the first, few propositions set forth in the first needed revision (an important exception is the rural-urban context of political participation). Findings have been subtly enriched, however, since there is more detail than before. The study of political participation has also been extended to new areas; important subject matter, long neglected, has come under scrutiny (protest behavior is an example). We now also know more about cross-national variability in the meanings and the antecedents of various political acts. All these are noteworthy advances.

While almost thoroughly revised in content, the present edition retains the structure and organization of the first. In Chapter 1 we discuss the nature of political participation, various modes of political activity, and a model for understanding political behavior. Chapters 2 through 5 are given to a discussion of broad groups of independent variables that explain participation in politics. In Chapter 6 we explore the general question of the impact of participation on the functioning of the political system.

Although most of the data reported in the book are derived from published literature, some original research also is reported. It was derived from the Buffalo Survey, conducted from 1966 to 1968 by E. Cataldo, R. Johnson, L. Kellstedt, L. Milbrath, and A. Somit.

We extend our heartfelt thanks to those who have read and commented on portions of this manuscript: Jim Hottois, Jim Munro, Jim Russell, Guenther Kress, Ellen Flerlage, and Rajni Kothari. Chong Lim Kim did an excellent job in thoroughly reviewing the manuscript and in suggesting improvements. Don Freeman, Chairman of the Faculty of Political Science at the University of West Florida supported the search efforts of Goel; much of this writing would not have been possible without his encouragement and aid. We acknowledge secretarial assistance from Kay Trine, Karen Born, Sue Feltes, and Elara Barrick.

Lal Goel would like to extend appreciation to his wife, Shully, and his daughter, Anu, for their understanding and support; he regrets that he could not spend more evenings and weekends with them.

The authors have contributed more or less equally to the manuscript; hence, we share whatever praise or blame becomes our due.

L W M
M L G
August, 1976

Contents

Introduction

Politics could be defined very broadly as the adjustment efforts of humans attempting to coexist in an interdependent relationship. This would mean that every form of human society would have some form of politics, and in a certain sense this is true. We recognize this when we talk about ✓ politics in private associations such as churches, businesses, pressure groups, social clubs, and so forth. Although it is undoubtedly valid to say that politics enters into the governance of private groups, such a broad definition dulls rather than sharpens our analysis. When "politics" becomes ubiquitous or universal, it begins to lose its meaning. We need a definition that will distinguish political from nonpolitical behavior.

This distinction can most readily be made in the context of defining a political system. We shall adopt Dahl's definition: "A political system is any persistent pattern of human relationships that involves, to a significant extent, power, rule, or authority" (1963, p. 6). In every day life, we think of a political system as including not only formal government but also the pattern of human relationships that affect the decisions of that government. Thus, a political system includes certain organizations like political parties and pressure groups and also behaviors directed toward governmental decisions such as discussions about governmental policies and voting. Political behavior, then, is behavior which affects or is intended to affect the decisional outcomes of government. The politics of nongovernmental organizations are excluded from this definition. Behavior which affects the decisional outcomes of a church or a corporation, for example, even if it were typically political in form and content, would not be considered political behavior by this definition. Politics now can be defined as the process by which decisions about governmental outcomes are made.

Even by this narrower definition, it is fair to say that every human life is touched by politics. As the world becomes ever more populated and crowded, requiring human relationships to become ever more complex and interdependent, the impact of politics on human lives will become increasingly determinative. The adequacy of functioning of a political system may well be decisive for the happiness and well-being of the members of that society. Since the manner in which citizens participate in their political process is integral to the manner in which the system functions, the question of how and why persons become involved in politics is germane to the concerns of every man, as well as to the curious probings of social scientists.

Political participation may be defined as those actions of private citizens by which they seek to influence or to support government and politics. This definition is broader than most others; it includes not only active roles that people pursue in order to influence political outcomes but also *ceremonial* and *support* activities. People relate to their government in a variety of ways. Some persons take the system for granted and are concerned only to adjust their behavior to its demands; others want to improve or transform it. Some have only a passive relationship to the system, while others are very actively involved. To some, the system is frightening and confusing; to others, it is an object to be explored and conquered. Some focus their attention on what the system demands from them, while others focus on the benefits they derive from the system.

Social scientists now have a sizable body of evidence that helps to explain differences in the ways persons relate to the system. This book is an attempt to summarize the state of our knowledge about political participation. A summary, to be really serviceable, must integrate discrete facts into a somewhat comprehensive whole; thus, some sort of theory is required. Two initial steps toward such a theory are taken in the book. An inductive approach has been adopted: findings are examined and then sorted into propositions which, at least in some cases, form "islands of theory." Secondly, while the authors have not attempted to build a grand overall theory, they have set forth in Chapter 1 a model or sketch which suggests a way in which the variables associated with political participation may be related to one another. This sketch provides a common basis for thinking about political participation and also serves as a plan for presenting the empirical findings to follow. This model was not arrived at deductively from a set of assumptions and then imposed upon the data; rather, it was built up inductively from careful examination of the findings.

Although some attention is given to the functioning of the political system, the major concern of the book is to explain individual human behavior as it relates to the political system. Therefore, the human organism, rather than groups or the political system, usually is taken as the unit of analysis. Political system and political culture are important influences on individual political behavior, and we naturally expect differences in political behavior patterns from culture to culture (see Almond & Verba, 1963). At the same time, most social scientists assume that, at a basic level, human beings follow the same behavioral laws no matter what kind of culture they live in. We shall seek such behavioral laws holding across cultures as the analysis proceeds.

Research on political behavior has been extended to a variety of nations in recent years, but available evidence is not as comprehensive as one might desire. The greatest amount of evidence is on the political behavior of Americans. Most of the other data comes from Western Europe, and a selected number of Asian countries (in particular India and Japan), leaving only scatterings from the rest of the world. These limitations require the caution that the generalizations set forth in the book may apply to only modern democratic systems in the second half of the twentieth century, where participation is legally permissible and extended. We may speculate that certain generalizations will hold in other systems and at other times, but certainty will have to await much more comprehensive investigation.

This book is primarily addressed to college students of political science, although research scholars and general readers may also find it interesting; practicing politicians will find many helpful generalizations in these pages. It has deliberately been kept short so that it can be used as supplementary reading in college courses. The book presents an overview and synthesis of the findings on political participation, and concentration on this objective means that other considerations must be slighted. Exhaustive evaluations of methods and of the quality of evidence are not possible in the text.

The inventory of findings reported here consists of generalizations that are empirically based. Writings devoted to theorizing about political problems or philosophical issues are omitted. Rather than report the findings of any given study in full detail and in a single location in the text, findings are brought in to support points in the natural progression of the discussion. Since studies are cited many times, only author and date of publication are given in the text and footnotes; full citations can be found in the bibliography. The book is not a bibliographic essay on political participation, and the authors make no pretenses that every relevant citation is given for each proposition. We have attempted, however, to be comprehensive in reporting empirically supported propositions about political participation. Nearly all of the literature referenced here appeared in English language books and articles in leading social and political science journals.

In the text, propositions are distinguished by levels of confidence. Those in *italics* are propositions for which there is some evidence, but of which the authors are not as confident as they are of those propositions in **bold-face** type. In the latter case, there is generally more than one study in support of the proposition.

Chapter 1   Conceptualizing Political Participation

THE LEVEL OF ANALYSIS Clarity in social science research is facilitated by specifying a level of analysis. The distinction is usually made between macro and micro levels. In social science, the macro level refers to large social units such as a nation, or political system, or organization. The micro level refers to individuals and their behavior. "Micro" and "macro" are comparative rather than absolute terms, however, and in other sciences may have a different specific meaning. In biology, for example, "macro" means unusually large and "micro" means unusually small.

Although the emphasis in this book is on micro political behavior, some attention is given to macro characteristics as well. The behavior of the two systems is often interrelated; individual (micro) political behavior affects the behavior of the larger political system (macro); macro characteristics, in turn, affect micro behavior. The level of inquiry adopted by the analyst is determined partially by the kinds of questions he wishes to ask. The question, "How does a system of political parties affect the stability of a political regime?" requires a macro level of analysis. The major question for this book, "How and why do people get involved in politics?" requires emphasis on the micro level. Certain questions require a bridging of the two levels. Two such questions for this book are: "How do the characteristics of the political system affect the manner and extent of citizen participation in politics?" and "How do the participation patterns of citizens affect the functioning of the political system?"

DECISIONS ABOUT PARTICIPATION Taking any political action generally requires two decisions: one must decide to act or not to act; and one must also decide the direction of his action. For example, a person not only decides to vote or not to vote, but also decides whom to vote for. Usually, the decision to perform in action like voting precedes the decision about the direction of the action, but the time sequence could be reversed. Sometimes, a person decides that he likes a candidate or a party before he makes up his mind to cast a vote. Certain actions do not involve a directional choice; for example, one cannot choose the government to which one wishes to pay taxes (without changing one's residence).

Decisions to act in a particular way often are accompanied by a third decision about the intensity, duration, and/or extremity of the action. Persons may lend political support mildly or vigorously, in a single instance or repeatedly. This third choice is intimately related to the other two. A person who takes vigorous and sustained political action very probably is strongly attracted in a certain direction. The very fact that he feels intensely makes it more likely that he will participate. This book focuses mainly on decisions to act or not to act and on decisions about the intensity and duration of the action.

Decisions about the direction of political action are properly another topic, and the book would be unduly expanded and complicated if an attempt were made to cover them here. Research findings about directional political choices are quite voluminous; furthermore, they are difficult to summarize, since the directions are specific as to setting and time. Generalizations applicable in one setting very likely are not applicable in other settings. For example, explanation of the factors leading some persons to prefer Eisenhower and others to prefer Stevenson in the 1956 presidential election in the United States has little generalizability to the choice the voters made between candidates in the 1960 or 1964 presidential elections.

Settings have one thing in common, however—the concept of *status quo*. Persons can defend or try to change the *status quo*. Its defenders often are called conservatives, and those trying to change it often are called liberals. Liberal-conservative contention about what should be done with the *status quo* is a familiar theme through many centuries of political writing. Unfortunately, many directional choices cannot be fitted to the general liberal-conservative dimension; they are even more specific as to setting and time and, therefore, are even more difficult to summarize.

We have learned to be very cautious in generalizing about liberal-conservative directional choices. Although rational deliberation plays some role in a person's choosing a liberal or conservative direction, the rational aspect of such a choice should not be overemphasized. We shall see that relatively few people have sufficient information or sufficient understanding of the political system to be able to make a completely rational political choice. Furthermore, personality predispositions incline a person to screen out uncongenial stimuli from the mass that impinge on his sensory system. Research evidence suggests that at least some persons have personalities which are inclined either liberally or conservatively (McClosky, 1958; Milbrath, 1962). Presumably, persons inclined liberally or conservatively would adopt a corresponding position with respect to the *status quo* no matter what setting or era they lived in.

But one can ask, in turn, where liberal or conservative personalities come from. In part, a liberal or conservative inclination comes from an environment: certain environments tend to produce liberals, and other environments tend to produce conservatives. It is a well-known generalization, for example, that lower-class environments tend to produce status-changers (liberals), and that upper-class environments tend to produce status-defenders (conservatives.) But environment does not seem to account for all the variance in political personality; persons coming from very similar environments may have quite different personalities. This suggests that heredity also is a factor inclining some persons liberally and others conservatively. It is likely that there is a very complex interaction between heredity and environment which produces a personality inclined in a certain political direction. Social scientists, at this point, have only a very dim understanding of that interaction.

Many other factors can intervene between personality inclination and choice of political direction. Pressures from family or peer groups are very important. Predominant community beliefs tend to structure the way a person sees his political world. The presence of a certain configuration of information about a current political choice (in contrast to an alternative configuration of information) can strongly influence that choice.

The complex interaction of these multiple factors influencing direction of political choice produces decisions that may seem rather inconsistent to the political analyst. Studies of the American electorate show, for example, that a "liberal" position on foreign policy (internationalism in contrast to isolationism) is not related to a "liberal" position on domestic economic policy (welfare state in contrast to laissez faire). These two positions, in turn, seem to show no correlation with a "liberal" posture favoring integration in contrast to segregation (Campbell, et al., 1960). In the United States, the issue of the welfare state versus laissez faire most clearly and consistently distinguishes the Democratic (liberal) party from the Republican (conservative) party. It is only in this very limited way that the two American parties can be characterized as liberal or conservative. If the political setting should change, one could anticipate that labels about the political direction of a party might also change.

The point of this short digression concerning the factors involved in making choices about political direction is to suggest to the reader the complexity and magnitude of the problem of trying to explain such choices. It would take us too far afield to attempt a full explanation here. The reader need only be aware that a choice to take action nearly always requires a second choice about direction. Most of the findings to be discussed in this book are valid, no matter what directional choice the political actor makes.

ROLES IN GOVERNANCE   It is obvious that people relate to government in a wide variety of ways. In order to understand the multiple ways persons do to their polity, it will be helpful at this point to begin with an abstract and general statement on the nature of government and the roles people play in it.

If one were to actually look at a government, and especially were one to try to relate to it, one would find only people. The people who comprise a government are tied together in a set of structured roles (we have special names for them such as mayor, governor, legislator, bureaucrat).

These roles exist in the minds of the political actors. There are many institutional constraints (constitutions, laws, role expectations, and so on) to insure that the actors play their roles in accepted ways.

In a similar sense, people who are not in government, but who are relating to government in one way or another, also are playing roles and acting in structured ways. The linkages between individuals and a polity are largely ideational or conceptual; most people act toward government in ways that they believe are appropriate for them to act.

Because of their distinctive structured roles, we can differentiate official decision-makers on the one hand from ordinary citizens on the other. All individuals, however, are playing roles. Various communications, acts, and shared expectations tie them together into a working system. In most societies a third set of structured roles are developed to facilitate the efforts of individuals as they attempt to make inputs into the official decision-making process. These roles are played in community institutions and include such familiar institutions as political parties, interest groups, informal power structures, economic institutions, and the mass media. Not all of these structures will be found in every society, but we believe that at least some of them will be found in each even though the institutions may be designated by different names and they may vary somewhat in their functions.

Community institutions can act as mediating agencies between the citizen and the government. While individuals may make an input (a letter, a personal conversation, a vote, and so on), directly to an official decision-maker, they also can route their inputs through a community structure by working in a political party, joining community or special interest groups, or writing a letter to an editor. These mediating institutions aggregate and articulate a mass of individual inputs; they often stimulate additional individual inputs as well.

INPUTS AND OUTTAKES   If we take governmental decision-making as the focus of inquiry, two sets of behaviors can be distinguished. Certain behaviors constitute *inputs* to the political system (voting, campaigning, contacting, protesting); other behaviors are *outtakes* or extractions from the system (services, public order, justice, economic opportunities). Systems analysts often speak of inputs and outputs when analyzing systems. We focus on the individual as he relates *to* the system; therefore we speak of inputs and outtakes. An input is something a citizen does to try to influence official decisions. In contrast, an outtake is something that an individual takes from the system such as a sense of justice, a sense of safety, a sense of being listened to, a sense of worth, a sense of freedom, and so forth. Outtakes can be expressed as a sense of satisfaction with such things as police protection, product quality, protection of civil rights, freedom to live where one wants, freedom of speech, employment opportunities, the elimination of poverty, and so on.

Outtakes can derive directly from governmental decisions, but more frequently they derive from the broader societal context. The distinction between inputs and outtakes can characterize the orientations or postures of individuals as well as characterize specific acts; some individuals emphasize outtakes in their orientation to the system and others emphasize inputs. It would be an oversimplification to classify inputs simply as costs and outtakes simply as benefits; many inputs carry auxiliary rewards (e.g., pleasure in voting), and many outtakes carry auxiliary costs (e.g., court costs in seeking justice).

Most empirical research on political participation has emphasized input behavior and orientations. Outtakes have come under research scrutiny only recently (Milbrath, 1968, 1971a, b, c). Outtake analysis can be applied to a wider range of political systems in that citizens take satisfactions and dissatisfactions from the decisions made in all political systems: developed and developing, democratic and totalitarian. In contrast, the scientific study of input behavior can only be pursued effectively in democracies where that behavior freely occurs. Therefore, the outtake conceptualization can provide us with an analytic category for more general comparisons across a variety of political systems. Outtakes are closely akin to life satisfactions and constitute, in our judgment, the appropriate basis for evaluating the quality of life in any given polity.[1]

Since this book is a summary and synthesis of findings in the area of political participation to date, our primary focus will be on the citizen behaviors and orientations labeled here as inputs. Perhaps future books can give greater attention to outtakes.

CHANGING VIEW OF POLITICAL PARTICIPATION: THE MODES
The conceptualization of political participation has been undergoing

---

[1] Recent studies of subjective indicators of quality of life are a welcome first step in this direction (see Campbell, Converse & Rogers, 1976).

important changes. Until recently most survey studies of political participation confined their inquiry to a relatively limited set of political acts.
Most asked whether a person had voted or not and some went on to ask
about such behaviors as attendance at political meetings or rallies,
working for a party, making a monetary contribution, and seeking public
office. The behavioral acts investigated belonged solely to electoral
politics. Because many of these acts were oriented toward winning
elections, the notion that political participation is unidimensional became
generally accepted. Political acts could be hierarchically organized from
the least difficult to the most difficult; if a person performed a more difficult
act, he was likely to perform those that were less difficult as well.

In the first edition of this book (1965) political participation was viewed
as unidimensional. The American public was divided into three broad
categories of participation intensity: (1) *apathetics,* persons who are
withdrawn from the political process (about one-third of the American
adult population); (2) *spectators,* persons who are minimally involved in
politics (about 60 percent of the American adult population); and
gladiators, persons who are active combatants (5 to 7 percent). The
terms gladiators, spectators, and apathetics were taken from an analogy
to the roles played at a Roman gladiatorial contest. A small band of
gladiators battle to please the spectators, who in turn cheer, clap, and
finally vote to decide who has won the battle (election). The apathetics
don't even watch the show.

In two recent studies this conceptualization of political participation
has been modified by acquiring much richer data sets. In one study,
teams of researchers from Austria, India, Japan, the Netherlands,
Nigeria, Yugoslavia, and the United States collaborated in a cross-
national comparative study of political participation under the leadership
of professors Sidney Verba and Norman Nie (Verba, Nie & Kim, 1971;
Verba & Nie, 1972).[2] The second study was conducted by Lester Milbrath, Everett Cataldo, Richard Johnson, Lyman Kellstedt, and Albert

---

[2] The cross-national research effort led by Verba and Nie has been publishing reports of
their results since 1971 and the major cross-national comparative volume is due to appear
soon. The first report (Verba, Nie & Kim, 1971) contained data from the United States, India,
Japan, Austria, and Nigeria. Later reports (e.g., Nie & Verba, 1975) also include data from
Yugoslavia and the Netherlands. This current study follows from, but should not be confused
with, an earlier five-nation study (Almond & Verba, 1963) which included Germany, Britain,
Italy and Mexico as well as the United States.

Somit in the Buffalo, New York area from 1966 to 1968 (Milbrath, 1968, 1971a, b, c). Both these studies took a much broader view of political participation, and through cluster and factor analysis[3] both discovered "modes" or "styles" of political participation. Fundamental to this discovery is the notion that political participation is multi-dimensional. Political acts are distinguished not only in terms of how difficult they are, but also in that they represent different styles by which citizens attempt to relate to government and politics. Our confidence that these modes really exist is enhanced by the finding that the modes that were discovered are quite similar in the two studies even though they were designed and analyzed independently and the specific questions asked differed in format and content. The modes of participation first reported in Verba, Nie, and Kim (1971) held for all the countries where their collaborators were conducting similar studies: Austria, India, Japan, Netherlands, Nigeria, and (with some modifications) Yugoslavia. This similarity across national cultures increases our confidence that these modes characterize participation in most democratic political systems. A brief description of each of these modes follows.

Voting It is theoretically significant that both the international and Buffalo studies found voting to be a separate mode of participation from party and campaign activity. In the Buffalo Survey, (1968), voting clustered with other patriotic acts: "love my country"; "show my patriotism by flying the flag"; "pay all taxes"; "respect the police"; "support my country in wars I don't agree with." This clustering indicates that voting is more an act by which the citizen affirms his loyalty to the system rather than an act by which he makes demands on the political system; in the Buffalo survey persons emphasizing this mode are called "patriots." A person casting a vote rarely believes that it will make an important difference to the political outcome. It is more likely that a person votes out of a sense of civic duty, a sense of a common social norm, and because it is a way of living up to his own definition of himself as a good member of the community. The act of voting does not require as much information and motivation as do most other political activities. Many people vote who are not politically involved, and conversely some who are involved may not

---

[3] Factor analysis is a statistical method for simplifying a correlation matrix. It shows how a group of items (behaviors, reactions, responses) cluster or "go together." It can be used to derive a typology empirically, in contrast to a typology which is conceptually derived and then imposed on the data.

bother to vote. In much of the literature on political development and modernization it has been a common practice to operationalize political participation and mobilization by measuring voting turnout (see Lerner, 1958; Deutsch, 1961; Lipset, 1960; McCrone & Cnudde, 1967, among others). The weak relationship between voting and other forms of participation as evidenced by the discussion above should caution researchers against taking voting as a valid indicator of mass mobilization.

Party and Campaign Workers The comparative international study and the Buffalo survey were almost identical in finding "party and campaign activists" as a type separate and different from the voters. In the Verba and Nie study the following items fell on this factor: persuade others how to vote, actively work for a party or candidate, attend a political meeting or rally, contribute money to a party or candidate, membership in political clubs. In the Buffalo Survey (1968) the following items clustered on this factor: participate in a political party between elections as well as at election time, take an active part in a political campaign, give money to help a party or candidate, work to get people registered to vote, join and support a political party, try to convince people to vote your way, be a candidate for public office, join groups working to improve community life. There is great overlap in the content of the items. Because the factor stood out so clearly in both studies we have high confidence that it is a basic mode of relationship between individuals and the polity. This cluster of activities had been given almost exclusive attention in early studies of political participation and is the basis for the earlier belief that political participation is unidimensional.

Only a relatively small proportion of people take a "party and campaign activist" posture toward the political system; such activists constitute about 15 percent of the United States population (the percentage engaging in any specific act ranges from 3 to 35, see Figure 1-1, p.18. Similar proportions have been found in several other countries. These people are the "gladiators" in political contests; they do most of the work while the majority of the population sits in the spectator grandstands and decides who has won the contest (by voting for their favorite).

Community Activists Community activists were delineated as a type in all the countries of the Verba and Nie study. (Only one community activity item was included in the Buffalo Survey and this was insufficient to form a type.) The following items loaded heavily on this factor: formed a group to deal with a social problem, worked with an existing group to deal with a social problem, number of active memberships in organizations concerned with public issues, contacting public officials about a social problem. In many ways community activists are similar to party and campaign activists; they both follow a general activist pattern and they both have a high level of psychological involvement in community matters. The main difference is that community activists are much less concerned with party and campaign politics than are party activists. Approximately 20 percent of Americans in the Verba and Nie study (1972) were isolated as community activists.

Contacting Officials Contacting is very specific as to situation and time; the person contacts a government official because he is concerned about a given narrow issue that directly affects him—school taxes, road work, social security check, etc. Persons emphasizing this mode usually are not intensely involved in political matters. Particularized contacting is weakly related to other modes as well as to the general dimension of activism. This mode of participation is hardly political in nature, and Verba and Nie refer to it as "parochial" participation. Only a small fraction (4 percent) of the American citizenry fell into this category (Verba & Nie, 1972). Questions about particularized contacting were not included in the Buffalo Survey.

The next two modes to be discussed emerged only in the Buffalo Survey; questions that might have disclosed these types were not included in the Verba, et al. cross-national study, probably because their conceptualization of participation was narrower than that used in the Buffalo Survey.

Protestors In recent years we have witnessed a rising frequency of protesting inputs to the polity, particularly by blacks, students, and women (in many previous studies it wasn't even deemed important to ask about such inputs). A small but readily detectable proportion of people do take a protesting posture toward the political system. The following items clustered on the protesting factor in the Buffalo Survey: join in public street demonstrations, riot if necessary to get public officials to correct political wrongs, protest both vigorously and publicly if the government does something that is morally wrong, attend protest meetings, join in a protest march, go with a group to protest to a public official, and refuse to obey unjust laws. With the exception of the last item, the proportion of

Table 1-1. Percentages Who Believe It Wrong to Engage in Various Protest Activities, by Race.

	Blacks	Whites
Join in public street demonstrations	21	62
Riot if necessary to get public officials to correct political wrongs	62	83
Attend protest meetings	8	29
Join in a protest march	14	52
Going with a group to protest to a public official	8	19
Refuse to obey unjust laws	21	41

Data are derived from the Buffalo Survey (1968).

whites engaging in such activities ranged from 1 to 5 percent; the proportion of blacks ranged from 5 to 19 percent. Refusing to obey unjust laws was somewhat more widely accepted with 14 percent of whites and 23 percent of blacks reporting that they had done it "fairly often."

It is clear that the great majority of both blacks and whites feel little responsibility to engage in protest activities. Even more striking are the sizeable percentages who believe it is wrong to protest and demonstrate (see Table 1-1). For each activity, the percentage who believe it is wrong is greater among whites than it is among blacks. This contrast is particularly striking for two items: "join in a protest march" where 52 percent of whites but only 14 percent of blacks believe it is wrong, and "join in public street demonstrations" where 62 percent of whites believe it is wrong but only 21 percent of blacks believe so. It is clear that whites and blacks live in very different political cultures. Not surprisingly, 83 percent of whites and 62 percent of blacks believe that it is wrong to riot in order to correct political wrongs. In contrast to most patriots, who see a moral conflict between protesting and being patriotic, most protestors see nothing wrong or unpatriotic about protesting. Among blacks, there was a positive correlation between protesting and being patriotic.[4] More information on the special characteristics of protestors will be given in later chapters.

---

[4] A positive correlation indicates that two variables move in the same direction; a negative correlation that they move in opposite directions. Correlations may vary from .00 to 1.0; the stronger the correlation the closer the relationship. Correlations at or near 0 indicate little or no relationship.

Communicators The factor analysis in the Buffalo Survey showed that a number of inputs clustered on what might be called a "communication" factor. It contained the following items: keep informed about politics, send messages of support to political leaders when they are doing well, send protest messages to political leaders when they are doing badly, engage in political discussion, inform others in my community about politics, make my views known to public officials, write letters to the editors of newspapers. Each of these activities requires a verbal interchange between the citizen and other members of the community. The communicator mode of relationship between the individual and the polity seems to require a high education, a high level of information about politics, and a high level of interest in politics. "Communicators" tend to be more critical of government than "party activists" or "patriots" but generally do not use protesting activities to express their critical views. Many people feel poorly equipped to compose or send messages to political leaders; thus, one finds much higher levels of responsibility to engage in these activities than the levels of actual performance. The feeling of verbal incapability is one reason why it is mainly the highly educated and well informed who choose the communicator mode. Persons without high verbal facility simply shy away from these activities. These acts vary a good deal in difficulty, thus, the percentages performing them also vary considerably. About 70 percent report that they keep informed, about 40 to 45 percent engage in political discussion "fairly often," but only 10 to 20 percent send messages.

Verba and Nie broke down the entire United States population into participant modes. They isolated one group of people (about 22 percent of the United States sample) who were inactive on every dimension; those who did not vote, those who did not contact, those who did not join groups, and those who did not campaign. The inactives formed a smaller component of the Buffalo sample due to the fact that the Buffalo team inquired into "communication" and "patriotic" inputs (which Verba and Nie did not). Since a high percentage of people make "patriotic" inputs, there was only a handful of persons in the Buffalo Survey who could be classified as inactive on every dimension (only 3 to 5 percent). Thus, whether one finds a sizable portion of the population to be totally inactive depends on one's definition of relevant activity. Nearly everyone is making some kind of political input (even if it is merely being patriotic and law abiding). If one adopts a more stringent definition, and excludes patriotic and support activities from participation, it is correct to say that from one-fourth to one-fifth of the United States population is completely inactive.

On the opposite extreme, Verba and Nie found about 11 percent of the United States sample to be active on every one of their dimensions. They called these persons "complete activists." They scored higher on every "mode of participation" than even the persons who "specialized" in a particular mode. (Keep in mind that Verba and Nie did not inquire into unconventional participation.) They were characterized by high psychological involvement in politics, by being skilled and competent in politics, by their willingness to take sides in political conflict, and by their civic mindedness. They were disproportionately from the higher socioeconomic strata of the population; they were particularly characterized by higher levels of education. Such a group of complete activists also was isolable in the Buffalo Survey. They did not rank high in protesting, however, since their access to public decision-makers already was so good that they had no need to resort to protesting. While they made "patriotic" inputs regularly (as did most people), they were not as distinctively high on the patriotic inputs as they were in the more active modes of participation.

The modes of relationship between individuals and the policy are summarized in Figure 1-1. The modes or styles for inputting to the political system are somewhat related to the beliefs people hold about what the government should do for them. The input/outtake patterned relationship has only been studied in Buffalo, but further research may show that something like it holds elsewhere. *Protestors* seemed to be more demanding of government than other types; in 1968, they especially were demanding, among other things better protection for civil rights and better economic opportunities. *Community activists* wanted a better community but turned more often to voluntary action in private groups (as opposed to the government) to achieve it. *Party and campaign workers* showed no particular emphasis in outtake posture. *Communicators* liked to observe and discuss what goes on in government and politics, and were quite critical of it; theirs could be called a watchdog posture. *Contact specialists* sought special responses to personal needs rather than a general social change to help solve their problems. *Patriotic supporters* preferred conventional government which would not be very active but would provide them with justice, security, order, and leadership of which they could be proud.

On a second dimension of Figure 1-1, some inputs may be char-

Figure 1.1. Modes Relating Individuals to the Polity.

	MODES	INPUTS — DEFINING ITEMS	OUTTAKE POSTURE
ACTIVE / UNCONVENTIONAL	PROTESTORS	Join in public street demonstrations (3%) Riot if necessary (2%) Protest vigorously if government does something morally wrong (26%) Attend protest meetings (6%) Refuse to obey unjust laws (16%) (They are also active on other modes.)	Demand very active government; particularly protect civil rights and provide economic opportunities
CONVENTIONAL	COMMUNITY ACTIVISTS	Work with others on local problems (30%) Form a group to work on local problems (14%) Active membership in community organizations (8%) Contact officials on social issues (14%) (They also vote fairly regularly.)	Use voluntary community activity rather than government to provide welfare
	PARTY AND CAMPAIGN WORKERS[a]	Actively work for party or candidate (26%) Persuade others how to vote (28%) Attend meetings, rallies (19%) Give money to party or candidate (13%) Join and support political party (35%) Be a candidate for office (3%) (They also vote regularly.)	No particular outtake posture

COMMUNICATORS	Keep informed about politics (67%) Engage in political discussions (42%) Write letters to newspaper editors (9%) Send support or protest messages to political leaders (15%) (They also vote fairly regularly.)	Observe, discuss, and criticize governmental performance; watchdog posture
CONTACT SPECIALISTS	Contact local, state, and national officials on particularized problems (4%) (They are inactive otherwise.)	Seek special response to personal needs rather than general social conditions
PASSIVE SUPPORTIVE VOTERS AND PATRIOTS	Vote regularly in elections (63%) Love my country (94%) Show patriotism by flying the flag, attending parades, etc. (70%) Pay all taxes (94%)	Conventional Limited Government Provide public order, security, leadership, justice
APATHETIC INACTIVE	No voting, no other activity (22%) No patriotic inputs (3-5%)	

a Percentages for these modes are based mostly on a national survey of the American public conducted in 1967 (Verba & Nie, 1972); percentages for the remaining modes are based on the Buffalo Survey (1968).

acterized as active in contrast to other inputs which may be characterized as passive supportive, and still others as apathetic. A third dimension in the figure suggests "conventionality" of inputs. We have labeled the protesting posture as "unconventional," and all other modes as "conventional." In using this terminology, we are merely conforming to current political science usage, not making any moral judgments. Conventional forms of participation are those activities which are regarded as "normal" and/or "legitimate." It is, of course, true that standards about "normality" and "legitimacy" differ from culture to culture and over time. The protesting mode is certainly more conventional at the present time than in earlier decades and is more conventional in United States black culture than white culture.

It is important to think about these modes of participation as patterns of emphases and not as discrete or separate behaviors. Both sets of data (Verba, Nie & Kim, 1971 and Buffalo Survey, 1968) showed that although the correlations between activities within the same mode are much higher than between activities across different modes, there is some positive correlation among all activities. This point is true even for protests and other unconventional behaviors. Many who protest see it as just another weapon to be used in political battle and also engage in conventional behaviors like campaigning and voting. Of course, some people believe protesting is wrong and refuse to take that step even though they may be very active in conventional ways. Therefore, even though citizens tend to concentrate their activities by mode, there is a tendency for persons active in one way to be active in other ways as well. In this sense, these recent rich data sets still are compatible with a unidimensional view of political participation where citizens are viewed as generally active or generally inactive. Voting and particularized contacting are more likely to be associated with the inactive end of the general activity dimension.

Figure 1-2 is a sketch combining the general dimensions of political involvement with the several modes of activity. As one moves up the tree, the level of activism increases. Activists are of different types: communicators, community activists, party and campaign workers, and protestors (shown as different branches of the tree). The modes of activity are not completely separated; this is shown by the lines that join these modes. A small proportion of citizens partake in all activities; these are the "complete activists" at the peak of the tree. (Some "complete ac-

Figure 1-2. Hierarchy of Political Involvement.

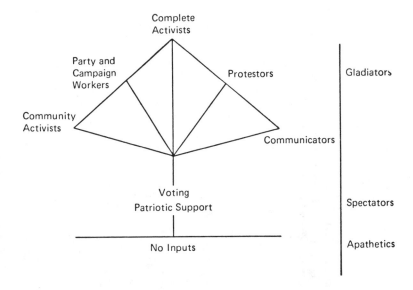

tivists" might refuse to protest or perhaps they are so influential they don't need to.) The figure suggests that there are not only gladiators and nongladiators, but that there are several different types of gladiators. Recent advances in research are not so much a rejection of the unidimensional model of participation, as they are a further elaboration and explication of it. We now have more detail than before.

A caveat needs to be entered here. In subsequent chapters we will focus on independent variables which explain, cause, or correlate with political participation as a broadly generalized dependent variable. If a given independent variable correlates differently with different modes of participation, that will be noted. The reader should remember, however, that in the vast proportion of the literature, political participation is treated as an undifferentiated phenomenon. For this reason we have had to treat political participation as a unitary activity in many of these pages, even though we would have liked to treat each mode of participation separately. Since unconventional participation, like protesting, has only recently been studied, we are not sure in many cases whether it should be

Table 1-2. Percentages of Citizens Active in Various Ways in Seven Countries.

	Austria	India	Japan	Netherlands	Nigeria	United States	Yugoslavia
	1	2	3	4	5	6	7
Voting							
Regular voters[b]	85	48	93	77	56	63	82
Campaign activity							
Members of a party or political organization[c]	28	5	4	13	a	8	15
Worked for a party[d]	10	6	25	10	a	25	45
Attended a political rally[e]	27	14	50	9	a	19	45
Communal activity							
Active members in a community action organization[f]	9	7	11	15	34	32	39
Worked with a local group on a community problem[g]	3	18	15	16	35	30	22
Helped form a local group on a community problem[h]	6	5	5	a	26	14	a
Contacted an official in the community on some social problem[i]	5	4	11	6	2	13	11
Contacted an official outside the community on a social problem	3	2	5	7	3	11	a

Particularized contacting							
Contacted a local official on a personal problem[j]	15	12	7	38	2	6	20
Contacted an official outside the community on a personal problem	10	6	3	10	1	6	a
Number of cases	1769	2637	2657	1746	1799	2544	2995

[a] Not asked.
[b] Vote regularly in both local and national elections.
[c] Formal membership in political parties in Austria, India, and the Netherlands; in political clubs in the United States and Japan; in the League of Communists in Yugoslavia. Item not asked in Nigeria.
[d] Worked for a political party in an election. In the Netherlands refers to displaying or distributing posters or leaflets. In Yugoslavia refers to any electoral activity.
[e] Refers to attending an election meeting or rally. In Yugoslavia refers to attending a voters' meeting.
[f] Active member of an organization that is in turn active in community affairs. In Yugoslavia refers to taking part in a formally organized community action.
[g] Refers to working with an informal group on some community matter. In Yugoslavia refers to taking part in an informal community action. In Austria refers to cooperating with others to bring community problems to the attention of officials.
[h] Helped form a group such as mentioned in 9 above.
[i] In Yugoslavia this item contains contacts both in and out of the community.
[j] In Yugoslavia this item contains contacts both in and out of the community.
Source: Sidney Verba and Norman H. Nie, "Political Participation," in Fred I. Greenstein and Nelson W. Polsby, eds., *Handbook of Political Science* (Reading, Mass.: Addison-Wesley, 1975), 4: 24-25.

included as part of a general proposition on political participation. If we are reasonably confident the proposition would not apply to unconventional participation we will insert this parenthetical notation: (n.a. unconventional participation).

HOW MUCH PARTICIPATION IS THERE? Table 1-2 presents information on the proportions of people active politically in various ways in seven nations. The percentages should be compared cautiously across nations because similar activities are not equivalent in meaning. Take the simple act of voting, for instance. Only 63 percent of the American citizenry reports regular voting as compared with 85 percent in Austria, 93 percent in Japan, and 77 percent in the Netherlands. The lower proportion of turnout in the United States does not indicate greater voting apathy there, but does reflect stricter registration regulations. Voting is more difficult in the United States than in most other democratic nations (see Chapter 5 for more information on this), and requires greater personal involvement in politics in order to exercise one's franchise.

A few broad patterns are obvious in Table 1-2. In all seven nations, voting is the only behavior which a majority of the citizens utilize. Most other political acts are engaged in by a fraction of the population, often a very small fraction. The behaviors requiring more time, energy, skill, or money tend to be left to the gladiatorial elite in all these nations. The division of society into the "rulers and the ruled" seems to hold for most nations. Based on data in Table 1-2 as well as on those gathered in the University of Michigan election studies over the years, the following profile of the American public can be offered. Only about 8 percent belong to a political club or organization. About 10 to 12 percent make monetary contributions, about 10 to 15 percent contact public officials, and about 15 percent display a button or sticker. Around 25 to 30 percent try to proselytize others to vote a certain way, around 30 percent have tried to work on some community problem, and from 40 to 70 percent vote in any give election.

A CONCEPTUAL DIAGRAM OF POLITICAL BEHAVIOR VARIABLES So far, we have been discussing ways of classifying and describing political behavior. Now we will try to think about its roots. We want to understand why people perform political acts and why they choose to perform some acts and not others. Description and explanation are not totally separate enterprises, but a shift to an emphasis on explanation leads to a search for relationships between variables that an emphasis on classification often does not.

Figure 1-3 shows a conceptual diagram that is useful for thinking about the causes of behavior. Designed to analyze behavior at the individual level, the model is largely based on concepts developed by learning theorists in psychology. Although it is not irrelevant to the analysis of group or organizational behavior, more serviceable models could be developed for them. The diagram incorporates a time dimension. Those factors to the left of the diagram are presumed to have had their effect on behavior earlier in time than those factors to the right, which are presumed to precede behavior immediately. The explanation of the diagram is most parsimonious if we begin at the right and work back from decision and its immediate antecedents to factors that affect behavior at progressively earlier points in time.

Behavior is by definition continuous: there is no such thing as not behaving. Deciding to do nothing (make no change) or to sleep are still modes of behaving. An organism does not have the option of choosing not to choose. For analytical purposes, however, continuous behaving might be sliced into arbitrary units of time that can be called decisional units. The behaving organism constantly is choosing to do some one thing rather than another. The analysis of the factors that produce political behavior must begin with the immediate factors that produce a given decision.

The decision of an organism about its next act may be seen as a function of the interaction between the stimuli coming from the environment and the particular pattern of predispositions possessed by the organism at a given point in time. At any moment, several predispositions may be competing to take command of the organism, and several stimuli are available in the environment with the potentiality of interacting with those predispositions. The difficult task for the analyst of human behavior is to try to understand why a given set of stimuli and predispositions take precedence over several competing sets. Before speaking directly to that point, it is necessary to discuss the nature of predispositions and to introduce two concepts: a threshold concept and a selective perception concept.

Predispositions have been categorized analytically into three types in Figure 1-3: physiological and psychological needs, beliefs, and attitudes. This particular breakdown is most serviceable for explaining political behavior, but for other types of behavior, another classification might be

Figure 1-3. Model for Analysis of Individual Behavior.

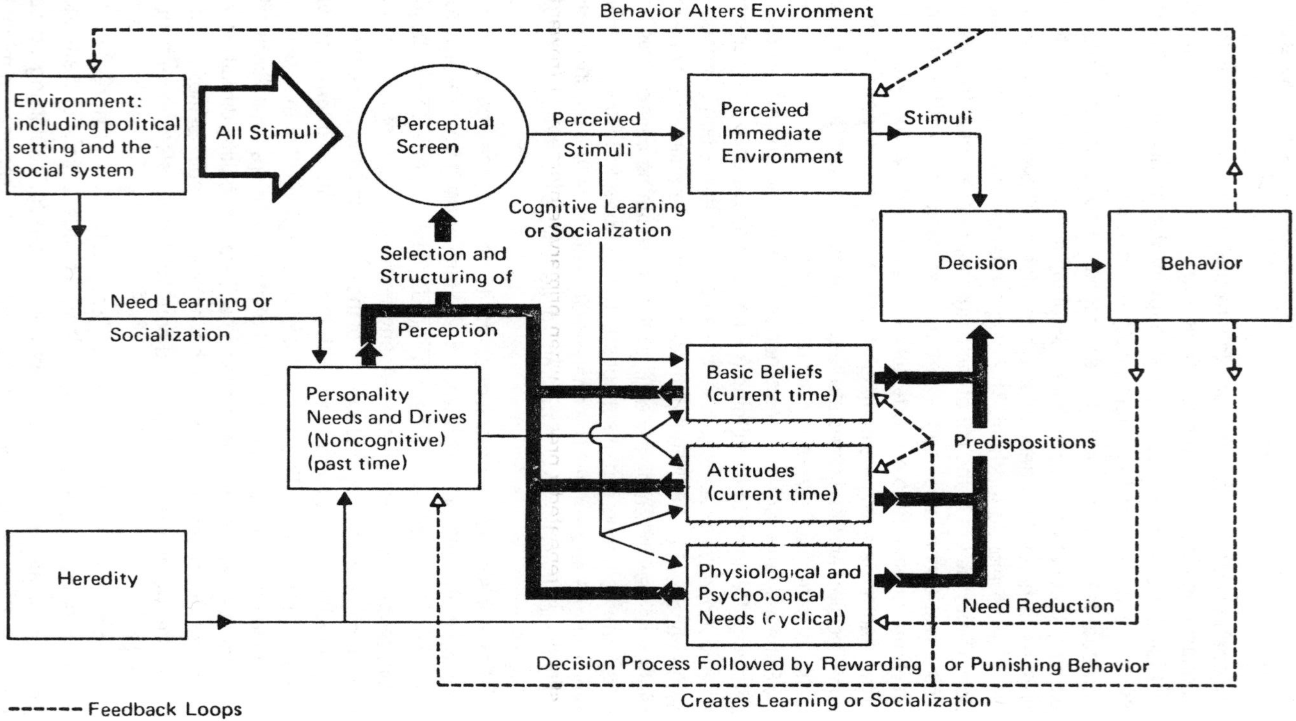

Environment: including political setting and the social system

All Stimuli

Need Learning or Socialization

Perceptual Screen

Selection and Structuring of Perception

Perceived Stimuli

Cognitive Learning or Socialization

Perceived Immediate Environment

Stimuli

Decision

Behavior

Behavior Alters Environment

Predispositions

Need Reduction

Basic Beliefs (current time)

Attitudes (current time)

Physiological and Psychological Needs (cyclical)

Personality Needs and Drives (Noncognitive) (past time)

Heredity

Decision Process Followed by Rewarding or Punishing Behavior

Creates Learning or Socialization

- - - - Feedback Loops

more useful. The strength of a given predisposition is a function of the needs of the organism and of the amount of reinforcement that predisposition has received. Maslow (1943) has listed five main categories of human needs: (1) physical (food, water, sex, sleep, etc.); (2) safety (order, predictability of the environment); (3) love, affection, belongingness; (4) self-esteem; (5) self-actualization.[5] Some of these needs, especially the physical ones, rise and fall in strength cyclically. At times of great physical need, the organism becomes completely absorbed in filling that need. It is only when these needs can be satisfied somewhat routinely or readily that the organism can turn to social and political behavior. This tendency for physical needs to override all others when they are not satisfied is the main reason they are included as part of the predispositional complex in a diagram (Figure 1-3) which is primarily oriented toward analyzing social and political behavior.

The strength of more strictly political predispositions, such as beliefs and attitudes, is largely a function of a learning mechanism called reinforcement. If an individual performs a certain act and is rewarded for it, the predisposition to perform that act is reinforced. If the reward helps to satisfy a basic human need, such as that for food or affection, we say the predisposition has received a primary reinforcement; thus, rewards that satisfy basic human needs are known as primary reinforcers. If a certain stimulus is repeatedly present when primary reinforcement (reward) is received, the stimulus itself becomes rewarding; this is called secondary reinforcement. (The reader is reminded of Pavlov's classical experiment with a dog who heard a bell each time food was given him; eventually the dog salivated at the sound of the bell even though no food was present.) This principle of secondary reinforcement is very important, because many social behavior patterns are established by it. In addition, the concept helps us understand another very important mechanism, to be discussed shortly, called selective perception. If a certain behavior pattern has been reinforced again and again (the principle holds for both primary and secondary reinforcement), that behavior pattern, or predisposition, is said to have developed habit strength. The greater the habit strength, the greater the likelihood that that habit or predisposition will take command of the organism when several habits or predispositions are competing for command.

[5] For a stimulating discussion of the way these needs affect political behavior, see Davies (1963), especially Chs. 1 and 2.

Figure 1-3 sets forth beliefs and attitudes as important political pre-dispositions. Both beliefs and attitudes are based on cognitions. Beliefs are defined as cognitions with an extra feeling of credibility which distinguishes them from cognitions which are not believed. I can cognize myself taking a trip in a spaceship to the moon, but I do not believe I will take such a trip. It is the *feeling* of credibility that makes a cognition believable; the cognition doesn't have to be true by some objective standard. People believe many things about which they have very poor information. Beliefs are expectancies and are close to what was called habit strength above. Attitudes are defined as cognitions with feelings of either attraction or repulsion attached. (Psychologists call this attraction-repulsion relationship valence.) A person may feel a duty to vote, or he may enjoy discussing politics, or he may feel an obligation to support his party with money or work. In these examples there is a positive valence between actor and object. There also can be a negative valence between them; a person may dislike door-to-door campaigning, he may be frightened of making speeches, he may dislike reading about politics.

Many cognitions are both beliefs and attitudes simultaneously. A person may believe very strongly that he is afraid to make a speech, that his party will win, or that it is his duty to vote. In fact, there is a tendency for persons to believe or expect those things they like or value. But it also is possible to have beliefs which are affectively neutral. One believes such things as "two plus two equals four," "there is an Africa," "steel is strong and hard," without necessarily having feelings of either like or dislike for them. Contrariwise, it is possible to like or dislike things one does not believe: "I would like to fly like a bird." Both beliefs and attitudes are included in the diagram because it is important to be aware that cognitions are affected by two kinds of feelings—credibility or incredibility and like or dislike. Another reason is that beliefs and cognitions have been relatively neglected in political behavior research, while there is already a good deal of research on attitudes. It is important to emphasize that political behavior is very dependent on the cognitions, and their credibility, that political actors hold about the political system in which they operate.

A threshold concept is helpful in understanding how predispositions compete to command the organism. The strength of a predisposition needed to take command of an organism is relative to the strength of the stimulus calling up the predisposition. Take, as an example, a person who has played mainly a spectator role in politics. None of the stimuli encountered in his daily environment have been strong enough to surmount his predispositional threshold and elicit active inputs to the system other than voting. The action of a personal friend in becoming a candidate for office, however, changes his personal environment. A request from his friend to help out in the campaign is sufficient to surmount his threshold and elicit new active political inputs. The stimulus which breaks the threshold is one which has previously received many primary reinforcements. The general predisposition to become active in politics has changed very little, but a particularly strong stimulus crosses the threshold. In this case, the stimulus not only acts upon the weak predisposition to become active in politics, but also activates a predisposition to help out a friend. A stimulus, then, need not be physically stronger or louder to activate a dormant behavior pattern (although the physical quality of the stimulus also is important); it may produce the relevant behavior by calling up additional predispositions until their combined force is sufficient to take command of the organism.

Returning to our example, suppose the man has some rewarding experiences while participating in his friend's campaign; he receives both primary and secondary reinforcement. The primary reinforcement strengthens his predisposition to campaign. The secondary reinforcement makes the stimuli associated with campaigning more attractive; they start to carry secondary rewards. The next time a political campaign starts up, a personal request may not be needed to elicit campaign behavior. The stimuli coming from the campaign will seem stronger to him, the strengthened predisposition to campaign will have lowered the stimulus threshold, and this is sufficient to get him to volunteer his services without a personal request.

The threshold concept is intimately related to a second concept we shall call the selective effect of predispositions upon perceptions. It is essential to the psychic economy of organisms that they perceive selectively. They have a perceptual screen which passes some stimuli and blocks others (see Figure 1-3). An organism would be overwhelmed if it attempted to attend to every stimulus impinging on its sensory organs. An organism may shift attention from one stimulus to another rather rapidly, but at any given instant the focus is upon relatively few.

How does the organism select the stimuli it will attend to? The answer to that is so difficult to study that psychologists speak of it as the "black box" which their methods cannot penetrate. Very generally, we can say that the choice of the stimulus seems to be a function both of the strength of the stimulus and of the strength of the predisposition with which that stimulus interacts. Very intense stimuli (loud sounds, bright lights, penetrating odors) are likely to get through the screen no matter how hard the individual tries to attend to something else. Also, stimuli that have been secondarily reinforced will be attractive and more likely to pass through the screen than those not so reinforced.

Stimuli also are screened for credibility. The judgment about credibility largely depends on how well the stimulus fits with the tightly woven pattern of cognitions already held as credible. Rokeach has told of hearing on a newscast one day that a camera had been invented that would take a picture of something that wasn't there; he rejected it as incredible. Later, he read that it took pictures of the heat remaining on a given spot after the object creating the heat had been moved. This fit into his pattern of believed cognitions, and he could accept the new invention as credible.[6] Credibility is determined not only by fit with things already believed but also by what a person wishes to believe. It is a natural human failing to perceive selectively and to distort perception so that it bolsters cherished beliefs.

The stimulus attended to also depends on the state of the organism, so to speak. A strong predisposition will incline an organism to pick up stimuli relevant to that predisposition. This interaction can be illustrated by the example of the man campaigning for his friend. One evening after dinner, he is calling on voters door to door. As the evening progresses, his earlier satiation with food gives way to hunger. Stimuli associated with food, such as the smell of food or the sight of a restaurant sign, which earlier in the evening were ignored, now become relevant. The predisposition to eat interacts with the sight of a restaurant, and the man turns away from campaigning to eat a hamburger. With partial satiation, the predisposition to campaign once more takes command, until increasing fatigue inhibits the response. The organism must allow sleep to take over and replenish the predisposition for campaigning.

The way that an individual selectively attends to stimuli is in many ways analogous to the way a radio tuner functions. If the tuner responded at once to all the stimuli in its environment, it would produce an unintelligible garble. If the set is tuned to an appropriate frequency and the gain (volume control) is set sufficiently high, a usable response is emitted. Similarly, the human organism must be tuned to a stimulus (have a

---

[6] Rokeach (1960), Part I, on the theory of belief systems, is very good.

relevant predisposition), and the predisposition must be strong enough to lower the threshold so that the stimulus can cross it. The strength of the stimulus needed to activate a radio is relative to the gain setting (predisposition level); a strong stimulus activates the receiver at even a low gain setting, but a higher gain setting is needed for a weak signal. If the environmental stimulus ceases, the receiver ceases to respond. Similarly, the human organism cannot make a given response unless the appropriate stimulus calling it forth is available in the environment. If several stimuli are at about the same frequency (desirability), the stronger crowds out the weaker.

It was asked several pages back why a given set of stimuli and predispositions take precedence over several competing sets. With the threshold and selective perception concepts in mind, the answer should now be more intelligible. It is a function of the need of the organism, the stimuli available in the environment, and the strength of the various predispositions relevant to those stimuli. The organism responds only to stimuli that are present. It selects from those stimuli according to its needs and according to the strength of various competing predispositions, as these have been built up through numerous past reinforcements. Social science has not advanced sufficiently for us to be more precise at this time.

One can gain a bit more understanding, however, by asking where and how predispositions are developed. What are their roots? Figure 1-3 shows that beliefs and attitudes are a product of three factors: (1) personality needs and drives; (2) cognitive learning (getting to know the world one lives in); and (3) learning which comes from behaving and then being rewarded or punished for that behavior. Physiological and psychological needs are developed partially from heredity and partially from personality needs and drives. The cyclical intensity of physiological needs is affected by the behavior of the organism in filling those needs; thus, a need-reduction arrow is drawn from behavior to that predispositional box.

Moving back a step in time, personality needs are a product of heredity, of need learning or socialization coming from the environment, and of rewards or punishments following from the various decisions of the organism. The reader will note that affective need learning has been conceptually distinguished from cognitive learning in the diagram; in real life, however, the two kinds of learning take place simultaneously.

Often, when explaining social and political behavior, we distinguish personality factors from environmental factors. (Such a distinction separates Chapter 3 from Chapters 4 and 5 in this book.) According to such a distinction, personality would include all five of the following boxes on the diagram: heredity, personality needs and drives, physiological and psychological needs, beliefs, and attitudes.

Environmental impact on behavior is indirect, meaning that it is always mediated by personality. In past time, it has had its impact by forming the personality and belief system of the actor. Rewards and punishments, by which learning takes place, had come out of the environment. In addition, environment had produced nearly all the stimuli (the only exception being kinetic stimuli from inside the organism) for cognitive learning. In current time, environment provides the stimuli from which the individual selects his perceived environment; thus, current environment also is mediated by personality. Personality is not totally determinative, however, since it selects only from stimuli presented. Environmental stimuli not only incite action but also provide information about boundaries, barriers, norms, and costs which help the organism to choose among alternatives.

The behavior model presented in Figure 1-3 is dynamic. The current behavior of an organism feeds back and has an impact on its future behavior (feedback loops are dotted lines on the diagram). Behavior alters the environment and thus changes the stimulus complex presented to the organism. In a discussion situation, for example, sending a message to one or more of the other actors usually stimulates a new message back to the first actor. An actor can move from one setting to another and thereby alter his stimulus complex. In a more long-range sense, lending or withholding political support partially determines whether a given set of officials wins an election; this surely has an impact on environment. Behavior also can alter the organism's internal environment by satisfying a drive; when satiation occurs, the drive-fulfilling behavior ceases.

Another way that behavior feeds back and affects future behavior is through the learning mechanism. Nearly all decisions have rewarding or punishing consequences through which the organism learns habits, beliefs, attitudes, and drives. The complex mechanisms by which learning occurs are a central theoretical preoccupation of modern psychology, and a thorough description of them would be too elaborate for inclusion here. We can say, however, that an explanation of political behavior must include an examination of the stimuli present, of the impact of personality

Figure 1-4. Simplified Map for Analysis of Environmental and Personal Factors Affecting Political Participation.

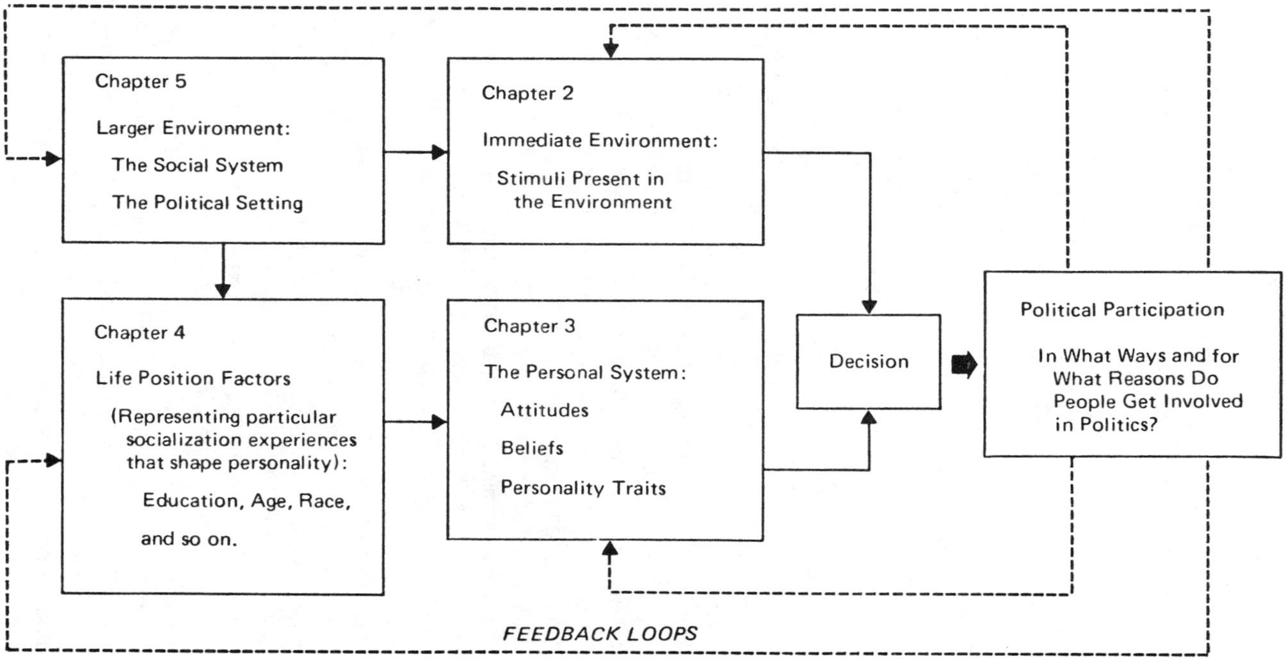

on selecting from those stimuli, and of the needs and predispositions competing for command of the organism. When we examine connections between environmental factors and political behavior, either we are indirectly measuring the impact of environment in shaping personality or we are seeing how the current environment presents opportunities and barriers to the actor. Finding the key to full understanding lies in our ability to unravel the complex learning process that mediates between the person and his environment.

The conceptual diagram sketched in Figure 1-3 does not have the predictive power expected of a full-fledged model. It does not, for example, enable us to predict which precise set of antecedent factors will produce one complex of predispositions and which set is needed to produce a differing complex. The major utility of the diagram is in locating and tentatively relating the variables that seem to determine behavior.

For purposes of structuring and organizing subsequent discussion, we have drawn in Figure 1-4 a simplified version of the model shown in Figure 1-3. The reader should keep the diagram in mind as he reads the subsequent chapters, because their organization is based on the categories of variables shown here. The variables have been given unequal research attention (scholars tend to do the easy things first), so the coverage is somewhat uneven.

We shall begin with the variables close to behavior in current time. Chapter 2 examines participation as a function of the stimuli impinging on political actors. The two classes of variables are the stimuli present in the environment and the stimuli the organism passes through its perceptual screen. Chapter 3 deals with participation as a function of personal factors: attitudes, beliefs, knowledge, and personality traits. In Chapter 4, the impact of life position (demographic) variables (age, sex, education, race, residence, and so on) is examined. These variables are shorthand ways of talking about the differential impact of environment on learning; persons in the different categories have grown up in different environments. These variables can also be considered as a summary index of variation in the socialization experiences. Such experiences generate sets of attitudes conducive to or inhibitory of political involvement. Chapter 5 is devoted to the discussion of participation as a function of the larger social and political environment, the level of modernization, and the political setting. In Chapter 6, a modest attempt is made to see what these findings mean for the functioning of the political system.

Chapter 2   Political Participation as a Function of Stimuli

The conceptual diagram (Figure 1-3 in Chapter 1) indicates that before a political action can occur, the political actor must pick up relevant stimuli from the environment. Stimuli likely to be perceived as political make up only a small part of the total available. Persons vary considerably in the number they receive. A general proposition relating stimuli and political participation appears repeatedly in the research findings: **the more stimuli about politics a person receives, the greater the likelihood he will participate in politics, and the greater the depth of his participation** (Allardt & Pesonen, 1960; Almond & Verba, 1963; Berelson, Lazarsfeld & McPhee, 1954; Campbell, 1962; Campbell, Gurin & Miller, 1954; Katz, 1957; Kyogoku & Ike, 1959; Lazarsfeld, Berelson & Gaudet, 1944; Lipset, 1960; Marvick & Nixon, 1961; Pesonen, 1961; Rokkan & Campbell, 1960). Evidence supporting this proposition comes from at least twelve different studies and eight different countries: Finland, Germany, Italy, Japan, Mexico, Norway, Great Britain, and the United States.

This proposition should not be read to mean that reception of political stimuli causes political participation; it means only that the two are closely associated. We shall see later that **persons with a positive attraction to politics are more likely to receive stimuli about politics and to participate more.** Other research evidence suggests that *exposure to stimuli about politics increases the quantity and sharpness of political knowledge, stimulates interest, contributes to the decisiveness of political choices, and firms up attachment to a party or candidate* (Berelson, Lazarsfeld & McPhee, 1954). There seems to be a circular pattern of relationships here that current research evidence does not enable us to untangle. Does an individual expose himself more to stimuli about politics because he is more interested in politics than others, or does he become more interested in politics as a result of lots of talk about politics in his environment? We know only that persons with high interest in, knowledge about, and exposure to politics are more likely to participate actively in politics.

Stimuli available in the environment of a political actor may come from the mass media, from campaign literature, from meetings, or from personal conversations. The tendency for those picking up more stimuli about politics to be more likely to be active in politics seems to hold regardless of the source of the stimuli. Personal contact and informal conversations are especially important stimuli for persons who are only marginally interested in politics. Several studies, from several countries, show that **persons participating in informal political discussions are more likely than nondiscussants to vote and participate in other ways in the political process** (Karlsson, 1958a; Kitt & Gleicher, 1950; Marvick & Nixon, 1961; Pesonen, 1961; Rokkan & Campbell, 1960).

The number of stimuli received and perceived as political is a function of two general factors: the number of stimuli about politics physically present in the environment and the operation of a person's perceptual screen, which picks up or shuts out stimuli about politics. We shall consider each of these general factors in turn.

EXPOSURE TO STIMULI AS A FUNCTION OF THEIR PRESENCE IN THE ENVIRONMENT It is a truism that the greater the number of political stimuli available in the environment, the greater the likelihood that an individual will pick them up. The technological revolution in the mass media of communications has made political stimuli readily available to nearly every citizen of modern industrialized countries. Furthermore, the day is almost at hand when ubiquitous political stimuli, via the mass media, will be widely available in less developed areas. Whether the medium be radio, television, or newspapers seems to make little difference, except in countries with a high rate of illiteracy. Studies in the United States have shown that as media attention shifted from radio to television, more and more people received the greater proportion of their political information from television (Campbell, Gurin & Miller, 1954; Campbell, et al., 1960). Yet, the level of political interest and political activity remained approximately the same (Campbell, 1962). Technically, it is very easy now for candidates to reach a mass audience; an estimated 80 million Americans watched the first Kennedy-Nixon television debate in the campaign of 1960. This technology also makes it easier for citizens to become surfeited with political information. Thus, the problem of getting messages through to citizens may be no less complex than before.

The number of stimuli about politics available in the environment builds up cyclically to a climax just before an election and then declines. Political campaigns are made up almost totally of messages in one form or another. *As campaign messages increase, informal discussion about the messages also increases* (Berelson, Lazarsfeld & McPhee, 1954); thus, campaigns have an accelerator effect on the total political stimuli available. In addition, at campaign time most parties make some attempt to contact at least some of the citizens personally about their vote intention. Personal-contact campaigns require a great amount of volunteer effort, and the nationwide coverage in the United States is generally less than 20 percent.[1] The impact of personal contact is significant, however; **several studies show that citizens contacted personally are more likely to vote and to be interested in the campaign** (see Chapter 5).

Many societies also launch "get-out-the-vote campaigns" at election time. These presumably activate or reinforce citizen-duty beliefs and have at least some impact on the political activity level of the society, but we do not have really good evidence about which types of appeals are most successful. So many factors influence a citizen's decision to vote

[1] Data are from the 1952 and 1956 election studies of the Survey Research Center, University of Michigan.

that it is difficult to measure the independent contribution of a get-out-the-vote campaign.[2]

Even though political stimuli are generously available, there are important differences in their level from one environment to the next. We can speak here of the over-all politicization level of an individual's environment. **Middle-class persons are exposed to more stimuli about politics than working-class persons** (Berelson, Lazarsfeld & McPhee, 1954; Eulau, 1962; Lazarsfeld, Berelson & Gaudet, 1944; M. Miller, 1952; DiPalma, 1970; Verba & Nie, 1972). **Men move in environments having more stimuli about politics than women do** (Berelson, Lazarsfeld & McPhee, 1954; Lazarsfeld, Berelson & Gaudet, 1944).

Since persons tend to interact with other persons of about their own level of educational attainment, and since persons with higher education generally are more involved in and talk more about politics, a more highly educated person encounters more stimuli about politics than one not so well educated (Almond & Verba, 1963; Berelson, Lazarsfeld & McPhee, 1954; Converse & Dupeux, 1961; Converse & Dupeux, 1962; Lazarsfeld, Berelson & Gaudet, 1944; Lipset, 1960; M. Miller, 1952). *Political conversation flows most naturally and freely when persons of the same sociocultural level interact* (Berelson, Lazarsfeld & McPhee, 1954); ease of interaction is especially characteristic of "in-groups."

The most closely knit in-group of all is the family, and family experience has a profound impact on a person's exposure to political stimuli and on his activity level in politics. **Children growing up in a home with a high incidence of political discussion and a high intake level for political stimuli are more likely to maintain a high level of exposure to stimuli about politics when adults** (Berelson, Lazarsfeld & McPhee, 1954; Almond & Verba, 1963; Marvick & Nixon, 1961; Rokkan & Campbell, 1960).

What little evidence we have suggests that the kinds of differences shown in politicization levels of personal environments for different sectors of society (class, sex, urban-rural, education, group membership) very likely are found in other political cultures as well as in the United

---

[2] Some ingenious experiments attempting to measure this factor on the local level were carried out by Eldersveld (1956), Eldersveld & Dodge (1954), and Gosnell (1927).

States (studies from seven countries were cited above). There seem, however, to be overall differences between national cultures as well. The five-nation survey showed that *persons living in Italy and Mexico tended to encounter many fewer stimuli about politics than persons living in Germany, the United Kingdom, and the United States* (Almond & Verba, 1963). A comparative study showed a greater incidence of newspaper reading in the United States than in France (Converse & Dupeux, 1962). Part of the difference vanished when statistical controls for education (higher in the United Stated) were applied, but highly educated Americans more universally read newspapers than highly educated Frenchmen. These two studies suggest that **politicization levels are different from country to country** and that the level in the United States is higher than in most other Western countries, although the level in Britain is close behind.

EXPOSURE TO STIMULI AS A FUNCTION OF A PERSON'S PERCEPTUAL SCREEN Even persons living in the same environment expose themselves to differing numbers of stimuli about politics. This could only mean that some persons are picking up the available stimuli, whereas others are shutting them out. The operation of an individual's perceptual screen was discussed in Chapter 1. A point made there bears repeating here: the perceptual screen operates to protect the organism from an overload of stimuli. Overload can occur in two ways: the total amount can be so excessive that all messages are garbled (like a radio tuned to several stations at once); or the stimuli hammer so incessantly that the senses are dulled (like the villagers' reaction to the boy who cried wolf too often).

There are important individual differences in the ability to encode political messages and in the ability to sustain political interest. Therefore, the likelihood that the perceptual screen will let political messages through is a function of personal abilities and needs. The screen also operates to protect the individual from stimuli which threaten his security system. Uncongenial or threatening messages either may be shut out entirely or may be distorted to soften the potential damage. The operation of a given person's perceptual screen is unique to his personality. Despite this uniqueness, aggregates of persons follow certain discernible patterns.

Persons who are attracted to politics (interested, concerned, curious, intense preferences) **expose themselves more to stimuli about politics than those not so attracted** (Allardt & Pesonen 1960; Berelson, Lazarsfeld & McPhee, 1954; Lane, 1959; Lazarsfeld, Berelson & Gaudet, 1944; Pesonen, 1960; Milbrath, 1971b). This proposition has been found almost universally in studies gathering the relevant data. It is so close to being a truism that few researchers bother any more to investigate it or report it. The relationship is important, however, in that any effort to increase the political information level of the populace must find some way to gain and maintain the interest of citizens. Disinterested and surfeited persons do not pick up political stimuli. Persons not attending to politics are called "parochials" in the five-nation study; their incidence is much greater in Italy and Mexico than in Germany, the United Kingdom, and the United States (Almond & Verba, 1963, Ch. 3).

A related proposition is that **persons with strong preferences for a party or candidate pick up more political stimuli than those with weak preferences** (Allardt & Pesonen, 1960; Campbell, Gurin & Miller, 1954; Campbell, et al., 1960; Lazarsfeld, Berelson & Gaudet, 1944). **Even if his mind is made up, the strong partisan exposes himself to more stimuli about politics than the undecided,** who, objectively, may need more information (Lazarsfeld, Berelson & Gaudet, 1944; Milne & Mackenzie, 1954). The partisan is not really interested in messages from both sides; **primarily, partisans pick up messages from their own side** (Lazarsfeld, et al., 1944; Milne & Mackenzie, 1954; Pesonen, 1960).

Additional evidence that the disposition to seek political stimuli is a personality trait comes from the finding that **political information-seeking behavior is cumulative** (Berelson, Lazarsfeld & McPhee, 1954; Katz, 1957; Lane, 1959; Lazarsfeld, Berelson & Gaudet, 1944; Pesonen, 1960; Pesonen, 1961; Scheuch, 1961). **The same persons have high exposure to several different kinds of media, and their high exposure continues throughout the surge and decline of political campaigns.** The behavior is cumulative in another way; **persons exposing themselves highly to political stimuli also expose themselves highly to nonpolitical stimuli** (Berelson, et al., 1954; Katz, 1957; Lane, 1959; Lazarsfeld, et al., 1944; Pesonen, 1960; Pesonen, 1961; Scheuch, 1961).

Persons pick up or seek stimuli about politics for a variety of purposes: to fill a need for knowledge, to satisfy their curiosity, to help solve problems, to fulfill the sense of duty that a good citizen must be informed.

But why do some persons deliberately shut out stimuli about politics? Research evidence on that question is relatively inadequate. The theory set forth in Chapter 1 leads to speculation that the perceptual screen shuts out stimuli as a way of protecting the personality (ego) of the individual. **Persons who lack education and sophistication about politics tend to shut out political stimuli** (Almond & Verba, 1963; Berelson, Lazarsfeld & McPhee, 1954; Converse & Dupeux, 1961; Converse & Dupeux, 1962; Lazarsfeld, Berelson & Gaudet, 1944; Lipset, 1960; M. Miller, 1952) as a way of protecting themselves from messages which they do not understand and cannot absorb. **Persons of middle age,** presumably with greater understanding of politics, **expose themselves to more stimuli about politics than persons of young ages do** (Berelson, Lazarsfeld & McPhee, 1954; Lazarsfeld, Berelson & Gaudet, 1944). *"Busy" persons,* who perceive themselves as having no spare time for politics, *protect themselves from political stimuli which are irrelevant to their pressing concerns.* If political stimuli are present in excessive numbers, some must be shut out to make the others intelligible. Messages which threaten the ego must be shut out or distorted so that their potential damage is diminished.

Evidence presented by one scholar suggests why certain persons hesitate to discuss politics: *persons with weak egos shun the clash of political argument because of the threat of deflation of their ego* (Rosenberg, 1954-1955; Rosenberg, 1962). Contrariwise, *persons with high self-esteem welcome political discussion and expose themselves readily to political stimuli. Some persons believe they will lose friends or opportunities for business success if they discuss politics.* Not all exposure to stimuli about politics requires engaging in a discussion; thus, the propositions are not directly on the point of this section. However, the more general point is relevant: many persons perceive politics as threatening and may well be inclined to shut political stimuli out of their lives.

Political stimuli also may be shut out because they are lost in the general competition for a given individual's attention. Persons attend to only one message at a time, and the choice of message to be focused on is dependent on the predispositional complex of the reacting individual. A predisposition to select out political messages rarely has highest priority for ordinary citizens. At campaign time, the predisposition may be high for those who are interested in politics. Exciting or unique political events stand out enough so that even some of the disinterested pick up messages about them. As a rule, however, ordinary political stimuli do not compete adequately with other possible messages for the attention of the average citizen. Only a small proportion of the population have learned to pick up and enjoy political messages; their predisposition complex gives such messages high priority. By and large, these same persons are those most likely to become active in politics.

Chapter 3   Political Participation as a Function of Personal Factors

The conceptual diagram (Figure 1-3 Chapter 1) isolates five "personal" factors, three of which have been related in research to political behavior: attitudes, beliefs, and personality traits. (There has been almost no research relating heredity or physiological and psychological needs to political behavior.) Beliefs and attitudes are "up close" to behavior. Personality is a more general background factor or disposition which feeds into a cognitive framework and finds expression as beliefs and attitudes.

It is virtually impossible to measure any of these personal factors directly; their presence and character can only be inferred from behavior in response to a stimulus. Typically, an experimenter or an interviewer gives some sort of verbal stimulus to a respondent and then measures or records the behavior that stimulus elicits. In the case of an attitude measure, he may read a series of statements to the respondent and ask him to agree or disagree with them. The inferential leap from response to attitude seems to be justified so long as one can be reasonably certain that the respondent is not lying. Personality traits are measured in much the same way as attitudes, except that a longer and less certain inferential leap is required. The stimuli used in personality measures ask about behavior in certain kinds of situations; they also ask for attitudes and beliefs. From these bits of evidence, the presence or absence of a trait is inferred.

Because of these measurement difficulties, it is important for the reader to keep in mind a distinction between a theoretical conceptualization of a factor and its operational definition (measuring instrument). A researcher always has a theoretical conception of a factor in mind as he works with it. For example, it may be a concept like "effectiveness." A major challenge facing him is to try to devise a measuring instrument (a scale, an index, an item) which will create in the mind of his respondent the same kind of concept that is in his own mind. This process is called operationalizing, and the measure he creates can be called his operational definition of his concept. It is a well-known fact that words don't always mean the same thing from person to person, and thus it is almost impossible to duplicate accurately a theoretical concept in a measuring instrument. The researcher works by trial and error to sharpen the measuring instrument so that it is the closest possible approximation to his theoretical concept. He knows he is getting closer when the measure seems stable in repeated applications over time, and when it relates to other variables in a manner that his theory leads him to expect. But there is always the possibility that the measure he has created is, in reality, somewhat different from his theoretical conception of the factor. This difficulty affects the following discussion in two ways.

Many times it seems, theoretically, that a very close relationship should exist between two variables, but the correlation shown in the data is relatively low. This can mean that the actual relationship is much lower than expected, but it can also mean that the measuring instruments are so imperfect that no higher relationship could be found. Thus, every finding is subject to two interpretations: that the real world is accurately mirrored in the data, or that the measuring instruments are so poor that the data do not reflect the real world. For example, one might hypothesize, theoretically, that persons with dominant personality traits would be more likely to become active in politics than persons who are less dominant. When a dominance scale is administered to a group of actives and nonactives, there seems to be no difference between the two groups on the incidence of dominant personalities. Does this mean that dominants are not more likely to enter politics than nondominants, or does it mean that the scale does not measure dominance, as had been supposed? The challenge to the social scientist is to try several approaches and extract knowledge from such imperfect data.

Difficulties in operationalization also affect the classification of variables into the sections of this chapter. Despite our theoretical effort to distinguish attitude, belief, and personality, many operationally defined variables overlap our conceptual boundaries. A given variable is discussed under a particular heading because the main emphasis of what is measured fell in that category. No effort is made to justify particular classifications, since that is not crucial to the intellectual enterprise of this book. The reader also will encounter several instances of interrelationship of beliefs, attitudes, and personality traits. In certain cases, it is difficult to sort out cause from effect.

PARTICIPATION AS A FUNCTION OF ATTITUDES AND BELIEFS   In Chapter 1 we made a conceptual distinction between attitudes and beliefs. The distinction was made to alert us to areas of inquiry that might be overlooked if we did not distinguish the two kinds of feelings. One's belief system generally is larger than one's value (attitudinal) system, and by focusing only on statements with valences a research study might miss many items of importance. For example, a respondent's belief about how his government functions may be much more important for understanding his political behavior than knowing whether or not he dislikes or likes the way it functions. An impoverished understanding of what an individual can do *vis-à-vis* the government not only will be highly determinative of an individual's political behavior but may well shape his general attitude toward the government. If one focuses on a study of beliefs, one is likely to pick up both values and beliefs; an exclusive focus on values or attitudes, however, increases the likelihood that important beliefs will be overlooked.

The belief-attitude clarification discussed here is meant to alert future researchers about the importance of this distribution. Beliefs, and cognitions which underlie both beliefs and attitudes have not been widely researched in behavioral studies; there usually is more research on attitudes. Because the belief-attitude distinction has seldom been followed by other researchers, it will be difficult in the following pages to classify particular predispositions into beliefs, and others into attitudes. Perhaps, in fact, such an exercise at this time is a bit premature.

Psychological Involvement Psychological involvement refers to the degree to which citizens are interested in and concerned about politics and public affairs. We can think of psychological involvement as being placed along a continuum. At one pole are those persons who are completely absorbed in the political conflicts surrounding them. At the other extreme are individuals who are totally preoccupied with their private lives and who have little interest in or care for public issues. During election times, the level of psychological involvement for most citizens increases dramatically.

Just as psychological involvement is a central variable determining exposure to political stimuli, so is it a central attitudinal variable relating to participation in politics. At least a dozen studies spread over different cultures (the relationship is so regular that many authors do not bother to report it) have shown that **persons who are more interested in and concerned about political matters are more likely to be activists** (Berelson, Lazarsfeld & McPhee, 1954; Campbell, Gurin & Miller, 1954; Campbell, et al., 1960; Janowitz & Marvick, 1956; Kuroda, 1967; Lazarsfeld, Berelson & Gaudet, 1944; Milbrath, 1971b; Eldersveld & Ahmed, 1976; Matthews & Prothro, 1966; Inkeles, 1969; Verba & Nie, 1972; Nie, Powell & Prewitt, 1969; Goel, 1975). In general, psychological involvement relates more strongly to campaign, community and protest activities and less strongly to voting and contacting (Verba, Nie & Kim, 1971; Buffalo Survey, 1968). This differentiation by modes is to be expected. Voting is less dependent on involvement in politics; many individuals vote because of patriotic sentiments, traditional commitments, and group pressure rather than personal involvement. In comparison with other political activities, particularized contacting also requires little involvement because as mentioned earlier the contactor usually acts to resolve a private need that has little relevance to broader social issues.

Some data from the Buffalo Survey (1968) which show a relationship between psychological involvement and modes of political participation are set forth in Table 3-1. "Interest in politics" was measured by a simple question which read "Generally speaking, how interested are you in politics—very much, somewhat, or not at all?" (We discussed the meaning of the various modes of political participation in an earlier chapter.) The reader can see that interest in politics is positively related to all forms of participation, but that it explains more of the variance in the electoral and the communications modes. It is also evident that persons living in the white community are more dependent on personal motivation for becoming active in politics, whereas in the black community social pressures and group associations are more significant for mobilizing people. Protesting is an exception to this point; interest in politics more likely stimulates protesting among blacks than among whites. This is because many whites would refuse to protest no matter how interested they might be in politics. (See Table 1-1 p. 15.)

Table 3-1. Modes of Political Participation Related to Interest in Politics, by Race (Pearson Correlations).

	Party & Campaign Work		Frequency of Participation in Communication Activities		Protests		Voting & Patriotic Activities	
	Black	White	Black	White	Black	White	Black	White
Interest in politics	.34	.50	.35	.55	.21	.15	.15	.17

Data are derived from the Buffalo Survey (1968).

As might be expected, **those with intense preferences for a party, a candidate, or an issue are highly inclined to be interested in politics** (Berelson, Lazarsfeld & McPhee, 1954; Campbell, Gurin & Miller, 1954; Campbell, et al., 1960; Pesonen, 1960: Verba & Nie, 1972; Sheth, 1975).

Why is it that some persons become highly involved psychologically in politics, or have intense preferences (or both, since they are highly correlated), while others do not? The difference stems partly from differences in social position and partly from differing personality development. Personality correlates are treated later in this chapter; only social-position factors are discussed here. **Persons of higher socioeconomic status (SES), especially higher education, are more likely to become highly involved psychologically in politics than persons of lower status** (Degras, Gray & Pear, 1956; Berelson, Lazarsfeld & McPhee, 1954; Campbell, Gurin & Miller, 1954; Campbell, et al., 1960; Converse & Dupeux, 1961; Eulau, 1962; Lazarsfeld, Berelson & Gaudet,

1944; Matthews & Prothro, 1966; Milbrath, 1971b; Verba, Nie & Kim, 1971, all five nations; Alford & Scoble, 1968; Goel, 1975).

> Perhaps the surest single predictor of political involvement is number of years of formal education. There are apathetic college graduates and highly involved people of very low educational level but the over-all relationship of education and political interest is impressive. It is impossible to say with confidence why it is that formal schooling makes people more responsive to political stimulation. One may surmise that education tends to widen the scope of one's acquaintance with political facts, to increase capacity to perceive the personal implications of political events, or to enlarge one's confidence in his own ability to act effectively politically. Whatever the precise nature of the educational process, it has clear effects on political interest (Campbell, 1962 p. 20).

It is traditional in most cultures that politics is primarily a concern of men, and that women should fall in line with them politically. The social changes wrought by modern industrial societies are eroding this sex difference, but the impact of tradition is still highly visible. **Men are more likely to be psychologically involved in politics than women** (Benney & Geiss, 1950; Berelson, Lazarsfeld & McPhee, 1954; Lazarsfeld, Berelson & Gaudet, 1944). This difference is more pronounced at the lower educational levels than at the upper, where it is nearly obliterated in modern industrial societies (Campbell, et al., 1960, p. 498; Rokkan & Campbell, 1960). In the United States, females seem somewhat more oriented to candidates than are men; there is no difference between the sexes on the intensity of their partisanship (Almond & Verba, 1963; Campbell, Gurin & Miller, 1954; Campbell, et al., 1960), In Germany, Britain, Mexico, and Italy, women are less likely than men to feel psychologically involved in politics, and this difference is especially striking in Italy (Almond & Verba, 1963; Degras, Gray & Pear, 1956).

Some studies have shown that *older persons are more interested in politics than younger* (Berelson, Lazarsfeld & McPhee, 1954; Lazarsfeld, Berelson & Gaudet, 1944). This relationship may be a function of length of identification with a party, length of residence in a community, and the acquisition of property and family responsibilities. Mere aging would not seem to produce increased interest. A study in Greenwich, England, in fact found no relationship between age and political interest (Degras, Gray & Pear, 1956).

Sense of Civic Obligation   A sense of obligation to participate in politics is another important political attitude relating to participation. The sense of civic obligation is very strong in the United States: in different surveys, 80 to 90 percent of the sample indicate adherence to this norm (Campbell, Gurin & Miller, 1954; Campbell, et al., 1960; Dennis, 1970; Milbrath, 1968). In the Almond-Verba five-nation study, Americans were found to be ahead of Britons, Germans, Italians, and Mexicans in voluntarily mentioning voting in response to an open-ended question on the part an ordinary person should play in his community. The comparative percentages were: United States, 40; United Kingdom, 18; Germany, 15; Italy, 2; Mexico, 1. Some other surveys, however, asking specifically about voting, have found voting duty to be much higher in these democracies. For example, in a study of Stockport, England, 82 percent regarded voting as a duty (Rose & Mossawir, 1967). The sense that voting is a duty may also be taking hold in other nations where people have had a comparatively shorter experience with democratic institutions; in Japan, for example, between 40 to 50 percent of respondents in different samples reported that voting is a duty (Richardson, 1974).

Feeling a duty to participate carries over strongly to political actions: several studies show that **persons feeling a duty to participate in politics are more likely to do so** (Campbell, Gurin & Miller, 1954; Campbell, et al., 1960; Marvick & Nixon, 1961; Mayntz, 1961; Milbrath, 1968; Alford & Scoble, 1968; Dennis, 1970; Kuroda, 1965b).

Data from the Buffalo Survey in Table 3-2 illustrate these generalizations. Before discussing the contents of the table it will be necessary to describe how the data were gathered. Possible inputs that a person might make to a political system were printed on separate small cards. Respondents were asked first to sort the cards into four groups: "Things you do regularly," "Things you do fairly often," "Things you seldom do," and "Things you never do at all." When all the cards had been sorted, they were shuffled and the respondents were then asked to sort the cards again, but this time in terms of their felt responsibility or obligation to perform each act. The four sorting categories were: "Things you feel it is essential for you to do," "Things you have an important responsibility to do," "Things you have some responsibility to do," and "Things you feel

Table 3-2. Sense of Responsibility to Participate and Frequency of Participation.

Items	Black		White		Behavior-Responsibility Correlations	
	Behavior	Felt Responsibility	Behavior	Felt Responsibility	Black	White
Participate in a political party between elections as well as at election time	19%	35%	19%	30%	.44	.48
Keep informed about politics	61	74	75	77	.45	.52
Vote in elections	83	95	81	95	.42	.42
Send Messages of support to political leaders when they are doing well	18	38	17	37	.31	.41
Send protest messages to political leaders when they are doing badly	15	37	11	34	.26	.43
Protest both vigorously and publicly if the government does something that is morally wrong	25	49	26	41	.42	.44
Join in public street demonstrations	11	14	3	4	.62	.54
Riot if necessary to get public officials to correct political wrongs	5	14	2	5	.49	.39
Take an active part in political campaigns	19	36	15	27	.44	.50
Engage in political discussion	42	48	46	38	.46	.53

Table 3-2. (continued)

Items	Black		White		Behavior-Responsibility Correlations	
	Behavior	Felt Responsibility	Behavior	Felt Responsibility	Black	White
Teach my children the importance of give and take in the democratic way of life	76	82	72	83	.61	.47
Pay all taxes	92	97	94	96	.28	.40
Be a candidate for public office	7	14	3	9	.30	.37
Inform others in my community about politics	34	40	26	34	.48	.54
Teach my children to participate in politics beyond voting	39	56	33	54	.48	.50
Have undivided loyalty and love for my country	93	94	93	94	.45	.51
Personally see to it that my children understand and accept the responsibilities of citizenship	75	81	75	83	.57	.40
Join and support a political party	44	56	35	49	.48	.49
Be a calming and informing influence in my own community	48	58	44	54	.52	.50
Actively support community organizations	56	73	52	60	.48	.52

Data are derived from the Buffalo Survey (1968).

you have no responsibility to do." The first sorting may be labeled as the "behavior" sort and the second as the "felt responsibility" sort.

The percentages in the table report those who fell in the two top categories in each sort, i.e., those in the "regular" and "fairly often" categories on behavior, and those in the "essential" and "important" categories on felt responsibility to participate. Race was such an important variable that separate scores were reported for blacks and whites. A readily visible pattern in the table is that the percentages feeling a responsibility were higher in most cases than the percentages acting. On all items there was a positive correlation between felt responsibility to participate and actual reported participation—majority of coefficients being in the .40's and .50's. Certain inputs were almost universally believed to be a citizen's duty: vote, keep informed, pay taxes, and have undivided loyalty to the country. Some other input items were rejected by an overwhelming majority: join in public demonstrations, riot if necessary to get a public official to correct political wrongs, and be a candidate for public office.

Feelings of citizen duty are instilled by the political socialization process and have their roots both in society and in personality. Data from Almond and Verba's five-nation study clearly indicate that some political cultures more thoroughly instill this sense of duty than others. Almond and Verba checked carefully to make sure that the differences found between countries were not simply a function of differences in education, status, or role between the countries. Statistical controls for education, occupation, and sex were applied to the national differences in sense of duty, and the latter persisted despite these controls (Almond & Verba, 1963, pp. 176-177).

Social-position factors within a nation also have an impact on civic duty feeling. The citizen-duty attitude relates to many of the same social-position variables as the psychological involvement attitude. **Upper-socioeconomic-status persons, especially those with higher education, are more likely to develop a sense of citizen duty** (Almond & Verba, 1963; Dennis, 1970; Campbell, Gurin & Miller, 1954; Campbell, et al., 1960; Eulau, 1962). Some scholars have speculated that middle-class society especially facilitates the development of civic conscience and duty. Not only does the middle class instill duty to society as a value in its children, but conformity pressures within that stratum help to enforce the code (Riesman, 1950; Lane, 1959).

In the United States, differences in civic duty no longer can be clearly traced to race (Milbrath, 1968; Dennis, 1970). Earlier studies found that black persons growing up in the American South were less likely to develop a sense of duty (Campbell, Gurin & Miller, 1954). In the United States, sex or age differences do not seem to affect the development of a sense of civic duty (Almond & Verba, 1963; Dennis, 1970; Campbell, Gurin & Miller, 1954). In Germany, Britain, Mexico, and Italy, however, men are more likely to develop a sense of civic obligation than women (Almond & Verba, 1963, p. 177).

Why is it that some persons so define themselves and their role that it includes the responsibility to be interested in, informed about, and actively participate in political affairs? These beliefs are learned in the formative years and come about partly as a function of the milieu in which a person grows up and partly as a function of the basic personality of the individual. The impact of social status on participation is mediated almost totally through the socialization process; persons from a higher status have been taught to be interested in politics, to keep informed, and to shoulder a responsibility to participate. The role training coming from the environmental milieu interacts with basic personality factors which operate differentially to produce different role conceptions for different individuals. A personality which is basically sociable, aggressive, and competent can accept the role training from the social milieu which says that a person should be politically active. Persons who feel shy or incompetent, and who withdraw from social combat, are more likely to reject the role model of the political participant.

The environmental milieu is not only important for training in political participation but also presents the stimuli and opportunity for participation. Some environments simply have more stimuli about politics available and thus increase the probability that persons living in that environment will participate. It is also true, however, that persons who define their social role as including political activity are more predisposed to pick up political stimuli and will sense an opportunity to participate that others with a lower predisposition would not pick up.

In summary, then, political participation is a learned social role which predisposes a person to select out and act on political stimuli thereby inducing much higher rates of participation than persons who do not accept political activity as part of their self-definition.

Party Identification   Two decades of research have shown that party identification is a fundamental explanatory variable for the level as well as the direction of electoral participation in the United States. Developed by scholars at the University of Michigan, the term measures the degree of psychological attachment or commitment to a political party. The importance of party identification lies in its stability over long periods of time. Party identification represents a long-term force in contrast to candidate and issue preferences which are short-term forces (Campbell, et al., 1960; Campbell, et al., 1966). The concept of party identification has been extended to the study of electoral behavior in several European and Asian countries (Converse & Dupeux, 1962; Campbell & Valen, 1961; Butler & Stokes, 1969; Converse, 1969; Kothari, 1970). However, cross-national comparability of the concept has been questioned by some on the grounds that party identification is unstable, and that its psychological content is meager and poorly developed in many non-American cultures (Shively, 1972; Eldersveld & Kubota, 1973).

When party identification is correlated with political activity, more than a dozen studies in six or more nations have shown that **persons who strongly identify with or intensely prefer a political party (any party) are more likely to participate actively in the political process** (Campbell, Gurin & Miller, 1954; Campbell, et al., 1960; Campbell & Valen, 1961; Valen & Katz, 1964; Marvick & Nixon, 1961; Pesonen, 1968; Matthews & Prothro, 1966; Sheth, 1975; Buffalo Survey, 1968; Goel, 1975; Verba, Ahmed & Bhatt, 1971; Verba & Nie, 1972; Butler & Stokes, 1969). The impact of partisan attachments on political participation seems to be independent of the impact of socioeconomic variables; *at all levels of education or income, those who are strong partisans are more active than the weak partisans or the independents* (Verba & Nie, 1972).

The impact of party identification on participation varies a great deal with the mode of activity. It correlates most strongly with voting and electoral activities, but only minimally with communal activities or with particularized contacting of government officials (Verba, Ahmed & Bhatt, 1971; Verba & Nie, 1972; Buffalo Survey, 1968). This pattern is to be expected, for both voting and electoral work are partisan activities and would therefore clearly benefit from partisan enthusiasm. In contrast, both communal activities and particularized contacting tend to be non-partisan in nature. In the Buffalo Survey, protestors were found to score only slightly higher than the average on strength of party identification.

As might be expected, **those with intense partisan preferences are also highly likely to be interested in politics** (Berelson, Lazarsfeld &

McPhee, 1954; Campbell, Gurin & Miller, 1954; Campbell, et al., 1960; Pesonen, 1960). Strength of partisan preference seems to be a function of other variables, too. **Older persons tend to have stronger party preferences than younger** (Campbell & Valen, 1961; Valen & Katz, 1964). Like the relationship between age and interest in politics this age-partisanship relationship seems to be more a function of the length of time a person has been exposed to party influences than of aging per se. A subordinate proposition is that *in countries with a recently developed party system there will be no age-partisanship relation at the outset since all age groups presumably are equally exposed to party socialization* (Converse, 1969). In support of the above proposition Eldersveld and Kubota (1973) found no consistent relationship between age and party strength of identification in India and Japan.

Unlike the positive correlation between SES and certain other psychological orientations (e.g., involvement, duty, and efficacy), *strength of party identification and status are somewhat negatively correlated.* In the Verba & Nie United States study (1972), 43 percent of the lower-status citizens reported strong party identification, compared with 34 percent in the middle-status group and 31 percent in the upper-status group. Since strength of party identification and political participation are positively associated, and since a greater proportion of the lower-status citizens have strong party identifications, could we argue that the lower socioeconomic sectors of society participate at higher levels than might be expected from their status alone, as a result of the strength of their partisan feelings? Or stated more generally, do strong partisan attachments tend to modify the socioeconomic based differences in participation? Rokkan and Campbell (1960) have shown that this is indeed the case in Norway where parties are class-based and the worker and farmer parties are effective in mobilizing their respective groups. In contrast to Norway, parties in the United States are broad-based (they draw support from divergent classes); as a result, they are less successful in helping narrow the participation gap between upper- and lower-status citizens (Rokkan & Campbell, 1960).

Verba and Nie (1972) have done extensive research on whether or not strong partisan attachments modify socioeconomic differences in participation. Their findings in support of Rokkan and Campbell's earler studies showed that this relationship depends on the nation under inquiry. In the United States, for example, strength of party identification has only a modest influence: it does appear to act to reduce the disparity between different socioeconomic groups in relation to the simple act of voting, but not in relation to the more demanding acts (Verba & Nie, 1972). A similar pattern prevails in India (Nie & Verba, 1975). On the other hand in Austria, Japan, and the Netherlands, strong party attachments help narrow the gap considerably (Nie & Verba, 1975).

The nature of the party system in each country largely accounts for these national differences. In those nations where parties substantially reduce the participation disparity between the upper- and the lower-class groups, parties are aligned with particular class or ethnic groups rather than being broad based. In Austria, for example, the farm segment is clearly linked to the Austrian People's Party, and blue-collar workers are more closely affiliated with the Austrian Socialist Party. Similar group-based parties exist in Japan and the Netherlands. Conversely political parties in the United States are broad based and heterogeneous in character, and therefore do not contribute much in reducing disparities between classes. Similarly in India, the Congress Party is dominant and draws support from virtually all segments of the population.

In addition to party preference, candidate and issue preferences are also related to the level of political participation. Several studies have shown that **persons with intense preferences for candidates or issues are more likely to be active in politics** (Campbell, Gurin & Miller, 1954; Campbell, et al., 1960; Marvick & Nixon, 1961). *If a person's issue preferences pull in different directions* (one issue toward one party and another issue toward another party), *the likelihood of his participation in politics is lessened* (Campbell, Gurin & Miller, 1954; Campbell, et al., 1960). Conversely, *congruence in direction of political attitudes* (alignments in the same direction for party, candidate, and issues) *increases the probability of participation* (Lane, 1959; Lipset, 1960).

Group Identification   Another attitudinal variable similar to party identification is a feeling of identity with a group. Group identification is a sense of belonging, plus an awareness of the salience of one's group. Group identification can become a belief system leading to greater political activity. The most vivid example of this phenomenon is the deliberate attempt by American blacks to build group feelings so as to enlist their energies for political action in the 1960s and 1970s. Recall the group cry for "black power" or that "black is beautiful." American whites do not manifest a comparable group feeling. Evidence indicates that **persons who exhibit strong group identification, participate more actively** (Verba & Nie, 1972; Verba, Nie & Kim, 1971; Buffalo Survey, 1968). As mentioned earlier, blacks generally are somewhat less likely to participate than whites in politics (especially true in the past); but if one considers those blacks who regard their "blackness" as salient, they are more likely to participate. Although higher socioeconomic blacks tend to be more conscious of their black identity, the relationship between group feelings and political participation seems to be independent of the influence of socioeconomic factors.

In a study of Southern blacks in the United States, a related concept—"racial pride and confidence"—correlated significantly with political participation. "Feelings of racial inadequacy do not seem appreciably to reduce Negro voting rates, but they do diminish the frequency with which Negroes participate beyond the voting stage. A sense of racial inferiority is largely incompatible with high levels of political activism" (Matthews & Prothro, 1966, p. 298). Similar data pertaining to a deprived group in India, the untouchables, support these generalizations (Verba, Ahmed & Bhatt, 1971).

Political Efficacy Feelings The feeling of political efficacy is one of the most widely discussed concepts in political science. Developed by the Survey Research Center at the University of Michigan, the concept continues to be employed as a predictor and/or correlate of a wide variety of behaviors and orientations, among them political participation in conventional and unconventional modes. Political efficacy is the *feeling* that one is capable of influencing the public decision-making process. When a person *believes* that he can influence government officials or public issues, he is said to be subjectively efficacious or competent. The political efficacy concept also appears under such guises as "political competence," "civic competence" and "citizen efficacy" and inversely as "political incapability," "political futility," and "political powerlessness." These terms will be used interchangeably below.

Two somewhat different operationalizations of the concept have been popular in the literature, one developed by the Michigan team (Campbell, Gurin & Miller, 1954), and the other by Almond and Verba in their five-nation survey (1963). Whereas the Michigan scale tended more to tap the belief that institutions are responsive to citizen pressure, the scale developed by Almond and Verba highlighted the belief that the respondent himself has the personal capacity to wield influence. The Michigan team used five "agree–disagree" items: (1) "I don't think public officials care very much what people like me think"; (2) "The way people vote is the main thing that decides how things are run in this country"; (3) "Voting is the only way that people like me can have any say about how the government runs things"; (4) "People like me don't have any say about what the government does"; and (5) "Sometimes politics and government seem so complicated that a person like me can't really understand what is going on." In the Almond-Verba operationalization, a hypothetical situation was presented to the respondent: "Suppose a regulation were being considered by (town or village government) that you considered very unjust or harmful. What do you think you could do?" If the respondent answered that he could do something, he was queried about "the likelihood that he would do something," about "the likelihood that he would succeed," and whether "he had actually done anything to try to influence a decision."* (See Appendix for full language.)

The relationship between feelings of efficacy and conventional political participation is among the most widely documented ones. It has been found over and over again that **persons who feel efficacious participate at a higher level than those who lack such feelings.** The evidence comes from many different national samples taken at different times (Agger, Goldstein & Pearl, 1961; Almond & Verba, 1963, all five nations; Campbell, et al., 1960; Erbe, 1964; Dahl, 1961; Di Palma, 1970; Finifter, 1970; Barnes, 1966, Italian data; Muller, 1970a; Dean, 1960; Olsen, 1969; Goel, 1975, Indian samples; Thompson & Horton, 1960; Welch, Comer & Steinman, 1973, Nebraska Mexican-American sample; Dennis, 1970; Tessler, 1972, North African study; Sallach, Babchuk & Booth, 1972; Hamilton, 1971; Baker, 1973, Germany; Matthews & Prothro, 1966; Verba & Nie, 1972; Lane, 1959; Milbrath, 1971a; Cataldo & Kellstedt, 1968). With the exception of only a few studies (Sallach, et al., 1972; Olsen, 1972), most research shows a positive correlation even

---

* In a secondary analysis of the five-nation data, Muller (1972a) has demonstrated that there are at least two dimensions to the concept of political competence, and that these dimensions can be defined cross nationally by equivalent measures. In a similar fashion, Converse (1972) discusses two forms of political efficacy in the Michigan Survey Research Center scale: (1) trust in system responsiveness, and (2) personal feelings of political competence.

after variation due to socioeconomic variables has been taken into account. Thus a sense of efficacy is shown to be a powerful independent determinant of political activism.

Although a feeling of efficacy facilitates participation in nearly all types of political activity, some variation can be discerned. Generally, efficacy scales show a stronger relationship with gladiatorial activities—campaigning, community involvement, writing letters, joining a club—than with spectator activities—voting, wearing a button, flying the flag (Verba & Nie, 1972; Milbrath, 1971b). This is to be expected, for spectator activities do not depend on personal motivation to the same extent as more demanding activities do. Protestors score above the average on sense of efficacy and self-esteem (Milbrath, 1971b; Hunt & Goel, 1976). This finding calls into question a common view that protesting stems from feelings of powerlessness and isolation (Ransford, 1968).

If feelings of efficacy increase political participation, might it not also be true that opportunities for participation increase one's sense of competence. This point has been argued by several authors and seems highly plausible (Dahl, 1961; Muller, 1970a; Barnes, 1966; Almond & Verba, 1963). Favorable interactions with authorities are likely to enhance one's sense of political competence; unfavorable interactions could lead to feelings of futility. It is hard to infer causality in social science research. The safest inference is that **political participation and subjective competence are positively related. An increase in the level of one is accompanied by an increase in the level of the other.** Perhaps, as Dahl (1961) hypothesized, participation in politics and feelings of efficacy feed on each other, producing a circularity of effects. Persons with middle-class resources are more likely to participate in politics and more likely feel efficacious about political action. Their political participation probably increases their sense of efficacy, and their sense of efficacy, in turn, probably increases their participation. In contrast, persons with working-class resources are less likely to participate in politics and less likely to feel efficacious about political action. Their failure to participate contributes to their sense of political impotence, and their lack of a sense of efficacy increases the probability that they will not participate (Dahl, 1961). This reasoning receives indirect support from another study, which found that *persons who were personally contacted by a canvasser were more likely to feel efficacious than those not so contacted* (Eldersveld, 1956).

What factors tend to develop a sense of efficacy in a person? Several studies have shown that attitudes of efficacy are acquired early in childhood and form part of a child's general sense of mastery over his environment (Easton & Dennis, 1967; Almond & Verba, 1963). **Persons able to participate in family affairs while young are more likely to develop feelings of efficacy in later life** (Almond & Verba, 1963). A number of scholars have investigated the connection between social factors and efficacy. The evidence is overwhelming that **feelings of efficacy are disproportionately found among those with higher objective social positions,** i.e., higher education, higher income, and higher occupational status. The positive relationship between education and sense of competence is particularly striking and holds in a variety of cultures (Almond & Verba, 1963, all five-nations; Campbell, Gurin & Miller, 1954; Campbell, et al., 1960; Dahl, 1961; Litt, 1963; Lane, 1959; Finifter, 1970; Barnes, 1966, Italian sample; Nandy, 1974, Indian data; Goel, 1975, Indian samples; Di Palma, 1970; Olsen, 1969; Thompson & Horton, 1960; Erbe, 1964; Agger, Goldstein & Pearl, 1961; Milbrath, 1971b; Verba & Nie, 1972).

The relationship of race to political efficacy should be intrepreted cautiously. Studies have shown that in general blacks exhibit a greater sense of powerlessness than whites; but this relationship is mainly a function of education, for when comparisons are made between races for the same educational categories, blacks feel no less efficacious than whites (Finifter, 1970; Buffalo Survey, 1968). Women have been found to feel less competent than men, and less critical of the operation of the political system (Almond & Verba, 1963; Finifter, 1970; Campbell, Gurin & Miller, 1954; Olsen, 1969). Age does not show a consistent relationship to a sense of efficacy.

In several countries *a greater percentage of respondents has been found to feel efficacious in relation to local government than to national government* (Almond & Verba, 1963, all five nations; Goel, 1970b, 1975). This difference reflects the proximity and general accessibility of local government in comparison to national government. Some evidence also suggests, however, that this generalization may not apply to minorities in the United States, like Mexican-Americans and blacks who may view local government as oppressive (Welch, Comer & Steinman, 1973).

Certain personality traits and attitudinal variables have been correlated with efficacy, as well. **Persons who are psychologically involved** in politics, and who score high on political information, are more likely to have developed a sense of efficacy (Verba & Nie, 1972; Lane, 1959; Buffalo Survey, 1968). A sense of efficacy is part of a general personality syndrome which includes such traits as self-esteem, ego strength, sociability, and personal control. A lack of feelings of efficacy often is associated with alienation: persons who feel powerless are also likely to feel estranged from the political system, and to distrust both political institutions and their leadership. This is a topic of the next section.

Alienation, Cynicism, Distrust Alienation has been thoroughly discussed by such famous social and political thinkers as Marx, Durkheim, and Weber. In Europe in the nineteenth century Marx was concerned about the dehumanization of individuals in an economic system where the means of production were separated from their ownership. Durkheim used the term "anomie" to describe the effects of social disintegration and loss of values in nineteenth century French society. Weber extended Marx's idea of "separation" to the modern professional worker in a bureaucratic system. In recent years in America many social scientists have built on these theories to interpret modern American society (Erich Fromm, 1955; David Riesman, 1950; Robert Merton, 1957; and C. Wright Mills, 1951).

Whereas earlier sociological studies in Europe and the United States focused on the fate of the individual in the wake of industrialization and materialism, political science studies have been more concerned with the fate and survivability of regimes. Most of this literature appears under such terminology as political efficacy, legitimacy, diffuse support, trust, and system allegiance. In a 1967 article, Easton and Dennis listed some thirty articles and books dealing with political efficacy and its correlates. Our examination disclosed that that list can be considerably updated. Alienation also has been studied extensively as a correlate of political violence.

It is not easy to define alienation; the difficulty stems from the fact that alienation is an extremely fashionable concept loosely used to refer to all sorts of negative attitudes about society in general and the political system in particular. Several writers have attempted to dissect the concept into its component parts. For instance, Seeman (1959) outlined five components of alienation: powerlessness, meaninglessness, normlessness, isolation, and self-estrangement. Finifter (1970) presented a four-fold scheme: specifically political powerlessness, political meaninglessness, political normlessness, and political isolation. Similar approaches to the subject matter appear in works by Dean (1960); Neal and Rettig (1967); Olsen (1969); Allardt (1970); Gamson (1968); and Nandy (1974).

Political alienation may be defined as deep-seated and relatively enduring feelings of estrangement, rejection, negativism, and unhappiness with the political system or its salient parts. People who feel alienated reject the political system as unworthy of their support. In contrast, allegiant citizens evaluate the system positively and believe that it has a proper claim to their obedience and support. Two referents of political alienation may be specified: (1) alienation with respect to the regime (normlessness), and (2) alienation with respect to the existing government and the leadership and/or the policies that they pursue (cynicism). Each variant will be discussed in turn.

Political Normlessness Normlessness or anomie is usually defined as a lack of or conflict among norms. Political normlessness is a questioning or rejection of the basic principles and institutions of the political system. It is a feeling that the rules of the game (constitutional order) are a sham, fraudulent, or unworkable for solving societal problems. In a democratic political system, anomic persons perceive that elections and partisan conflict are meaningless, and may believe that elections and parties do more harm than good. Normlessness occurs in other polities with different norms, but different criteria would be used to discover anomic beliefs. Thus, in a communist-type system, rejection of the Communist Party as the control institution suggests alienation. *The "transitional" or emerging polities, where old values have broken down but the new ones have not taken a firm hold, are likely to contain many more anomic citizens than the more established, modern polities* (Dean, 1960; Struening & Richardson, 1965; Keniston, 1965; Nandy, 1974; Finifter, 1970; Di Palma, 1970).

No completely satisfactory measuring scale for this concept is available. A short anomie scale developed by Srole (1956) has been used in several studies, but it lays heavy emphasis on personal life situations rather than on attitudes toward political objects.[1]

---

[1] The reader may wish to consult the measuring device developed by Citrin, et al., (1975)

Political Cynicism and Distrust Another variant of alienation consists of feelings of distrust in the government and political leadership of the country. "Trusting" citizens are more likely to believe that governmental activity tends to improve conditions, that politics is not all dirty, and that public officials work for citizen welfare. In contrast, "untrusting" citizens tend to feel that people are often manipulated by politicians, that a country's leadership is corrupt and self-serving, and that special interests wield too much power. Arthur Miller defines political trust this way:

> Political trust can be thought of as a basic evaluative or affective orientation toward the government . . . the dimension of trust runs from high trust to high distrust or political cynicism. Cynicism thus refers to the degree of negative affect toward the government and is a statement about the belief that the government is not functioning and producing outputs in accord with individual expectations (A. Miller, 1974a, p. 952).

The level of political trust is more likely to fluctuate than feelings of normlessness. Political trust rises in "good" times and decreases in "bad" times. For example, during and after the Watergate scandal in the United States, the level of political trust was sharply eroded. Yet most people continued to believe in the basic soundness of the American system of government, which helps explain the smooth transition of power from the Nixon administration to the Ford administration in 1974. A prolonged period of distrust can, of course, lead to questioning and even rejection of constitutional norms (i. e., to normlessness as used here).

Political cynicism has been measured several ways; as one example, the University of Michigan Center for Political Studies has regularly used a battery of five questions to measure political cynicism: (1) "How much of the time do you think you can trust the government in Washington to do what is right?"; (2) "Would you say the government is pretty much run by a few big interests looking out for themselves or that it is run for the benefit of all the people?"; (3) "Do you think that people in government waste a lot of the money we pay in taxes, waste some of it or don't waste very much of it?"; (4) "Do you feel that almost all of the people running the government are smart people who usually know what they are doing, or do you think that quite a few of them don't seem to know what they are doing?" and, (5) "Do you think that quite a few of the people running the government are a little crooked, not very many are, or do you think hardly any of them are crooked at all?" Through factor analysis, and Guttman scaling techniques, these five items have been demonstrated to form a single dimension (A. Miller, 1974a).*

Normlessness toward a regime and cynicism toward leaders although interrelated, are conceptually distinct. Individuals may accord legitimacy to the regime but distrust leaders. Support for institutions is to be distinguished from support of leaders, for as Gamson (1968) says, "It is possible for individuals simultaneously to feel high confidence in political institutions and alienation toward the incumbents who man them." Readers are alerted that the distinction we have made is not readily visible in much of the literature; "political distrust," "cynicism," "lack of faith in the system" are often used to include both distrust of the basic system and of the leadership in charge at a particular time.

The important question is: How do these orientations affect political participation? The answer to this question will be discussed first by examining the relationship between alienation and *conventional* political participation, and then between alienation and *unconventional* political participation. When one considers the first relationship, studies show *that negative evaluations about the political system are associated with low levels of political action* (Dean, 1960; Almond & Verba, 1963; Di Palma, 1970; Thompson & Horton, 1960; Templeton, 1966; Agger, Goldstein & Pearl, 1961). This generalization needs to be qualified to some degree, however.

Erbe (1964), using a second-order partialling operation on data drawn from three midwestern towns found that the correlation between alienation and political participation disappeared when SES and involvement in nonpolitical organizations were held constant. This finding should not be interpreted to mean that alienation does not affect participation in politics; it could mean simply that environmental factors like organizational participation and SES are important for developing alienated or nonalienated attitudes. Another set of studies suggests that persons living in communities with urban political machines are more likely to develop cynical attitudes toward political participation. *The longer the residence*

---

*The interested student may also wish to consult a somewhat more elaborate operationalization of a trust scale by Muller (1970b). He constructed a pool of 24 items to measure the degree to which government officials as well as the police and the courts were perceived as using power "honestly, justly, and benevolently."

in the machine-dominated city, the greater the cynicism (Levin, 1960; Litt, 1963).

In another sample drawn from a midwestern city, Olsen (1969) correlated two measures of alienation ("incapability" and "discontentment") with political participation. Those who felt incapable were less likely to act politically, but discontentment showed no relationship. Finifter's analysis (1970) of a national probability sample showed no significant association between "perceived political normlessness" and political activism. Similarly, in another analysis of national election data, cynical respondents did not show any less involvement in presidential and congressional campaigns than those who scored high on a trust in government scale (Citrin, 1974).

How do we account for these dissimilar, if not contradictory, findings? One explanation lies in the conceptual vagueness about the independent variable; alienation has been defined and measured differently by researchers, thus making comparability hazardous. Another reason may lie in the changing socioeconomic correlates of political alienation. Several studies have shown that lower SES positions, especially lower levels of education, are positively correlated with alienation and distrust (Agger, Goldstein & Pearl, 1961; Thompson & Horton, 1960; Templeton, 1966; Kornhauser, Sheppard & Mayer, 1956). Lower SES, as we know, is associated with lower participation rates. However, recent evidence from the United States suggests even though a strong relationship between low status and alienation may have characterized the 1950s and earlier decades, in the sixties and seventies *the alienated are as likely to come from higher SES groups as from the lower ones* (Schwartz, 1973; Citrin et al., 1975; Aberbach & Walker, 1970). Whether this development will become an enduring feature of American society is, of course, still to be seen.

Almond and Verba (1963) have popularized a unitary conception of modern man: those who are educated, knowledgeable, subjectively efficacious, and politically participant are also more allegiant as well as more benign toward political authorities.[2] These findings, however, are not universally applicable. In a study of six developing nations (Argentina, Chile, former East Pakistan or Bangladesh, India, Israel, and Nigeria),

---

[2] Di Palma's analysis (1970) of the same data (which were gathered in 1959–1960) also corroborated that "system commitment," "system satisfaction," and "system proximity" are orientations more commonly prevalent among people with high education, high-status occupations, and high income.

Inkeles (1969) found that the "participant" or "good citizen" was more hostile and less patriotic. He defined "good citizen" as a person who is informed and interested in politics, is more likely to identify with the national state in competition with the primary social units, participates in civic matters, and supports the use of rational rules as a basis of government. Inkeles found a strong correlation between education and good citizenship. However, the good or the participant citizen is not necessarily more satisfied, more loyal or less hostile.[3] Thus the relationship between socioeconomic factors and political satisfaction is time- as well as context-bound. No simple explanation to account for these differentials can be advanced. Obviously, the socialization process that goes on in schools and colleges has something to do with it. The economic position of the educated persons in relation to other members of the society also may have some relevance. A depressed economic condition among the educated can lead to the anti-system bias. Unhappiness with particular government policies is also a source of political dissatisfaction. The conduct of the Vietnam War and the Watergate scandal in the United States are obvious cases in point.

In the United States, not surprisingly, **blacks are more distrustful of politics than are whites;** this is true at all socioeconomic levels (Citrin, et al., 1975; Aberbach & Walker, 1970; Buffalo Survey, 1968; Finifter, 1970; A. Miller, 1974a). In general, *women tend to be less cynical of government and politics than men* (Almond & Verba, 1963; Finifter, 1970). Age shows no uniform pattern with alienation. In a study conducted in the San Francisco Bay Area, Citrin et al. (1975) found that age correlated positively with political trust; the older the person the more trustful he was of government. This finding contradicts two earlier studies which showed that older persons were more likely to feel cynical and alienated from politics than younger persons (Agger, Goldstein & Pearl, 1961; Kornhauser, Sheppard & Mayer, 1956). It is conceivable that over the decade of the sixties young people moved from political trust to cynicism.

The five-nation study showed differences in alienation by national political cultures. The highest percentages of alienated persons were found in Italy and Mexico; Great Britain and Germany were at an inter-

---

[3] The lack of a relationship between high status and positive orientations toward the political system in India has also been reported by Eldersveld, Jagannadham & Barnabas (1968), and Goel (1970b), and in Japan by Kuroda (1965b) and Richardson (1973).

mediate level; and the lowest percentage was in the United States (Almond & Verba, 1963, p. 99). Political alienation seemed to be related to general attitudes of social trust and distrust; those who had faith in people tended also to exhibit politically relevant trust (p. 285). Persons living in Great Britain and the United States were most likely to have attitudes of social trust, Germans were the next most likely, while the Italians and Mexicans were least likely (p. 267). The close correspondence between attitudes of social trust and political trust most clearly held in the United States and the United Kingdom; in the other three nations there was less correlation between social and political trust (Almond & Verba, 1963, p. 287).*

Americans have traditionally shown a high degree of confidence in their political system and its leadership. Top leaders, such as supreme court justices, cabinet members, and senators, are usually accorded high status (Bell, Hill & Wright, 1961). In another study, "politicians" were near the bottom of the scale, ahead only of used-car salesmen (Rotter & Stein, 1971). These studies suggest that in the recent past the American public perceived its top leaders more as "statesmen" than as "politicians." McCloskey (1964) showed that nine out of ten Americans agreed that "I usually have confidence that the government will do what is right." In a 1964 Wisconsin survey, about two out of three respondents reported support for the American party system by agreeing to "democracy works best where competition between parties is strong" (Dennis, 1966).

These support and trust levels in the United States, however, have been dramatically eroding from the mid-1960s onward. On several indicators, political cynicism has increased, as the data reported in Table 3-3 demonstrate. The sharpest decline in trust took place between 1972 and 1974, an obvious consequence of the Watergate scandal. Analysis of data by the Michigan Center for Political Studies also reveals that the rise in cynicism is related to the discrepancy that many Americans have come to feel between their policy preferences and those that the government pursues. Right and left extremists are more cynical than those Americans who prefer centrist policies (A. Miller, 1974a).

Comparable data from other nations are hard to find. In India, about half the respondents in a 1969 four-state survey accorded legitimacy to the Indian system of government (Nandy, 1974). A Gallup poll in India in 1967

---

* The close correspondence between social and political trust was not found in two American studies (Aberbach & Walker, 1970; Schwartz, 1973).

Table 3-3. Level of Political Cynicism in the United States, 1964–1974.

Percentage Who Feel That	1964	1966	1968	1970	1972[a]	1974[a]
Government in Washington can be trusted only some of the time	22	31	37	44	45	61
Government is run by a few big interests	29	34	39	50	53	65
People in government waste a lot of tax money	46	—	57	69	66	74
Public officials don't know what they are doing	27	—	36	44	40	45
Quite a lot of public officials are crooked	28	—	25	31	36	45

Data are adapted from Arthur Miller, "Political Issues and Trust in Government: 1964–1970," *American Political Science Review*, 68:3 (September, 1974), p. 953. The data are based on election surveys conducted by the University of Michigan Center for Political Studies.
[a]Figures for years 1972 and 1974 were received via personal communication with Arthur Miller.

showed a little more than half the respondents feeling that they can do something to counteract an unfair local regulation (Goel, 1970b, 1975). In Japan, inconsistent patterns were found by Richardson (1974); in general, evaluation of specific political leaders was higher than of politics in general. Japanese citizens were more satisfied (41 percent) with the performance of local government than with national government (13 percent). On a regime-related question, nearly 80 percent of the electorate in one major city felt that the vote was "an important basic right" and a majority of the same group opposed the idea that "elections are meaningless" (p. 69). In a 1961 poll, 61.2 percent gave an efficacious response to the item, "The people's vote decides the operation of the nation's affairs," but in another survey only 30 percent said that "The people have some effect on the machinations of politics" (Richardson, 1974). Once again, caution is recommended in comparing percentages across nations; item wordings, respondent's frame of reference, and differences in the timing of surveys make comparison hazardous.

Alienation and Unconventional Political Participation Does alienation lead to protest and violence? From Marx to Marcuse writers have argued that alienation and estrangement are basic causes of revolutions.

Kornhauser (1959) contends in *The Politics of Mass Society* that individuals in an atomized mass society develop feelings of value loss and become vulnerable to, or "available for," extremist mobilization and radical political action. Rudimentary empirical data support this argument. Kerr and Siegel found that wildcat strikes were more common among isolated labor groups such as mining and maritime workers. These isolated occupational groups are believed to have weaker ties to the prevailing democratic norms so that discontent is more likely to be expressed through extremist action than through normal channels (Kerr & Siegel, 1954; Lipset, 1960). In a study of school bond issues, those who felt powerless and isolated in community affairs voted in lower numbers, but these people also were more likely to cast protest votes—a "no" vote on a bond issue being a protest against the existing power structure (Thompson & Horton, 1960).*

If alienation can induce radical action as well as apathy and withdrawal, additional evidence should be introduced to determine when one or the other will occur. It may be hypothesized that *when political distrust is combined with feelings of efficacy, the result is likely to be protest against the system; when, on the other hand, distrust is combined with feelings of inefficacy, the consequence is likely to be withdrawal from politics.*** The low efficacy–low trust combination likely leads to withdrawal from participation, for why get involved when one's actions have such a low probability of influence. Those who have both efficacious and trustful orientations are likely to choose conventional modes of participation because they are perceived as producing the desired outcomes. In contrast, the efficacious-mistrustful persons may be inclined toward radical action because such action is perceived as both necessary and possible. Those who trust political leadership but doubt their own capacity for political influence most likely engage in supportive and ritualistic activities (voting, flying the flag, enlisting, and so on). These hypothesized relationships between alienation, efficacy, and political participation are charted in Figure 3-5.

As shown previously, feelings of efficacy are positively correlated with SES. If such feelings are necessary for radical activism, it also is likely that

---

* Crain, Katz, & Rosenthal (1969) have argued for a modification of the Kornhauser hypothesis on mass politics by showing that even the pluralistic communities are not protected from extremism, as witnessed in the anti-water-fluoridation movements in the United States. For a critique of the mass society theory, also see Pinard (1968).

** This thesis is an adaptation of the one developed by Gamson (1968), who connected efficacy-mistrust to all forms of activism—conventional and unconventional.

Figure 3-1. Modes of Political Participation Related to Efficacy and Alienation.

		TRUST	
		HIGH	LOW
EFFICACY	HIGH	Active, Allegiant and Conventional Participation	Radical Action or Unconventional Participation
	LOW	Supportive, Patriotic & Ritualistic Participation (e.g., voting, joining a parade, enlisting, etc.)	Withdrawl from Politics

the better educated, the more sophisticated, the more informed (the higher SES persons) are more inclined toward protesting. Two factors may be responsible for the greater protest involvement of individuals with higher than average SES: such individuals are likely to feel less vulnerable to the social and economic reprisals which the system can bring forth against them; and such persons possess resources—education, organizational skills, information—which facilitate their participation in radical activities. The following review of literature demonstrates some support for this line of reasoning. (The generalizations below apply to both blacks and whites.)

In the Buffalo Survey (1968) which examined both conventional and unconventional political participation, protesting was found more frequently among blacks and among young people. A slight but consistent tendency was found for protestors to be of higher socioeconomic status (correlation about .20). The protestors felt slightly more efficacious (.12) and were more interested in political matters than the average. They were considerably more knowledgeable about the political world as well as more cosmopolitan than the average respondent in the sample. Many protestors saw no contradiction between protesting and being patriotic. Protesting

Figure 3-2. Selected Sociological and Psychological Characteristics of Protestors.

> More likely to be black
> Younger
> Slightly more likely to be male
> Somewhat higher status than average
> Somewhat more than average interest in politics
> Very high information level
> Slightly more than average efficacy
> Slightly more than average self-esteem
> Very dissatisified with government

Data are derived from the Buffalo Survey (1968).

and dissatisfaction with governmental performance were positively correlated; the protestors tended to view government as highly ineffective in performing its activities and also assigned it very heavy responsibility to solve many problems. These characteristics are summarized in Figure 3-2.

A study of black students in southern Negro colleges reveals a similar pattern. Students who took part in sit-ins and marches were not typical of the student body. The higher the socioeconomic status of the student's family, the more likely his participation in demonstrations. The typical protesting student was not depressed, withdrawn and uninformed, but optimistic, knowledgeable and confident; he was also more discontented with the lot of black people in general, as well as less trustful of the institutions which had produced these conditions (Matthews & Prothro, 1966, pp. 416–424; also see Orbell, 1967). In another survey, 503 adults in Waterloo, Iowa, were interviewed with respect to their readiness to resort to extremist tactics to register their disapproval of government policies. Distrust in political authorities and belief in the effectiveness of past violence correlated with readiness to protest. The largest single correlation (-.464) was that persons less trusting of leaders had greater potential for political violence (Muller, 1972).

The finding that political distrust may instigate radical action finds further support in a 1967 Detroit study. Positive answers to the question "Can you imagine a situation in which you would riot?" were more frequently given by cynical persons than by non-cynical ones. "Distrust clearly stimulates a willingness to engage in violence or favorable predis-

Table 3-4. Efficacy and Dissatisfaction Related to Political Participation[a].

| | | "Attended Civil Rights Rally" | | "Participated in a Demonstration" | | "Membership in NAACP" | |
| | | Efficacy | | Efficacy | | Efficacy | |
		Low	High	Low	High	Low	High
Relative deprivation (or dissatisfaction)	Low	10.4%	41.5	3.8%	17.1	6.4%	34.8
	High	20.6	40.5	15.5	28.2	10.1	18.8

[a]Table entries are percentages taking the action, percentages not taking the action are not shown.
Data are derived from Thomas J. Crawford and Murray Naditch, "Relative Deprivation, Powerlessness and Militancy: The Psychology of Social Protest," *Psychiatry,* 33:2 (1970), pp. 220-221. Data have been recombined and relabeled.

poses people toward voting for the extremist candidates" (Aberbach & Walker, 1970, p. 1213). Further corroboration is found in the Sears and McConahay (1973) study of self-claimed activists in the Watts riots of 1965. The respondents who admitted high activity in riots tended to be native born Californians rather than immigrants from the rural South, were somewhat better educated, more politically sophisticated, as well as more optimistic about the future and their own personal capabilities.

Some confirmation of the efficacy-mistrust and extremist-action hypothesis is provided by Crawford and Naditch (1970) in an analysis of the 1966 National Opinion Research Center survey of 1624 Negro men and women. Crawford and Naditch sought to relate feelings of personal efficacy (internal-external control) and dissatisfaction (relative deprivation operationalized by Cantril's self-anchoring striving scale[4]) with conventional and unconventional political participation. We will presume that relative deprivation is a rough indicator of political distrust, since it is normal for those who believe they are not so well off as others to blame it on the government and political leadership. If this assumption is valid, the data summarized in Table 3-4 are interesting. Of the measures utilized, "attending a civil rights rally" and "NAACP membership" are forms of conventional

---

[4] Cantril (1965) presents a picture of a ten-rung ladder to respondents and asks them to imagine the top of the ladder as the best possible life and the bottom of the ladder as the worst. They are then asked to judge where they personally stand on the ladder at the present time. See Appendix for details.

political participation; on both these measures, those high on personal efficacy and low on dissatisfaction have the highest percentage active among those engaging in each behavior: 41.5 percent for attending a civil rights rally and 34.8 percent for membership in NAACP.

In contrast, those having demonstrated are most likely found among those feeling efficacious dissatisfied.

Additional support for the efficacy-mistrust and extremist-action hypothesis is available. In one study, Schwartz (1973) analyzed data from several surveys and came to the following conclusion: When SES is controlled, the upper and middle classes (who tend to feel efficacious) are likely to express their alienation through vigorous action and the lower and working classes through withdrawal. He writes:

> Upper and upper-middle class individuals, for example, seem more likely to play out the alienation in active modes such as reformism or rebelliousness, because they have the resources and the relative economic and social invulnerability to do so and because they have learned norms of civic duty and participation that would make withdrawal, for example, a nonvalued option (Schwartz, 1973, p. 23).

In another study, a group of young black students was surveyed during and after the 1967 Detroit riots (Forward & Williams, 1970). Those who offered a favorable evaluation of the Detroit uprising had achieved a slightly higher grade point average, and came from better educated families than their counterparts. Psychological characteristics distinguished the young black militant from his cohorts; the young militants were more confident about their own capabilities and did not accept the stereotype that the ghetto conditions were a result of their own inherent weaknesses rather than outside forces. "Compared with non-militants, the riot supporters have very strong beliefs in their ability to control events in their own lives and to shape their own future" (Forward and Williams, 1970, p. 88).

This review of the literature supports the alienation-extremism hypothesis: **the likelihood of extremist action against the government will be highest when the level of trust in political institutions and its leadership is low.** This review also indicates that **those most likely to participate in unconventional, extremist behavior are not depressed, ignorant, and low class; instead they tend to be better educated,**

more sophisticated, more interested in politics, more knowledgeable about it, and more subjectively efficacious about their personal capabilities. (Support for these propositions comes from the studies reviewed above as well as from Fogelson, 1971; Masotti & Bowen, 1968; A. Miller, 1974a; Tomlinson, 1970b; Dizard, 1970; Muller, 1970b; Levy, 1970; Caplan, 1970; Eisinger, 1974; Kubota, 1975; Kaase, 1975; Citrin, et al., 1975.)

PARTICIPATION AS A FUNCTION OF PERSONALITY It is not easy to establish clear and reliable connections between personality and political behavior. This problem stems from two kinds of difficulties. First, it is difficult to measure personality: it is not accessible to direct measurement, it can only be inferred from behavior. Such inferences are complicated by lack of clear correspondence between manifestation and personality. Seemingly identical acts by different individuals may spring from different personality needs, and seemingly different acts may spring from the same personality needs.

Second, the impact of personality on behavior is mediated through beliefs and attitudes, which also are influenced by cognitions and cognitive learning. The relationship of all these variables, as the authors conceive them, can be seen in Figure 1-3 (p. 26). The "distance" of personality from behavior means that the impact of personality forces on behavior is often more latent than manifest; it may come forth strongly in some situations and have almost no influence in others. Robert Lane, one of the foremost scholars of personality and political behavior, takes this perspective:

> Some situations so clearly structure behavior; some roles leave so little room for personal choice; and some social norms are so unambiguous that personal differences have little effect upon behavior. On the other hand some situations afford considerable "scope" for personality to affect behavior. Among these are the following:
>   Situations where reference groups have politically conflicting points of view.
>   Situations at the focus of conflicting propaganda.
>   Current situations which for any individual are in conflict with previous experience.

Situations where social roles are ambiguous, strange, and unfamiliar.

Some types of behavior are less likely to offer scope for the expression of personal differences. These would, by and large, include the more conventional items, such as voting, expressing patriotic opinions, and accepting election results as final, at least temporarily. On the other hand, those types of expression which are more likely to reveal the idiosyncratic features of personality include:

Selection of the grounds for rationalizing a political act.

Selecting topics for political discussion.

Selecting types of political behavior over and above voting.

Expression of the probable consequences of participation.

Holding particular images of other participants.

Styles of personal interaction in political groups (Lane, 1959, pp. 99–100).*

Personality is a complicated, interrelated, and interacting system. The study of a complete personality, such as might be carried out by a psychoanalyst, is time-consuming and requires special training. Case studies of this type show rather convincingly how personality affects political behavior (Smith, Bruner & White, 1956; Lane, 1962), but the time costs of such studies are so great that it is difficult to get enough cases to arrive at generalizations that one can be confident would hold for the great mass of people. Furthermore, the personality dynamics leading to a political act are so complex as to defy succinct summarization. Consequently, no attempt is made in this book to summarize psychoanalytic or depth studies of personality and political behavior.

Personality also can be studied, in somewhat more piecemeal fashion, by using scales to measure specific personality traits. The methods of trait psychology enable one to administer scales and tests to large numbers of people and to establish statistical relationships between traits and behavior patterns. The discussion to follow depends mainly on

---

* Greenstein (1969, pp. 40–62) discusses a similar, albeit more elaborate, list of situations where personal variability is manifested in political behavior.

the findings of trait psychology. These are uneven in coverage: certain traits have been well investigated, while others are neglected. These findings also are difficult to interpret because of the measurement difficulties mentioned above. Failure to discover a relationship between a trait and behavior may mean that, in fact, there is no relationship, but also it may mean that the researcher's measuring tool does not measure what he hoped it was measuring. If a researcher finds no correlation between a cynicism scale and political activity, it may mean that, in reality, there is no relationship, but it also may mean that either his measure of cynicism or his measure of activity is faulty. Conversely, finding a relationship may not be proof of its existence; relationships can appear as an artifact of measurement bias, such as response set. One must question the assumption that a scale measures what the designer intended it to. In this section, syndromes of traits are discussed rather than specific scales. If similar results are discovered when similar, but not identical, scales are administered to different samples, one has increased confidence that a relationship does in fact exist between a trait and political behavior (Campbell & Fiske, 1959).

An examination of research studies indicates that the study of personality in relation to political behavior has not been a fertile undertaking, at least not so in comparison with the study of sociodemographic and attitudinal determinants. Whatever research is available is limited mostly to the first six categories in the following listing: (1) extraversion, sociability, friendliness, and the like; (2) ego strength, competence, self-confidence; (3) assertiveness, aggressiveness, dominance; (4) authoritarianism, dogmatism; (5) personality needs (Maslow's need hierarchy); (6) anomie, alienation; (7) achievement motivation, creativity; (8) flexibility, adaptability; (9) empathy, relational closeness; (10) morality, super-ego strength; (11) high energy level; and (12) planning, future orientation.[5] These are working categories and cannot be made exhaustive nor mutually exclusive. Even though we only discuss the first six categories in this book, a longer list is presented in hopes of stimulating further work on the remaining clusters. The anomie-alienation syndrome was discussed under attitudes; the other five will be discussed here. Two excellent books by Greenstein (1969) and Knutson (1973) have each made a plea for greater focus on personality related political behavior

---

[5] Some of the clusters are based on a list developed by Reddy and Smith (1972).

research, but perhaps it is too soon for these treatises to have had much generative impact.

Sociability, Extraversion   It has been observed many times that politicians are glad-handing extroverts. Does it follow that a sociable personality is a prerequisite for political action? Some scholars believe that man has a social need and that filling this need is an important motive for engaging in political actions (Davies, 1963, pp. 34–36). Sociability is here defined as a feeling of ease and graciousness in social relationships; normally, it is accompanied by the possession of effective social skills. A few studies have linked ease in social interactions with political participation. On the basis of limited research available, it can be concluded that **sociable personalities are more likely to enter politics and to take leading roles once they enter it** (Milbrath, 1960a; Milbrath & Klein, 1962; Kuroda, 1967). Participation in social groups is highly correlated with political participation. Gough (1952) found a significant correlation between extraversion and voluntary involvement in a study investigating participation in extracurricular activities among high school students. Martin and Siegel (1953) found that "gregariousness" was positively associated with group participation among a sample of male undergraduate students. In his study of Chilean voluntary organizations Smith (1966) found that various measures of extraversion were positively related with active participation among organization members.

A correlation between sociability and participation could be a mere artifact of the well-known correlation between SES and political participation since SES and sociability are highly correlated. The relationship between sociability and participation, however, continues to be significant even with SES controls. Sociability should be called a necessary but not sufficient condition for entering politics. Many sociable persons do not become active. The reverse is not true, however; a nonsociable person has a barrier to participation in socially interactive political behavior.

A study of opinion leaders found that gregariousness was related to public affairs opinion leadership (Katz & Lazarsfeld, 1955). Some scholars have suggested that while a sociable personality facilitates entry into politics, overly high social aspirations could lead a person away from politics toward more immediately gratifying social activities (Rosenberg, 1954–1955; also Lane, 1959).

Ego Strength, Self-Confidence Self-confidence is closely associated with a sense of civic competence or a feeling of political efficacy—traits that were discussed under attitudes. Persons who are generally self-confident also are likely to feel politically efficacious. Many of the findings discussed under civic competence also hold true here. In general, the conclusion of many studies is that **persons with a sense of confidence are more likely to assume political activist roles** (Lane, 1959; Campbell, et al., 1960; Rosen & Salling, 1971; Gore & Rotter, 1963; Buffalo Survey, 1968).

As might be expected, **persons growing up in an upper-middle or upper-SES environment are more likely to develop self-confidence and feelings of competence than those from a lower SES environment. This is especially characteristic of persons who achieve higher levels of education** (Campbell, et al., 1960; Dahl, 1961; Verba & Nie, 1972). The reader is reminded of Dahl's hypothesis, discussed earlier, that environment and feelings of efficacy have interactive effects on each other. Dahl found that if feelings of efficacy were controlled statistically, the relationship between SES and political participation was no longer statistically significant. This suggests that environment primarily affects political participation through shaping personality traits like sociability and ego strength (Dahl, 1961, pp. 291–292; also Nie, Powell & Prewitt, 1969).

It is also difficult to separate the effects of environment from those of heredity in developing feelings of confidence and effectiveness. The more generously endowed child, who is sensitive and analytical, learns to manipulate successfully the objects and persons in his environment early in life. If he is also well coordinated and successful athletically, his sense of mastery will be enhanced. The rewards of successful manipulation soon build a firm personality trait of self-confidence. A child of this type who also lives in a high SES environment is given many opportunities to encounter and master different types of situations; consequently, he has little fear of social, business, or political challenge. His low SES counterpart, who may be equally gifted, will have less broad familiarity with challenging situations.

One additional bit of evidence bears on this trait. One study found that *persons who score highly on the personal effectiveness scale are less likely to resent government* (Stokes, 1962). One can speculate that persons who feel effective in dealing with their environment also feel effective in dealing with government and, thus, are less inclined to resent government or to feel that it does not respond to their efforts.

Dominance, Manipulativeness, Power Drive It is often supposed that individuals with a personal need for status and power over others naturally gravitate to politics to fulfill their craving. Hobbes and Nietzsche built their political philosophies around this central assumption. In his early writings, notably *Psychopathology and Politics,* Harold Lasswell set forth his famous formula for the developmental sequence of political man. Restating the symbolism of his formula into verbal terms, he said that the private motives, which had been nurtured in the person's early life in the family (especially the motive for power), might become displaced onto public objects. These displaced private motives would tend to be rationalized in terms of the public interest and, thus, ordinary man became transformed into political man. Later Lasswell qualified his position, suggesting that power is a nonprimary motive; considering it the sole or major motive for entering politics was too inflexible an explanation. He thought it more likely that political leaders would seek such values as respect, rectitude, and wealth. If a person did enter politics only to seek power, he would be likely to be restrained by other political actors and might not rise above a lesser position (Lasswell, 1954).

The available empirical evidence on this point (for the United States only) suggests that *persons with high power motivation are not likely to enter politics* (other arenas, such as business or the military, provide better opportunities to dominate others), *and if they do, they are not likely to be very successful at it.*[*] A dominance scale was administered in three studies of political participation (Milbrath, 1960b; Milbrath & Klein, 1962; Jensen, 1960). Only a slight trend appeared for dominants to be more likely to become active in politics, and in only one study was the relationship statistically significant, and that just barely. A study of South Carolina legislators found them only slightly more dominant than a sample from the general population (McConaughy, 1950). A study of officeholders found no correlation between power motive and holding public office (Browning & Jacob, 1964). When only offices with high power or with a clear road to success were considered, the correlation was significant.

---

[*] Lane (1959, pp. 124–128) has an excellent discussion of the belief that political man seeks power and suggests why this supposed relationship is not borne out by the evidence.

The researchers also found a correlation between achievement motive and holding public office in political systems where the office had high achievement potential. In sum, the evidence suggests that a desire for dominance and power provides only a weak attraction toward general political action; only in special cases affording clear use of power (rare in politics) could power be considered a significant or primary motivation.

If additional evidence should confirm that power-hungry persons are not particularly likely to go into politics, how would one explain the lack of relationship? It is quite likely that a certain proportion of any population does develop strong motives for power and that some, but not many, do find their way into politics. A very strong power motive may be the outward manifestation of a deep need for reassurance and a cover for feelings of unworthiness and low self-esteem. We saw above that persons of low ego strength are not likely to enter politics. The person who attaches great importance to imposing his will on others is not likely to be very successful in democratic politics; he may alienate instead of attract followers. He may be unwilling to take orders or to serve menially as a way of working his way up in a political party.

Another factor is that the political arena is not a particularly fruitful place to find fulfillment for power needs; there is too little opportunity for direct satisfaction. The worlds of finance, industry, or the military may be more satisfying to a man with lust for power. For many people, the need for power is most visibly satisfied in primary relationships. Perhaps it is enough for such persons that they can be autocrats in their own homes. There are, then, many other environments, in addition to politics, where the need for power can be satisfied; many of them carry fewer uncertainties than politics.

The desire to manipulate is somewhat different from the desire for power. One study found politicals more willing to compromise than apoliticals (Hennessy, 1959). Another found law students planning to go into politics scoring higher on a manipulative scale than those not planning to enter politics (Agger, 1956a). There is no evidence that political actives necessarily have a desire or need to manipulate, but the willingness to manipulate and the ability to be successful at it probably facilitates entry into politics.

Authoritarianism, Dogmatism Revulsion from nazi-fascist experience before and during World War II has stimulated a great number of studies of authoritarianism[6] and has added a popular word to our vocabulary. All sorts of behaviors and persons are characterized as authoritarian, and this wide usage makes definition of the trait extremely difficult and somewhat arbitrary. An operational definition has not been agreed upon by the academic profession, either. There does seem to be consensus that authoritarians like to issue orders and receive complete and unquestioning obedience. They also tend to be submissive to and unquestioning of persons with authority over them. The central disposition that characterizes an authoritarian personality is the submission-aggression syndrome—submission to those who are above them, and aggression toward those who are below them. An incisive description of this trait in German folklore is caught by the symbolism, the bicyclist's personality—"Above they bow, below they kick" (Greenstein, 1969).

Despite the rash of studies, there is relatively little reliable evidence in the form of substantiated propositions about the impact of authoritarianism on political behavior. Part of the failure stems from inadequate operational definitions and other methodological difficulties. In the early versions of the Fascism (F) scale (the most widely used measure of authoritarianism, developed by Adorno, et al., 1950), all the items were scored positively and were heavily subject to response-set bias. Once this was discovered, new versions, with half the items worded so that they would be scored negatively, were developed. But even the new versions seldom showed a relationship to political behavior. Few attempts at scaling the items by Guttman (1950) techniques have been successful, suggesting that the items make up a syndrome rather than a single trait. After all these years of research, one is still required to say that the concept is not satisfactorily operationalized, no clear and precise definition of the trait (if it is one) can be given, and evidence about the relationship of the concept to political behavior is highly inconclusive.

Because of these factors, a review of the following findings relating authoritarianism to political participation should be taken with a grain of salt and with a wait-and-see attitude. The findings are interesting, even if they are not conclusive. Those relating authoritarianism to direction of

---

[6] Since the publication of *The Authoritarian Personality* (Adorno, et al., 1950), there has been a profusion of studies on the subject: a selected review of literature on authoritarianism through 1956 contained 260 bibliographic references (Christie & Cook, 1958). For a review of later additions, the reader should consult Greenstein (1969), Knutson (1972), and Sanford (1973).

political behavior (which are not reviewed here) are even more extensive than those relevant to political action, but they are no more conclusive.

Christie's version of the F scale with half its items reversed (Christie, Havel & Seidenberg, 1958) was included in the Michigan Survey Research Center's nationwide study of the American electorate in 1956 and, therefore, could be cross-tabulated with a campaign activity index. It showed no significant relationship to that index or to any of the specific political activities incorporated in it. Statistical controls for response set and for education did not succeed in bringing out a relationship. Two other studies found no relationship between authoritarianism and participation in politics (Harned, 1961; Hennessy, 1959).

In contrast, certain other studies show high authoritarians as disinclined to participate in politics. One reported high authoritarians scoring low on efficacy and being less likely to vote (Janowitz & Marvick, 1953). Another found no correlation between authoritarianism and likelihood of voting, but found a slight tendency for authoritarians to be less likely to campaign, to have a lower level of political interest, and to score lower on efficacy (Lane, 1955). A third study found high authoritarians less likely to join groups (we have already seen that group activity and political activity go together) and less likely to participate in politics. Unfortunately, this study used no SES or response-set controls, yet the early version of the F scale used is strongly biased by both factors (Sanford, 1950).

One scholar has suggested that the relationship between authoritarianism and political participation will vary by type of authoritarian being studied. Persons with authoritarianism operating at physical need levels are likely to be nonparticipants, whereas those motivated by unmet affection and esteem needs will take on activist roles (Knutson, 1972). (Psychic needs and how they are related to political participation are discussed below.) To say the least, the findings are ambiguous and inconsistent.

A psychological trait closely related to that of authoritarianism is that of dogmatism (Rokeach, 1960). Dogmatic persons are closed-minded, anxiety prone and have difficulty in incorporating new information. The dogmatism scale is also shown to be part of the psychological deprivation syndrome (Knutson, 1972). The relationship of this attribute to political participation should be of theoretical interest but only a little work has been done in this area. In one study dogmatism and political participation were inversely related: –.15 magnitude (Knutson, 1972). In another study, a sample of Italian legislators was compared with a nonrandom control group (Di Renzo, 1967). The legislators scored higher on dogmatism, suggesting a positive correlation between this trait and political activity. Because of the inadequate control group in the study, more convincing evidence is required before lending high level credibility to generalizations.

If additional data should confirm that high authoritarians are not likely to participate in politics, how could this be explained? Authoritarians, according to the theory, prefer an environment where status relationships are clear and stable, where it is accepted that one follows orders from above and receives obedience from those below. This kind of environment is much less likely to be found in politics than in some other environments, such as a corporate bureaucracy. The political world often is unstructured and ambiguous. This is especially characteristic of United States politics, which is much less structured by political parties than is true of many other societies. Persons who have a low tolerance for ambiguity are likely to be uncomfortable in politics, and it has generally been found that authoritarians have a low tolerance for ambiguity.

Politics often presents a situation in which one person is trying to convince another that he should do a certain thing; compliance usually is obtained by persuasion and not by the application of sanctions. Because of their personality, authoritarians tend not to be skillful or at ease in this type of social interaction. One study found a significant negative correlation between sociability and the F scale (Milbrath & Klein, 1962). All of the above factors suggest why authoritarians might be uncomfortable in democratic politics. Whether they would be attracted to extremist politics (many such movements have rigid leader-follower relationships) is difficult to say; there is no statistical evidence either way.

Personality Needs Maslow's theory of needs is another way of looking at the relationship of personality characteristics to political behavior. Maslow discussed five tiers of needs: (1) physical (hunger, sleep, sex, excretion, etc.); (2) safety; (3) affection, belongingness; (4) self-esteem, ego strength, and (5) self-actualization (the need for fulfillment of the self). Any of these needs can occupy the attention of an organism, but when a lower level need is activated, it tends to override higher level needs.

The concept of personality needs has been discussed by a number of

Table 3-5. Need Fulfillment and Political Participation.

| | Political Participation[a] | | | | |
	Low	Middle	High	Total	(N)
Psychically deprived[b]	36.6	37.4	26.1	100%	(273)
Low self-actualizers	33.3	40.8	25.8	100%	(120)
High self-actualizers	23.5	32.3	44.1	100%	(102)

[a]The political participation index used in the table consists of conventional political activities.
[b]"Psychically deprived" includes those persons categorized as primarily motivated by physiological, safety, affiliative, or esteem needs. The remaining subjects are classified as "low" or "high" self-actualizers depending on their score on that index.
Source: Jeanne Nickel Knutson, *The Human Basis of the Polity; A Psychological Study of Political Men* (Chicago: Aldine-Atherton, 1972), p. 236. Copyright © 1972 by Aldine-Atherton.

psychologically oriented political scientists (Lasswell, 1930; Lane, 1959; Lane, 1969; Davies, 1963; Bay, 1968). The first researcher to systematically apply the need hierarchy to political participation was Knutson (1972). Her study was based on a nonrandom sample of 495 adults in the state of Oregon. Several scales were developed to measure each of the personality needs. A major conclusion of the study is: *political participation is correlated with striving to fulfill higher-level psychic needs.* Those concentrating on needs at the base of the hierarchy are least likely to be active. Persons whose basic physical needs are unfulfilled spend their psychic energies coping with their environment and have little remaining energy or motivation to become active in the social and political arena. This finding casts doubt on theories which argue that the poor and the downtrodden are likely to revolt. Persons with basic needs filled but with unmet social and affectional needs begin to reach out and become active. They may be motivated to fulfill esteem needs (Lasswell, 1930; Ziller, et al., 1969). Those seeking self-actualization are most likely to participate (see Table 3-5).

Politics is only one arena where a person may seek self-actualization; he also may seek it in the arts, sports, charitable activities, etc. Higher rates of activity, which characterize those striving to fulfill higher level needs, generalize also to politics. It may be most important to know under what conditions a self-actualizer seeks fulfillment in politics rather than some other arena.

Conclusions The role of personality in attracting people to politics or keeping them out of politics probably is much more pervasive than the sketchy research evidence presented here can indicate. The available evidence suggests that persons with great neurotic or psychotic problems are not attracted to normal democratic political action. The chaotic, rough-and-tumble environment of competitive politics carries few rewards for thin-skinned, neurotic personalities. Such persons might be attracted to extremist politics under certain conditions, but there are no data specifying such conditions. This is not to say that political actives do not have neurotic needs—probably many of them do—but they usually have their impulses under control and clothe their motives with the garb of public interest. Their defense mechanisms are strong enough to withstand political shock and disappointment. A finding from the Evanston Survey, (Jensen, 1960), is relevant here: 83 percent of the party actives said they "enjoyed the challenge of politics," but only 42 percent of the cross-section of citizens thought they would enjoy it.

The data suggest that political gladiators are persons who are particularly well equipped to deal with their environment. They feel personally competent; they know themselves and feel confident of their knowledge and skills; their egos are strong enough to withstand blows; they are not burdened by a load of anxiety and internal conflict; they can control their impulses; they are astute, sociable, self-expressive, and responsible. Although they may desire to dominate and manipulate others, political gladiators do not seem to lean any further in this direction than persons in many other roles. Gladiators seem to glory in political battle and are self-sufficient enough to withstand the rough-and-tumble of partisan politics. The political arena is not a hospitable place for insecure, timid, and withdrawn people who do not have great faith in their ability to deal effectively with their environment.

Chapter 4   Political Participation as
A Function of
Social Position

The greatest quantity of research on political participation has related that behavior to social-position variables. In part, this is because social-position and other demographic variables are so visible and so readily measured. They are included in nearly every study as a matter of custom and convenience. A related reason is that social-position variables "stand for" many of the attitudinal and personality variables, discussed earlier, which are so difficult to measure. They also provide us with clues regarding the social definition of a person and suggest the type of socialization experience he has had. Social-position variables, such as class or place of residence, do not "cause" any specific behavior in the sense that they are requisites for, or the immediate antecedents of, given acts. Social conditions, however, do form personalities, beliefs, and attitudes which, in turn, do "cause" (are requisite to) specific acts such as participation in politics.

It is a simple matter, then, to find correlational relationships between social-position variables and political participation, but the reader should keep in mind that the effects of social-position variables must be mediated through personality, beliefs, and opinions. Social environment also can affect behavior through the stimuli which it presents to behaving organisms (this was discussed in Chapter 2). The reader should keep both channels of influence in mind throughout the following discussion.

SOCIAL POSITION TOWARD THE CENTER OR PERIPHERY OF SOCIETY A general way to discuss the relationship of social position to political participation is to plot social position along a central-peripheral dimension. This is superior for heuristic purposes to the more commonly used social class or socioeconomic status. For one thing, the center-periphery concept incorporates other variables in addition to SES, such as length of time at a given residence, amount of group activity, race and ethnicity and integration into the community. Another reason is that position on the center-periphery dimension is more than an objective fact, it is also a psychological feeling of being close to the center of things or of being out on the periphery. This feeling of closeness to or distance from the center is an important correlate of political participation. Feeling or perception is closely entwined with reality here; the person whose life circumstances have placed him close to the center (as determined by an impartial observer) is quite likely to *feel* closer to the center than is a person whose life circumstances have placed him on the periphery (as determined by an impartial observer).

There is no objective center which every observer would immediately recognize as such, and this means it is necessary to try to define the concept. Defining it one way might show a stronger relationship to political participation than defining it another. We shall look at several definitions advanced by scholars which differ in specifics but which have many similarities. The precise nature of the concept may still be a bit vague at the conclusion of that examination, but the broad outlines of the dimension will be visible, and that will be adequate for our purposes.

Lane has defined centrality largely in terms of communication (1959, p. 196). Centrally located persons are more accessible, more likely to be informed, partake in more discussions, belong to more organizations, are more likely to be opinion leaders.[1] A study of decision making in a

---

[1] This is similar to Berelson, Lazarsfeld & McPhee (1954).

housing project showed that apartment dwellers located at a crosspath or at the bottom of the stairs were more likely to become involved in a controversy over self-government for the project (Festinger, Schachter & Back, 1950). Another aspect of Lane's definition of centrality is that the centrally located person is liked by many others, especially other "central" persons. As a consequence, he is involved in many more interactions and receives many more communications.

Rokkan and Valen (1962) have defined communes in Norway, instead of people, as central or peripheral. Peripheral communes have many persons engaged in primary occupations such as fishing and agriculture, whereas central communes have more secondary (manufacturing) and especially more tertiary (service) occupations. Peripheral communes lost, and central communes gained population. Per capita income is lower in peripheral communes than in central communes. Peripheral communes have more small farms and less favorable tax rates because of many subsistence incomes. Peripheral communes are relatively isolated from existing transport networks. This is a reasonably good operational definition of centrality-peripherality in Norway, but one would expect other factors, as well, to be relevant in other societies.

Sociologists sometimes speak of the "underdog" in society (Knupfer, 1947); this is the socially and economically underprivileged. The operational definition of the underdog is essentially socioeconomic status: underdogs have low income, little education, low prestige, and feel that they have little power. They are similar to the persons discussed as alienated in Chapter 3. The underdog might be thought of as on the periphery of society, while the top dog is at the center.

Agger and Ostrom isolated a community role they termed "active advisor" (Agger, 1956b; Agger & Ostrom, 1956). Such persons are in close contact with the "top leadership" in the community. The characteristics of these active advisors are very similar to those generally defined here as persons near the center of society: they have higher educational attainment, membership in more groups, greater length of residence in the community, plan to continue to live in the community, read more out-of-town newspapers, associate more with school or governmental officials, are more likely to have held public office, are more likely to be men than women, and are not likely to be young persons.

Lazarsfeld and Katz developed the concept of "opinion leader" (Berelson, Lazarsfeld & McPhee, 1954; Katz, 1957; Katz & Lazarsfeld,

1955; Lazarsfeld, Berelson & Gaudet, 1944). Opinion leaders are important communication links in the message flows of a society. They attend
more to the mass media and communicate more with leaders; in turn,
when requested, they pass this information on to others who are not so
closely tied in to the communications system. They have many of the
characteristics of persons near the center: higher SES, strategic social
location (to receive and send messages), high integration into social
groupings, high competence (highly correlated with education), high
gregariousness, more activity in groups, greater interest in a subject
(public affairs), greater exposure to media, and they personify certain
values (are admired). The intimate relationship between position factors
and personality factors is illustrated by this listing of characteristics of
opinion leaders.

The general central-peripheral dimension should now be visible to
the reader. Persons close to the center occupy an environmental position
which naturally links them into the communications network involved in
policy decisions for the society. They become identified with the body
politic. They receive from and send more communications to other persons near the center. They have a higher rate of social interaction, and
they are active in more groups than persons on the periphery. This central
position increases the likelihood that they will develop personality traits,
beliefs, and attitudes which facilitate participation in politics. There are
many more political stimuli in their environment, and this increases the
number of opportunities for them to participate. (See Figure 1-3, Chapter
1 for a conceptual scheme of these relationships.)

One of the most thoroughly substantiated propositions in all of social
science is that **persons near the center of society are more likely to
participate in politics than persons near the periphery** (Agger, 1956b;
Agger & Goldrich, 1958; Agger & Ostrom, 1956; Berelson, Lazarsfeld &
McPhee, 1954; Buchanan, 1956; Campbell, Gurin & Miller, 1954;
Campbell, et al., 1960; Di Palma, 1970; Dogan, 1961; Glaser, 1959–1960;
Guttsman, 1951; Karlsson, 1958a; Katz & Lazarsfeld, 1955; Kitt &
Gleicher, 1950; Kornhauser, Sheppard & Mayer, 1956; Lane, 1959;
Lazarsfeld, Berelson & Gaudet, 1944; Lipset, 1960; Lipset, et al, 1954;
Marvick & Nixon, 1961; M. Miller, 1952; Pesonen, 1960; Riesman &
Glazer, 1950; Rokkan & Valen, 1962; Verba & Nie, 1972). *Persons near
the center encounter more stimuli enticing them to participate, and they
receive more social support from their peers when they do participate.*

Children growing up in homes located near the center are more likely to develop personalities, beliefs, and attitudes facilitating their entry into politics (Dogan, 1961; Guttsman, 1951; Marvick & Nixon, 1961). Furthermore, *persons at the center tend to recruit new political gladiators from their acquaintances at the center* (Guttsman, 1951; Kuroda, 1967). Decision-makers at the center are more likely to respond to communications coming from other persons near the center (Lane, 1959). *Persons near the periphery are less likely to send communications to the center* (Lane, 1959).

A corollary of all this is the finding that *stability in location and occupation across generations tends to increase political participation* (Lipset, 1960; Pesonen, 1961). This generalization probably is more true of persons in high-status positions than of low-status persons. A person in a menial position is unlikely to participate no matter how many generations were in the same position. The proposition is also more likely to hold for traditional societies than for highly mobile industrialized societies like the United States. Whether a person had the same occupation status as his father or had risen or fallen in status showed no consistent relationship to campaign activity in the Survey Research Center's 1956 election data.

SOCIOECONOMIC STATUS (SES) OR CLASS It will not be necessary, for our purposes, to distinguish status and class; they will be treated as roughly the same concept. Status or class differences imply not only that some persons have more of the goods of life than others, but also that some persons are looked up to more than others. Status differences are found in every society, even though the components of status and the ways of measuring it differ from society to society. What is valued and looked up to in one society may not be valued in another.

Yet, no matter what things are valued in status and no matter how status is measured, it seems clear that persons of high status are close to the center of society and persons of low status usually are on the periphery. Center-periphery, as defined above, is a broader concept than status, so the two are not identical, but the correlation between them is very high.

In Western industrialized societies in the mid-twentieth century, SES is generally conceived of as having three components: education, income, and occupation. These three components are themselves highly intercorrelated, but they are sufficiently different to warrant measuring them separately and including all three in a combined "objective" index of class or status. In a typical index of this type (different scholars use somewhat different weightings), persons who scored high on all three factors would be placed in the upper SES. Those who scored high on two factors but medium or low on one factor would be in the next rank. Those who scored high on only one factor would be in the next rank, and so forth. The index is called "objective" because the researcher places the respondent in a particular status after he has gathered the relevant data on the person.

In contrast, a "subjective" measure of class allows the respondent to select the class that he thinks he falls into. One of the first questions of this type might have read something like this: "Do you usually think of yourself as being part of the upper class, the upper-middle class, the lower-middle class, or the lower class?" Researchers soon discovered several difficulties with this type of question: (1) some people never thought about class; (2) few people had the pride to place themselves in the upper class; (3) almost no one had the lack of pride to call himself lower class. Modern survey researchers now use a series of questions reading something like this: "There is a lot of discussion about class these days. Do you ever think of yourself as belonging to a class?" "If you had to pick a class for yourself, would you say you are middle class or working class?" "Do you think you are in the upper part of the ____ class or just average ____ class?" A small percentage of respondents in the United States refuses to pick any class, sometimes insisting there are no classes in a democracy. Most respondents, however, give answers that are readily codable into one of the four categories produced by the questions: upper middle, lower middle, upper working, and lower working.

Naturally, some respondents "misperceive" their class when their judgment is compared to the scholar's "objective" measurement, but most correlations between the two types of measures are rather high. Most people do accurately perceive their class status. More importantly, subjective perception of class may be as significant, or more significant, an indication of behavioral predisposition than the person's "objective" status. People tend to take on the norms and behavior patterns of the class they aspire to join. As one might imagine, many people aspire upward and take on middle-class values; almost no one aspires downward. *Upwardly mobile persons may become active as part of their effort to move upward* (Dogan, 1961; Marvick & Nixon, 1961; Alford & Scoble, 1968). No matter how class is measured, studies consistently show that **higher-class persons are more likely to participate in politics than lower-class persons** (Agger, Goldrich & Swanson, 1964; Allardt & Pesonen, 1960; Campbell, Gurin & Miller, 1954; Campbell, et al., 1960; Connelly & Field, 1944; Dahl, 1961; Erbe, 1964; McPhee & Glaser, 1962; Tingsten, 1937; Nie, Powell & Prewitt, 1969; Verba & Nie, 1972; DiPalma, 1970; Goel, 1975; Alford & Scoble, 1968; Sallach, Babchuk & Booth, 1972; Olsen, 1972; Watanuki, 1972). This proposition has been confirmed in numerous countries. There are many explanations for this relationship. Persons with higher social position have greater participatory *opportunities*—they interact more frequently with those who are activist, and they receive greater political stimuli; they have the *resources*—information, skills, and competence; they possess requisite *norms*—feelings of obligation and duty that motivate them to participate; and they receive a boost from *facilitative structures*—legal rules and the workings of political institutions (party systems) which, in certain countries, favor their participation.

Socioeconomic status and political activity show different levels of correlation from nation to nation. Table 4-1 reports the correlations between political participation and socioeconomic status for ten countries. As one can see, the relationship is stronger in India and the United States than in the other eight nations. The high correlational value in India reflects the fact that participation is extremely depressed among the illiterates and the destitute; it has been found that those in the middle status are as active as those in the highest status (and sometimes more) (Goel, 1975; Eldersveld & Ahmed, 1976). This is in contrast to the United States where status has a consistent and sharp impact on activity. Why should political involvement differ so sharply by social stratification in the United States?—a society known for its egalitarian values. Several writers suggest that the answer to this apparent paradox lies in the way political parties are related to social class. As mentioned earlier, parties in the United States are heterogeneous, and do not recruit their activists within a single class. In contrast, many European political parties are closely allied with a given class or occupational group. The class-identified party usually does a good job of mobilizing its adherents. Thus, paradoxically, the very absence of class ideology and class parties in the United States makes it more likely that higher-class persons will partici-

Table 4-1. Correlation of Social Status and Participation in Ten Countries.[a]

Civic Culture Data		Cross-national Program Data	
United States	.43	India	.38
United Kingdom	.30	United States	.37
Italy	.28	Nigeria	.31
Mexico	.24	Netherlands	.18
Germany	.18	Austria	.10
		Japan	.07

[a]Verba and Nie say: "We present two separate sets of correlation because the data come from two different studies. In each column the measures are comparable, but not across the columns, because different measures are used. This explains the two different figures for the U.S.
"The data in the left column . . . are discussed in Nie, Powell and Prewitt, 'Social Structure and Political Participation'; those in the right column in Verba, Nie and Kim, *The Modes of Democratic Participation: A Cross-National Comparison.*"
Source: Sidney Verba and Norman H. Nie, *Participation in America: Political Democracy and Equality* (New York: Harper & Row, 1972), p. 340.

pate in politics, and has the consequence of giving political advantage to those groups who already are socially and economically advantaged (Verba & Nie, 1972; Rokkan & Campbell, 1960; DiPalma, 1970).

Studies in countries with status-polarized party systems (multiple parties that split along class lines) show that *political participation, especially voting turnout, is higher in communes which are homogeneous in politics, socioeconomic status, and economic activity* (e.g., all fishing or all manufacturing) (Allardt & Bruun, 1956; Allardt & Pesonen, 1960; Pesonen, 1960; Pesonen, 1961; Rokkan, 1962b; Rokkan & Campbell, 1960). In Finland, where both Swedish and Finnish are official languages, communes that are homogeneous in language have higher turnout (Allardt & Bruun, 1956). *In societies with residential segregation by SES* (SES homogeneity within political units), *the normal tendency for high SES persons to be more likely to participate is reduced* (Allardt & Bruun, 1956; Lipset, 1960; Rokkan, 1962b; Tingsten, 1937). One can guess that without status differences to inhibit their feeling of competence and importance, lower-class persons are more likely to become willing political workers. If this homogeneous group should also have its own political party (as we saw earlier is true of some areas in Norway), that party would recruit and train workers from within its own stratum (Rokkan, 1962b).

In general, *the impact of status on voting participation is higher in low-stimulus than in high-stimulus elections. Those persons with high internal motivation (associated with high SES) turn out even for dull elections.* In a study of Toledo, Hamilton (1971) found that the association between turnout and status was much higher in city elections (low-stimulus) than in presidential elections (high-stimulus).

Some persons have an indeterminate status; perhaps their education is high but their income is low, or vice versa. Perhaps they continue to live in a poor neighborhood when their educational and income achievements would enable them to move to a better one. Some scholars speak of such persons as having "cross-pressures" in their status and report that they are less likely to vote than persons who are not cross-pressured (Lazarsfeld, Berelson & Gaudet, 1944; Lenski, 1956; Lipset, 1960). Presumably, for persons in the United States the cross-pressure arises from the tendency for one aspect of their status to incline them in a Republican direction, while the other aspect of their status inclines them toward the Democrats. Some of them resolve the dilemma by not voting at all. No data were found relating cross-pressures in status to gladiatorial activity.

Countries with higher economic development have higher absolute rates of participation than countries at lower levels of development (Deutsch, 1961; Huntington, 1968; Almond & Verba, 1963; Nie, Powell & Prewitt, 1969; Needler, 1968; Nie & Verba, 1975; the studies cited under "modernization" in the next chapter are also relevant here). Pesonen (1961) reported that following a rise in the economic level of the underprivileged northern counties of Finland the level of political participation also rose.

Economic development of an area has the effect of enlarging the numbers in the middle and upper classes. **An increase in the socioeconomic status of an area increases political activity by slowly affecting the attitudes of the persons who have acquired new status** (Nie, Powell & Prewitt, 1969; Verba & Nie, 1972). There usually is a time lag. For example, areas in Indiana that changed from agricultural to industrial continued their old voting turnout rates for several elections thereafter and showed only a gradual increase in turnout as time passed (Key & Munger, 1959). The southern states in the United States are shifting rapidly from an agricultural to an industrial economy, but a rise in the percentage turnout at elections lags about a decade behind (Milbrath, 1965a). West Virginia, which was industrialized and became highly unionized around the turn of the century, but which is now having considerable problems with poverty and unemployment, continues to have one of the highest turnout percentages in the United States (Milbrath, 1971c; Johnson, 1971).

Economic modernization is a potent, if slow, force affecting political patterns. Studies in Norway and Japan show that *as patterns of employment shifted from largely primary economic activities* (fishing, agriculture, forestry) *to secondary* (manufacturing) and *tertiary* (services), *more and more persons who had formerly stayed outside the political process were mobilized into the electorate* (Masumi, 1961; Rokkan, 1962a; Rokkan & Valen, 1962). As these areas became more industrialized, more of the political contesting was carried out through political parties: party membership rose, parties took the job of candidate recruitment, and nonpartisan elections tended to fall into disuse (Masumi, 1961; Rokkan & Valen, 1962). As industrialization progressed in France, more and more persons with middle-class origins were elected to the French Assembly (Dogan, 1961).

We have little information about what happens to political participation during times of depression. During the Great Depression of the thirties, the number of persons offering themselves as candidates for public office in Indiana rose; later, during World War II, the number of candidates dropped off (Standing & Robinson, 1958). The researchers suggested that during periods of high unemployment the lure of public office (with its certain salary) substantially improves. Another scholar, after checking voting turnout figures over a considerable period of time, could find no relationship between depressions and voting turnout (Lane, 1959).

Although socioeconomic status affects all modes of participation, its impact is greater on some activities than on others. Voting and particularized contacting are related less strongly to SES than gladiatorial activities, especially communication activities. Voting requires little initiative and is not very dependent on skills, information, and psychological involvement. In addition, many persons are mobilized to vote by parties or groups. Particularized contacting is engaged in by people from all walks of life; it shows very little relationship to SES.

Socioeconomic status also is positively related to unconventional political participation (Milbrath, 1971b; Hunt & Goel, 1976). Those who engage in protests, or those who hold favorable views about extremist tactics, are no more socially underclass or psychologically underprivileged than the nonprotestors (Caplan, 1970; Tomlinson, 1970a & b; Eisinger, 1974; Cataldo, Johnson & Kellstedt, 1968; Schwartz, 1973; in addition, the studies cited under "alienation and unconventional political participation" and "personality needs" are relevant here). In an analysis of data from a Negro locality in Los Angeles, Tomlinson sums up the behavioral relationships:

> [Militants] are more likely to be brought up in an urban setting, somewhat better educated, long-term residents of the city (over 10 years), equally or more involved in religion, and in possession of a more positive self-image. They are as [sic] equally likely to be working as the non-militants and tend to be more sophisticated politically (Tomlinson, 1970a, p. 115).

Two different patterns of protesting have been found—one for blacks and the other for whites. Among American blacks, protest activity has become a "normal," accepted form of participation, and a majority of blacks perceive protests to be beneficial to their cause. Blacks appear to have developed "protest duty" feelings, similar to "voting duty" feelings in the larger public. Blacks are mobilized to protest by their community in the same way that voters are mobilized to turn out for elections by the larger community. Blacks live in a "culture of protest" (Milbrath, 1971b). In contrast, only a small proportion of whites approves of protests.

Also, black protest participants are not a fringe element of their community; instead, they are active in community groups and tend to be long-time residents. White protestors, on the other hand, although ranking higher in education and income than the general population, tend to be nonconformists and at odds with the views of the white community at large. In summary, whereas black protestors receive support from their community, white radicals protest in the face of strong community opposition (Eisinger, 1974; Milbrath, 1971b).

Income It is almost universally true that **the more prosperous persons are more likely to participate in politics than the less prosperous.** This finding is supported by many studies in and outside the United States (Agger & Ostrom, 1956; Campbell, Gurin & Miller, 1954; Campbell, et al., 1960; Connelly & Field, 1944; Dahl, 1961; Lane, 1959; Lipset, 1960; Milbrath, 1971b; M. Miller, 1952; Riesman & Glazer, 1950; Tingsten, 1937;

Matthews & Prothro, 1966; Verba & Nie, 1972; Olsen, 1973; Inkeles, 1969; Nie, Powell & Prewitt, 1969; DiPalma, 1970; Alford & Scoble, 1968; Erbe, 1964; Bennett & Klecka, 1970; Hamilton, 1971; Rosenau, 1974). Reference has already been made under SES to the impact of economic modernization of a nation on its overall level of political activity; in general, countries with a higher per capita income have higher participation rates.

In the American South, among the Negroes, income has a more powerful impact on their political participation than either education or occupation. The same number of years of schooling does not mean the same degree of education for Negroes and whites; nor do Negro and white ownership of a store or the practice of law or religion carry the same status. But "a thousand dollars of 'Negro income' means about the same as a thousand dollars of 'white income' " (Matthews & Prothro, 1966, p. 91).

Income relates differently to different measures of participation. Its greatest impact is on activities that require self-esteem (e.g., convincing others to vote a particular way) or that require financial well-being (e.g., donating money to parties). In the Verba & Nie United States study (1972), income was more strongly related to "communal" and "partisan" activities than to "voting" or to "particularized contacting." In India, the level of income showed no positive correlation with voting, but it did with gladiatorial activities (Goel, 1975); in Japan, Kuroda (1967) found no significant correlation between income and political participation. The relationship between income and unconventional political participation is similar to the relationship between SES and unconventional political participation. *Those at the bottom of the economic ladder are least likely to protest,* as most of their time and energy is consumed in eking out a living (Caplan & Paige, 1968; Caplan, 1970; Buffalo Survey, 1968). In a Milwaukee survey the mean income for black protestors was $6,790 as compared with $6,300 for nonprotestors, and among the whites the respective incomes were $8,320 and $7,310 (Eisinger, 1974).

Several reasons are given to explain the strong income-participation relationship. The most obvious reason is that differences in income are related to other socioeconomic and attitudinal differences. The more affluent are likely to have had higher levels of education, are more likely to interact with others in social and political groups, are more likely to be exposed to mass media and, therefore, are more likely to have developed attitudes and beliefs that encourage participation. Furthermore, in poor countries only the economically well-off can afford newspapers, radios, and televisions. In summary, then, active citizenship may be perceived as a sort of luxury which cannot be "afforded" by those who are struggling to fulfill their subsistence needs.

Education Among the socioeconomic variables investigated to explain political participation, education is about the most thoroughly researched factor. A widely documented research finding is that **people with higher levels of education tend to participate at a higher level than those with less education** (Agger, Goldrich & Swanson, 1964; Allardt & Pesonen, 1960; Almond & Verba, 1963; Degras, Gray & Pear, 1956; Berelson, Lazarsfeld & McPhee, 1954; Buchanan, 1956; Campbell, Gurin & Miller, 1954; Campbell, et. al., 1960; Converse & Dupeux, 1961; Dahl, 1961; Jensen, 1960; Key, 1961; Kuroda, 1967; Lane, 1959; Lipset, 1960; McPhee & Glaser, 1962; Milbrath, 1971b; Sussman, 1959; Woodward & Roper, 1950; Alford & Scoble, 1968; Matthews & Prothro, 1966; Di Palma, 1970; Inkeles, 1969; Nie, Powell & Prewitt, 1969; Verba & Nie, 1972; Verba, Nie & Kim, 1971; Olsen, 1973; Goel, 1970a, 1975; Sallach, Babchuk & Booth, 1972; Erbe, 1964; Barber, 1969; Kelley, Ayres & Bowen, 1967; Tessler, 1972; Rosenau, 1974). Although education is closely associated with SES, its effects have been found within all statuses and occupations. In addition, the relationship has been found to exist across cultures and nationalities, not only in the industrialized West but also in the developing nations of the world (see Inkeles's research on Argentina, Bangladesh, Chile, India, Israel, and Nigeria; Verba, Nie and Kim's report on Austria, India, Japan, Nigeria, and the United States; Goel's on India; Marquette's on the Phillippines; Tessler's on Tunisia; and Kuroda's on Japan). There are few studies, if any, which show the impact of education to disappear when other socioeconomic variables are controlled. Education emerges as one of the most powerful factors in stimulating fuller participation. The relationship holds for most modes of political activity, with the possible exception of voting, which will be discussed below.

Why does education have a consistently strong impact on political behavior in such a diversity of cultures? The most important reason is that differences in educational attainment are associated with differences in other social characteristics and psychological attributes. Persons with higher educations are more likely to have higher incomes, to be exposed to more mass media, to occupy higher status positions, to possess greater information about government and politics, to perceive higher stakes in politics, to feel more efficacious, and so on.

The five-nation study has done the most thorough research on the impact and the reasons for the impact of education on political behavior. The findings are very clear, they hold in all five nations, and they parallel many points already made in this book. The summary is so clear and inclusive that it deserves quotation at length. The chapter citations are to chapters in *The Civic Culture.*

> (1) The more educated person is more aware of the impact of government on the individual than is the person of less education (chapter 3);
>
> (2) The more educated individual is more likely to report that he follows politics and pays attention to election campaigns than is the individual of less education (chapter 3);
>
> (3) The more educated individual has more political information (chapter 3);
>
> (4) The more educated individual has opinions on a wider range of political subjects; the focus of his attention to politics is wider (chapter 3);
>
> (5) The more educated individual is more likely to engage in political discussion (chapter 4);
>
> (6) The more educated individual feels free to discuss politics with a wider range of people (chapter 4). Those with less education are more likely to report that there are many people with whom they avoid such discussions;
>
> (7) The more educated individual is more likely to consider himself capable of influencing the government; this is reflected both in responses to questions on what one could do about an unjust law (chapter 7) and in respondent's scores on the subjective competence scale (chapter 9).

The above list refers to specifically political orientations, which vary the same way in all five nations. In addition, our evidence shows that:

(8) The more educated individual is more likely to be a member—and an active member—of some organization (chapter 11); and

(9) The more educated individual is more likely to express confidence in his social environment: to believe that other people are trustworthy and helpful (chapter 10) (Almond & Verba, 1963, pp. 380–381).

Understanding the relationship between education and political participation requires one important qualification. The effect of education is *not* uniform across all forms of participation. It correlates most *strongly* and *clearly* with campaign activity, community participation, and communication activities. It also correlates positively to a small degree with protest behavior; several studies have found that protestors tend to be somewhat better educated as well as better informed than the average citizenry (Gary Marx, 1967; Tomlinson, 1970b; Caplan & Paige, 1968; Caplan, 1970; Buffalo Survey, 1968). In Milwaukee, Wisconsin, black protestors had an average educational attainment of 11.96 years, as compared with 9.89 years for nonprotestors; among whites the difference was even larger: 14.57 years for protestors and 10.96 years for nonprotestors (Eisinger, 1974).

An important exception to the familiar relationship between education and participation is its lack of a consistent impact on voting. Education correlates insignificantly, and sometimes negatively, with voting turnout. Goel's research on India showed a curvilinear pattern: turnout there increases with middle schooling but decreases with high school and college education (Goel, 1975; also Eldersveld & Ahmed, 1976). In the five-nation cross-national study, only in the United States was education found to correlate significantly with voting (.21); in India, the simple correlation was −.04; in Austria, −.09; in Japan, .03; in Nigeria, −.03 (Verba, Nie & Kim, 1971). A negative correlation between education and voting also has been found in urban Malaya and in the Japanese local elections (Rabushka, 1970; Richardson, 1966). In a study of primary elections in Toledo, Ohio, no meaningful association between education and voting was found, when occupation and income were held constant (Hamilton, 1971). Using the statistical technique of Multiple Classification Analysis on 1964, 1966, and 1968 United States national election data, researchers found education to be the strongest predictor of political efficacy, political interest, and political influence attempts, even when the concurrent effects of occupation and income were taken into account. On the other hand, it was less intimately related to voting turnout; in fact, when the concurrent effects of occupation and income were taken into account, education retained little direct influence on turnout (Bennett & Klecka, 1970).

Why don't the more educated vote in higher proportion in some cultures? One possible explanation is that in some countries higher levels of education do not lead to more patriotism, system-affection, political happiness, and a feeling that voting is a civic obligation. Data from India and Japan show that the more informed and knowledgeable citizens also are more hostile to the system and less patriotic (Inkeles, 1969; Goel, 1975; Eldersveld, Jagannadham & Barnabas, 1968; Richardson, 1973). The positive or negative feelings toward the political system are important because voting is a patriotic activity by which a citizen affirms his allegiance. Recall that in the Buffalo Survey (1968), voting clustered on the "patriotism" factor which included such other activities as "flying the flag," "paying all taxes," "respecting the police," and "supporting my country in wars I don't agree with." It is rare for an individual casting his vote to believe that his vote will make a difference to the outcome, or that it will benefit him in a personal way. It also can be argued that the act of voting is less dependent on personal factors like political interest, information, and feelings of efficacy, which are developed by education. Most political cultures encourage citizens to exercise their franchise even if they are not interested and involved in politics. On the other hand, participation in more demanding activities is difficult without personal motivation.

Another bit of interesting information is that the socialization process by which the more educated "naturally" assume more politicized roles may not work for members of an ethnic minority. In an exploratory survey of Mexican-Americans in Nebraska, little positive correlation was found between educational attainment and several dimensions of political participation "because the education process and other socialization agents do not prepare group members for political roles" (Welch, Comer & Steinman, 1973, p. 813). Minorities may not feel that behavior norms for the majority apply to them. Further research is needed for clarification.

In summary, then, we may state that educational attainment is a strong predictor of political activity. This has been found in a variety of cultures and it applies to most forms of participation. The only exception seems to be the absence of any consistent impact on voting.

Occupation Occupation is a somewhat more tricky variable to interpret than education or income. What kinds of occupational distinctions are meaningful, and how can one compute quantitative differences in occupation (as one can for income and education)? A traditional distinction, which is rather broad and vague, is between white-collar and blue-collar occupations, but the color of his collar is not a sure guide to the most relevant characteristics of a person's occupation. This distinction produces inconclusive results when it is related to political participation. Some studies (Allardt & Bruun, 1956; Alford & Scoble, 1968) show white-collar persons to be more likely to participate than blue-collar, while other studies (Jensen, 1960) show no relationship.

Another way of handling occupation is to rank the statuses of the various occupations. Occupations closer to the center usually are perceived as having higher status than those on the periphery. One way to create a status ranking is to have a random sample of citizens rate the prestige of various occupations. Such ratings have quite high inter-rater reliability, suggesting that there are widely shared beliefs about the prestige of occupations. A categorization based on such ratings was used to make an occupation status index for respondents in the 1956 election study. This index showed a clear tendency for higher-status persons to be more likely to be active in politics. Several other studies report that **persons of higher occupational status are more likely to participate in politics** (Agger & Ostrom, 1956; Berelson, Lazarsfeld & McPhee, 1954; Bonham, 1952; Buck, 1963; Campbell & Kahn, 1952; Connelly & Field, 1944; Dahl, 1961; Barber, 1969; Matthews & Prothro, 1966; Olsen, 1973; Erbe, 1964; Bennett & Klecka, 1970; Hamilton, 1971). In the United States, an analysis of the Michigan Survey Research Center election data indicates the following percentages of voting turnout in the 1964 presidential elections: professional and managerial (80 percent), other white collar (79 percent), farmers (79 percent), skilled and semi-skilled (69 percent), and unskilled (64 percent). Caution is recommended in using voting turnout data as a general indicator of political involvement, however.

In status-polarized societies, manual workers may achieve participation rates equal to or higher than those who occupy more prestigious positions (Rokkan & Campbell, 1960). This suggests an interesting hypothesis: *Status differences are less strongly associated to political participation in class-distinct party systems (e.g., Norway) than in heterogeneous party systems (e.g., United States).* In the class-based Norwegian party system the parties mobilize the lower status occupations to political activism, whereas the heterogeneous character of political parties in the United States depresses participation among the lower classes. A similar inference can be drawn from British data; the gradual weakening of the Labor party's distinctive identification with the working class has led to a discernible decline of electoral turnout in traditional working-class neighborhoods (Butler & Stokes, 1969).

One can also ask the question: "What is it about occupation that might facilitate or hinder political participation?" This is likely to produce a different type of categorization than that discussed above. Lane has suggested that these characteristics of jobs facilitate political participation: (1) the development and use of social and intellectual skills that might carry over to politics; (2) opportunity to interact with like-minded others; (3) higher than average stakes in governmental policy; (4) roles on the job that carry over to public service (1959, p. 334). A study of local party officials shows that a higher than normal percentage of them had come from occupations with "brokerage roles" (occupations requiring the person to relate smoothly with other people) (Bowman & Boynton, 1966).

The following four criteria, that theoretically seemed important in determining whether a person in an occupation would become active in politics, were used to create an index of occupational propensity toward politics.* (1) Does the job provide an opportunity (freedom of schedule and blocks of time) for political action? (2) Does the job require or develop skills (largely verbal) that can be transferred to politics? (3) Is the job sufficiently affected by political decisions that job occupants would feel it important to become active in politics to protect or enhance their position? (4) Does the position become vulnerable if the occupant engages in politics; in other words, might a job-holder have to pay a cost in anxiety or

---

*Robert Boynton collaborated with Milbrath on this research. Data were taken from the 1956 election study of the Michigan Survey Research Center.

defense if he should participate? Specific jobs were rated as high, medium, or low on each of the criteria by a board of judges. Simple weights were applied (1, 2, 3, with scoring for the last criterion reversed), and scores were summed for the four criteria. Lawyers, as an example, were scored high on the first three criteria, but medium on the last.

Inter-rater reliability was satisfactory, and the resulting index did correlate significantly with campaign participation. However, the overall correlation was no higher than that between occupation status and campaign participation. As might be expected from the criteria employed, the index showed a stronger relationship with gladiatorial activities than with spectator activities. At the highest ranks of the index, 38 percent of the persons had engaged in at least one gladiatorial activity compared with 14 percent for the entire sample. This pattern, for those on the top rank of the index to be much more likely to participate, held for each of the specific political acts included in the study. This difference in top-rank behavior suggests, although we would need more and better data to be confident, that a high rank on all or nearly all of the criteria are needed before a person feels that the door is wide open to gladiatorial activity.

In the Buffalo Survey (1968), Milbrath and his colleagues investigated further the vulnerability people might feel if they became active in politics. Respondents were asked if "the people at work would disapprove," if "friends and neighbors would disapprove," and "would you feel out of place?" Vulnerability to disapproval of people at work or among friends and neighbors showed no relationship to political participation. Feeling out of place, however, did significantly depress participation.

Turning now to somewhat more specific occupations, several studies show that **professional persons are the most likely to get involved in politics** (Anderson, 1935; Buck, 1963; Guttsman, 1951; Jensen, 1960; M. Miller, 1952; Nie, Powell & Prewitt, 1969; Schlesinger, 1957). This generalization seems especially true of political office-holding, being very evident for higher offices. It very probably would not hold for a setting where political activity, or the kind of office held, is not well respected. The Evanston survey showed professionals most likely to be active in politics, followed by businessmen, clerical, skilled, and unskilled workers in that order (Jensen, 1960). In Anglo-Saxon countries and in France, lawyers are especially likely to seek office and be active in other ways in politics; this pattern is not so prevalent in other countries, however. Almost half of the state governors in the United States from 1870 to 1950 (456 of 995) were practicing lawyers (Schlesinger, 1957). Occupations of members of the British Parliament have followed a trend away from landowning and toward professional occupations (Buck, 1963; Guttsman, 1951). There is a pattern in some countries for government employees to be very active politically (Lipset, 1960; Tingsten, 1937). Whether or not this occurs may depend on possible legal prohibitions against political activity by public employees. The Hatch Act (1940) controls the political activities of employees of the federal government in the United States*. Certainly, the public nature of their job means that government job-holders have an important stake in political outcomes.

Businessmen, compared to the rest of the population, tend to be quite active in politics, although there is variation from business to business and perhaps also from community to community. A study of the political activity of Philadelphia businessmen reported these findings: A high proportion vote and contribute money, as a matter of course (40 percent contributed money as compared to 10 percent for a national sample) (Janosik, n.d.). The percentage of businessmen who worked in a campaign (8 percent) was just a little higher than the national average (3 or 4 percent) and is a normal percentage for upper-middle SES persons. There were no public office-holders among these businessmen. They tended to have a positive attitude toward politics and politicians, tended to be optimistic about politics, and tended slightly to inhibit political discussion for fear of offending associates. Top business executives were more likely to be active in politics than middle- and lower-level executives. Another study of the effects of political training classes, designed to involve businessmen in politics, reported modest to poor results for the training (Hacker & Aberbach, 1962). The positive attractions to politics often did not compensate for the costs of political action (especially diversion of time and energy).

Most studies show laboring persons disinclined, on the whole, to become involved actively in politics. There are exceptions to this generalization in countries with strong working-class movements and parties. We saw above how effective the Norwegian labor party is in enlisting political activity from laboring men. In the United States, labor unions have some success in mobilizing their members for political

---

*At this writing, the Congress is considering a bill which seeks to liberalize some provisions of the Hatch Act.

action, but the result is not very impressive; this effort will be discussed later under group memberships. Certain aspects of a laboring man's job make it difficult for him to become active in politics, especially to undertake gladiatorial activity. He has a fixed work schedule, making it difficult to be free for meetings. His job usually does not emphasize or teach verbal skills that can be transferred to political action. The relevance of political outcomes for his income and job satisfaction is often not very clear.

PLACE OF RESIDENCE The size of the place of residence is an important independent variable for explaining political participation; behavioral studies usually include it as one of the explanatory factors. Even though there are a myriad of studies comparing urban with rural residence, there is no consensus regarding how and to what extent the size of community affects individual political action; especially, there is variation across national cultures.

At least two distinguishable trends can be seen in the literature. One version holds that urban living, as compared to rural, is conducive to higher involvement in politics. In the definitional terms of center-periphery discussed at the beginning of this chapter, urban dwellers are generally perceived to be closer to the center of most societies than the rural dwellers. This is largely due to the enhanced opportunity for interaction and communication that the urban dweller has when compared to rural people. Campbell comments on the isolation of American rural life:

> We . . . find very low levels of political interest and involvement among farmers in the United States. Despite the widespread ownership of automobiles and television sets by rural people, farm life in America is not only physically but socially remote. The typical farmer not only lives apart from his neighbors but has relatively little formal association with them. Most American farmers belong to no farm organizations and few of those who do express any great interest in them (Campbell, 1962, pp. 13–14).

It has been found in many studies in many western societies that **farmers are less likely to become active in politics than city dwellers** (Berelson, Lazarsfeld & McPhee, 1954; Campbell, 1962; Campbell, et al., 1960; McPhee & Glaser, 1962; Pesonen, 1960; Rokkan & Campbell,

1960; Rokkan & Valen, 1962; Tingsten, 1937, in all four Scandinavian countries). In addition to the communication disadvantages of the rural setting, another reason for the urban-rural difference is the striking difference in political activity levels of rural and urban women (Rokkan & Campbell, 1960). Women from families engaged in primary economic activity (agriculture, forestry, fishing) are much less likely to participate in politics. Women in a primary economy tend to stay close to home and often are involved in production. This not only leaves little time for politics, but also limits social interaction to family members (once again, social interaction seems to be a central variable). An additional factor is that primary economies tend to be more tradition-oriented, and it is a strong tradition to think of politics as "man's work." As a greater proportion of the economic activity in a locality becomes secondary and tertiary, the differences in participation between men and women are reduced. Women in urban areas in Norway are just as likely to vote as men, they are just as likely as men to take part in party affairs, and they are more likely to become candidates for office than rural women, even though urban men are still more likely to become candidates than urban women (Rokkan & Campbell, 1960; Rokkan & Valen, 1962).

Scholars in the field of modernization and political development also subscribe to the mobilization effects of urbanization (Deutsch, 1961; Russett, et al., 1964). But this conclusion is reached on the basis of aggregate data, where whole nations are compared. While it is true that *the more urbanized nations* (which are also more modernized) *have higher levels of participation, it may, nevertheless, not be true that within each nation, persons living in urban areas are more active than those living in the rural areas.*

The alternative perspective on urban-rural differences has shown, in a variety of studies, that there either is a lack of or a somewhat negative association between urban living and political activity, especially voting. The evidence comes from a diversity of cultures (Nie, Powell & Prewitt, 1969: data on United States, United Kingdom, Germany, Italy, Mexico, and India; Inkeles, 1969: data on Argentina, Chile, India, Israel, Nigeria, and Bangladesh; Cameron, Hendricks & Hofferbert, 1972: data on France, India, Mexico, Switzerland, and United States; Watanuki, 1972, Richardson, 1973, Kyoguku & Ike, 1959, and Chong Lim Kim, 1971: all four on Japan; Goel, 1975, on India; Kesselman, 1966, and Tarrow, 1971: on France; Marquette, 1971, on the Philippines; Robinson & Standing,

Table 4-2. Correlations between Political Participation[a], Urban Residence, and SES, with and without Controls, in Seven Nations.

	U.S.	U.K.	Germany	Italy	Mexico	India	Japan
Urban residence and participation scale	.068	−.023	−.022	−.002	.073	.035	−.193
Urban residence and participation with SES controlled	−.001	−.037	−.054	−.054	.046	.104	—
Urban residence and SES	.159	.040	.166	.175	.118	.339	.122

[a]Only conventional participation items are considered in this table.
Data for the United States, United Kingdom, Germany, Italy, Mexico, and India are adapted from Norman H. Nie, G. Bingham Powell, and Kenneth Prewitt, "Social Structure and Political Participation," *American Political Science Review* 63 (1969), pp. 364, 367. Data for Japan are adapted from Joji Watanuki, "Social Structure and Political Participation in Japan," 1972.

1960: the state of Indiana). Together these studies reported data from 15 different countries.

The lack of relationship between urbanism and political activity is strikingly brought out when the effect of colinearity with other variables—organizational involvement, social status, and so on—is neutralized. The following quote is representative of several of the research studies: "Our most striking finding is precisely that urbanism, despite its zero-order correlation, fails to meet the test of being an independent school of citizenship. Neither urban origin, nor the number of years of urban experience after age 15, produce significant increases in active citizenship when other variables are controlled. This is confirmed by many special matches" (Inkeles, 1969, p. 1140). The data in Table 4-2 demonstrate this pattern. Only in the United States, Mexico, and India is the relationship positive, and barely at that. In addition, when the effect of SES is partialled out, the relationship almost disappears (United States and Mexico), suggesting that whatever slight positive association does exist between urban residence and active citizenship is the result of the higher SES of urban dwellers.

The reason most often cited for the negative relationship between urban residence and participation is that in contrast to rural areas where an individual is a member of a small integrated community, the city resident is part of an atomized mass society. Politics in the city often become impersonal, complicated, and distant. Social relationships may become diffuse and less intimate, cutting down on the level of group activity. Contrary to the pattern in the United States where farmer dwellings tend to be isolated from others, rural communities in many European and Asian countries are organized into highly interactive homogeneous villages. Urban centers in these nations, on the other hand, have grown very rapidly and social life often is poorly organized.

Some scholars have argued that it is not the *size* per se of the community that is important for political participation but its *character.* Some communities are autonomous and well-defined; boundaries are clearly marked; they have functioning local government; most people living there identify with the community. Other communities do not have these characteristics. A general proposition is that *communities that are autonomous and well-defined have higher participation than amorphous and loosely-defined localities.* In accordance with this proposition, the suburban complexes adjacent to large cities in the United States (which are least well-defined as communities) should have the lowest participation rates, and small towns and rural villages should show above average rates of participation. This pattern emerges when the effect of SES is neutralized, for without such control, the suburbs rank rather high on participation because of their preponderance of high SES persons (Verba & Nie, 1972, Ch. 13).

Japan is an important example of a country where political participation and urban living are negatively correlated. Rural areas consistently have shown higher voting turnout than urban areas at all election levels. These differences range from 8 to 12 percent. Participation in other activities also is more common in rural districts than in the cities (Richardson, 1973; Watanuki, 1972; Kyogoku & Ike, 1959). Most of the reasons given for this finding suggest that urban persons are no closer to the center of Japanese society than rural persons. If anything, the tendency is in the other direction. Most urban areas, especially Tokyo, have grown very fast in recent years, and a large proportion of city dwellers is poorly integrated into their community. Rural areas show higher community integration; the houses are close together (not isolated, as farmhouses are in the United States); social interaction and group activity also are generally higher in the rural areas, and exposure to mass media and education has spread throughout Japan to incorporate rural areas.

One very important contributing factor to the above is the social structure of Japan, which is basically communal in character with high social involvement. Old and large landowning families are closely knit by kinship and friendship ties. There is an authoritarian tradition for the people to follow the political lead of the head of the clan; voting is taken as a sign of loyalty. These rural political machines are stronger than urban machines and are the basic strength of the conservative party in Japan. Rural people place more emphasis on the reputation and personality of candidates, whereas city dwellers must rely more on party labels as a guide to voting.

City areas in Japan have experienced a much higher percentage of candidates offering themselves for public office. Many of these candidates have little reputation and status and meager city background. This seriously increases the information demands and costs for city voters.

In Japan and India, some research evidence also suggests that urban living leads to greater political cynicism, negative views about politicians, and a lower sense of duty to vote. In contrast, rural residents tend to feel more dutiful, and less hostile (Richardson, 1973; Goel, 1975; Eldersveld, Jagannadham & Barnabas, 1968). As our theory leads us to expect, these negative feelings depress voting turnout in particular.

What can we make of the contradictory findings presented in this section? It seems to us that earlier researchers perhaps were looking at the wrong variable. It is not size of community but type of community that affects the degree of political participation. Communities with many high-status people will be more active than those with many low-status people. Communities where citizens feel integrated into community life will be more active than communities where people feel isolated from each other. Communities with a high level of communication will be more active than those where communication is poor. In some countries, at some times, these conditions are more likely to be found in urban areas; in other countries, or at other times, these conditions are more likely to be found in rural areas.

ORGANIZATIONAL INVOLVEMENT It is clear from many studies that **those who are organizationally involved participate in politics at rates far greater than citizens who are not so involved** (Lipset, 1960; Lane, 1959; Nie, Powell & Prewitt, 1969; Verba & Nie, 1972; Verba,

Ahmed & Bhatt, 1971; Milbrath, 1971b; Sallach, Babchuk & Booth, 1972; Alford & Scoble, 1968; Rokkan & Campbell, 1960; Olsen, 1972; Almond & Verba, 1963; Matthews & Prothro, 1966; Erbe, 1964, cites 14 studies). This close relationship occurs not only because many of the same social and personal characteristics lead to both social and political participation, but also because groups are important mobilizers of political action by their members. In addition, social participation broadens one's sphere of interests, concerns, interpersonal contacts, and leadership skills. The impact of associational membership on politics, of course, holds only if a particular organization permits or encourages political activity; some groups may have a norm favoring noninvolvement in politics (Jehovah's Witnesses is an example).

Education is an important variable stimulating participation in both nonpolitical and political groups. In a similar fashion, **men more than women, the middle aged more than the young or old, participate in voluntary groups** (an extended summary of these correlations is presented in Smith, Reddy & Baldwin, 1972). Since these very characteristics also lead to increased political participation an important question arises: is organizational involvement independently related to political participation or is the relationship *spurious,* i.e., a reflection of other variables that correlate significantly with both social and political participation? Several studies have examined this question and it is safe to conclude that **organizational involvement is a major independent predictor of political participation** (Erbe, 1964; Alford & Scoble, 1968; Nie, Powell & Prewitt, 1969; Verba & Nie, 1972; Olsen, 1972). The effects of social participation on political participation are cumulative. *The greater the number of one's affiliations, the greater the likelihood of one's participation in political activity* (Olsen, 1972; Buffalo Survey, 1968). In the developing nations, factory work experience has been found to be importantly related to active citizenship (Inkeles, 1969). Factory experience can be thought of as similar to organizational involvement in its consequences for the individual. Industrial organization emphasizes rational decision making, collective goals, and elevation to authority by virtue of "achieved" criteria (education and skills, not kinship). The factory in developing societies may socialize those working there toward modern values.

It is possible to speak of persons belonging to groupings even though there is no formal organization which they have joined. For example, it is common in politics to speak of ethnic minorities as groups, even though the accident of birth is the only criterion for membership. Despite their loose structure, these groupings have a discernible impact on political behavior, especially on the direction of the vote. Political commentators often try to predict how the "Jewish vote" or the "Polish vote," for example, is going to go in a forthcoming election. Most important for our purposes is the point made earlier that *persons living in communities that are relatively homogeneous with respect to these groupings tend to have a somewhat higher rate of political participation.* Living in such a homogeneous environment seems to increase a sense of political effectiveness, facilitates communication about politics, strengthens participatory norms, and deepens group identification.

Persons belonging to more than one group may find their groups pulling in different directions, or some groups may urge political action while others urge inaction. As discussed in Chapter 3, such persons may be thought of as cross-pressured. It has generally been found that **persons in group cross-pressure are less likely to participate than those not cross-pressured** (Degras, Gray & Pear, 1956; Fuchs, 1955; Lipset, 1960). Conversely, **persons belonging to groups that are homogeneous in political direction are more likely to participate** (McClosky & Dahlgren, 1959; McPhee & Glaser, 1962). **The family is a highly homogeneous group with a very high rate of interaction; its influence on participation patterns as well as on voting choice is very high** (Bowman & Boynton, 1966; Glaser, 1959–1960; Kuroda, 1967; McPhee & Glaser, 1962; Marvick & Nixon, 1961; Wahlke, et al., 1962).

Organizational mobilization is especially important for relatively deprived groupings such as Negroes in the United States, or the untouchables in India (Verba, Ahmed & Bhatt, 1971). The recent spurt of growth in membership and numbers of civil rights organizations in the United States has enormously increased the participation of Negroes in politics. Several studies also show that **Labor union members are more likely to take an interest in politics, to have stronger stands on issues, and to vote than are nonunion laboring persons** (Campbell, Gurin & Miller, 1954; Campbell, et al., 1960; Campbell & Kahn, 1952; McPhee & Glaser, 1962; Tingsten, 1937; Verba & Nie, 1972).[2]

---

[2] There are some exceptions: both in Illinois and Indiana samples, union membership had no impact on the likelihood of voting (M. Miller, 1952; Olsen, 1972).

Evidence suggests that group membership boosts the participation rate of lower-status individuals to a greater extent than similar membership does for higher-status individuals. Thus, organizations can become important channels helping to bring the lower strata of society into politics. Some individuals achieve a high level of political activity because of their personal characteristics: their education, skills, efficacy feelings, and so on. Others, who are without these necessary resources, also can reach high activism through affiliation and involvement with groups. Group activity can usually increase political action without concomitant increases in political information, efficacy, or attentiveness (Nie, Powell & Prewitt, 1969).

Organizational context also can be used to explain an interesting anomaly in the United States. The state of West Virginia has a higher voting turnout rate than its neighboring states; indeed, in the nation it ranks sixth from the top. West Virginia is characterized by low family income, low education, and high rates of unemployment. This high level of activity in a poor state is an exception to the general pattern. The explanation is that certain sections of the state were subjected to high unionization activity around the turn of the century (1890–1920). The union movement brought poor people to politics. The participatory tradition developed in that period has continued to be relevant to the present time (Johnson, 1971).

COMMUNITY IDENTIFICATION   It was mentioned several times above that persons who are well integrated into their community tend to feel close to the center of community decisions and are more likely to participate in politics. One evidence of this is that **the longer a person resides in a given community, the greater the likelihood of his participation in politics** (Agger, Goldrich & Swanson, 1964; Alford & Scoble, 1968; Allardt & Bruun, 1956; Birch, 1950; Birch & Campbell, 1950; Buchanan, 1956; Kitt & Gleicher, 1950; Lane, 1959; Lipset, 1960; Tingsten, 1937). Although length of residence correlates with voting turnout, it seems especially relevant to gladiatorial activities. A newcomer to town very likely begins to vote after a year or so, but it usually takes some additional time before he is drawn into party work. Only after a few years of testing will community residents be inclined to entrust party office to a newcomer or encourage his candidacy for public office.

Another bit of evidence is that *homeowners, who more likely have a stake in the community, are more likely to vote, and be generally involved in politics than nonhomeowners* (Alford & Scoble, 1968; M. Miller, 1952). A study of a Mississippi community found that persons who identified strongly with their community were more likely to feel that their vote had political impact, and they were less likely to perceive their community as run by a small elite not subject to popular guidance (Buchanan, 1956). It is curious, yet understandable, that persons most estranged from politics and their community are most likely to perceive their community as run by a small clique of autocratic rulers. Additional evidence relative to community integration comes from data relating age to participation: *young people are not likely to become enmeshed in politics until they have become established in a job, a home, and start to raise a family*—but that is the topic of the next section.

AGE Many studies the world over have found that **participation increases steadily with age until it reaches a peak in the middle years, and then gradually declines with old age** (n.a. unconventional participation). This finding receives added confidence by appearing in a variety of samples from many cultures (Tingsten, 1937; data from five countries; Campbell, et al., 1960; Lipset, 1960; Lane, 1959; Kuroda, 1967; Matthews & Prothro, 1966; Verba & Nie, 1972; Nie, Verba & Kim, 1974, data from five countries; Goel, 1975). In earlier studies, curves were plotted mainly for voting turnout, but recent evidence suggests that the curvilinear age-participation relationship is equally relevant to other modes of participation.

Strong evidence from the United States indicates, however, that when educational and sex differences of various age groups are taken into account, the decline in the voting rate of the elderly largely disappears (Glenn & Grimes, 1968; Riley & Foner, 1968). (Older persons in the United States are below average on education and more likely to be female.) Evidence also suggests that *age makes the greatest difference among the least educated persons; the best educated are likely to vote at all ages.*

For conventional activities other than voting, a similar curve has been reported in the five-nation survey of: Austria, India, Japan, Nigeria, and the United States (Nie, Verba & Kim, 1974). In each nation (with minor variations), participation rises in the early years, reaches a peak in the middle years, and declines in old age. The heterogeneity of these cultures gives us confidence in the validity of the findings. When the authors corrected for educational variation among different age cohorts, they found that the older groups participated around the average for all citizens. Thus, lower activity among the elderly largely reflects their lower educational attainment, and not a withdrawal from politics because of age. On the other hand, it seems clear that the young are genuine underparticipants in conventional activities.

The normal age-participation relation may not hold for blacks in the United States in current times. One study in the South found that Negroes under age thirty-five were more conventionally active in community affairs than older Negroes (Agger, Goldrich & Swanson, 1964). In another study of the South (Matthews & Prothro, 1966), the whites fit the normal pattern, but two factors distinguished the Negroes' political participation from that of the whites: (1) the peak of their political activity occurred at a much earlier age (in the forties) than it did for southern whites or for Americans in general, and (2) the level of activity for Negroes beyond age forty was very low (Matthews & Prothro, 1966). Obviously, some generational experiences particular to Negroes are at work here. Most of the older Negroes in the South grew up in a period of open political repression oftentimes officially sanctioned. Young militant Negroes fought hard for civil rights and opportunities to participate in politics; they have had some success. We may expect Negroes to more closely approach the national curve relating age to participation after the older generation has passed from the scene.

The variation of participation with age is perhaps best explained by position in the life cycle. **The most apathetic group are the young unmarried citizens who are only marginally integrated into their community.** Several studies have found that **married persons are more likely to participate in politics than single persons** (Allardt, 1956; Allardt & Bruun, 1956; Glaser, 1959–1960; Karlsson, 1958a; Lipset, 1960; Tingsten, 1937; Olsen, 1972). Other studies, however, found no relationship between marital status and political participation (Agger & Ostrom, 1956; M. Miller, 1952). Possibly the relationship of marriage to participation is confounded by the fact that it is difficult for a couple with young children to find time for politics. This factor is more important in determining gladiatorial participation than in determining voting. There is scanty evidence connecting the number and age of children to participation; analysis of the Survey Research Center's 1956 election data suggests that couples with young children participate less than couples with no children or with older children.

The full array of data suggests, then, that there are three intervening variables relating age to participation: integration with the community, the availability of blocks of free time for politics, and good health. Integration with the community develops gradually with marriage, job responsibility, and acquiring a family; thus, participation rises gradually with advancing age, leveling off at about thirty-five or forty. Young children and other confinements delay the full opportunity for participation, especially for young mothers. Finally, in the twilight years, physical infirmities probably account for a modest decline in participation.

We need to make one important qualification to the discussion presented here. Whereas conventional political activities correlate positively, or sometimes curvilinearly, with age, participation in protests, demonstrations and riots seems to be largely a youth phenomenon. Several United States studies have reported that **the militant, particularly the rioter, is most likely to be a young male** (Sears & McConahay, 1973; Tomlinson, 1970b; Caplan, 1970; Eisinger, 1974; Buffalo Survey, 1968). Available data are only from the United States, but the pattern may hold in other countries as well. Several factors may explain the overrepresentation of the young in militant behaviors: blocks of free time (for students and the unemployed); lack of integration into or rejection of community norms; invulnerability to economic and social reprisals (no jobs to lose, disdain for disapproving neighbors); and desire for reform of the system which puts them in those positions.

VARIATIONS BY SEX The traditional division of labor which assigns the political role to men rather than women has not vanished. The survey interviewer seeking respondents for a political study discovers after only a few house calls that there are significant remnants of the tradition in modern society. A favorite excuse for not wishing to be interviewed is to claim that the husband takes care of the family politics. The finding **that men are more likely to participate in politics than women** is one of the most thoroughly substantiated in social science (Agger, Goldrich & Swanson, 1964; Allardt, 1956; Allardt & Pesonen, 1960; Almond & Verba, 1963; Degras, Gray & Pear, 1956; Berelson, Lazarsfeld & McPhee, 1954; Birch, 1950; Buchanan, 1956; Campbell & Cooper, 1956; Connelly & Field, 1944; Dogan & Narbonne, 1955; Gronseth, 1955; Grundy, 1950;

Kuroda, 1967; Lane, 1959; Lazarsfeld, Berelson & Gaudet, 1944; McPhee & Glaser, 1962; Pesonen, 1960; Rokkan, 1962b; Tingsten, 1937, data from five countries; DiPalma, 1970; Matthews & Prothro, 1966; Olsen, 1973; Goel, 1975; Nie, Verba & Kim, 1974, data from five countries; Watanuki, 1972; Buffalo Survey, 1968). Data supporting this proposition come from more than a dozen countries. The only exception to this rule, known to the authors, has been reported in Argentina where one study showed female turnout to be a shade higher than male (83.7 percent versus 82.7 percent, Lewis, 1971).

In the United States, the voting rate of women is about 10 percent lower than that of men, although the gap is becoming gradually narrower. **The gap between men and women is widest among lower-status people, and narrowest among the upper-status.** At lower-status levels very few women participate but at higher levels, e.g., among college-educated women political participation rates are little different from those of college-educated men. There is little difference in sense of citizen duty between men and women in the United States. In fact, among the better educated, women are more likely to express a duty to participate. What distinguishes male political participation rates from female political participation rates is the male's sense of political efficacy; **men are more likely than women to feel that they are qualified to deal with the complexities of politics** (Campbell, et al., 1960). Feelings of efficacy are least common among poorly educated women.

Economic and social modernization is slowly eroding this sex difference, however. In the Almond and Verba five-nation study (1963), the United States led other countries in its overall rate of participation (except in voting, where the United States ranks lower). This higher participation rate was mainly due to the high rate of participation by American women. Comparison of participation rates across countries *for males only* shows the same level of participation in the United States, the United Kingdom, and Germany (e.g., almost exactly two-thirds of the males in each nation belong to organizations). In another cross-national comparison, the male-female gap was found to be the smallest in the United States and the largest in India, with Japan, Austria, and Nigeria falling in between (Nie, Verba & Kim, 1974). This suggests that feminine political roles continue to be defined rather narrowly in many parts of the world. In the southern United States, sex differences for all forms of participation and at all levels of education are more distinct among Negroes than among whites; Negro males are more active politically than females, notwithstanding the familiar dominant role of the mother in the Negro family (Matthews & Prothro, 1966). In India, the more modernized states have higher female voting turnout than the less modernized states (Goel, 1975). The participation gap between men and women likely will close further as literacy increases, incomes rise, women find jobs outside the home, and women's liberation movements progress.

RELIGION It is difficult to know if religion per se influences political behavior, because religious groupings tend to coincide with SES, ethnic, and racial groupings. It is virtually impossible to separate out religion from these other factors. In any case, religious differences in participation are slight. The general pattern found in the United States is that **Jews are slightly more active in politics than Catholics who, in turn, are slightly more active than Protestants** (Campbell & Kahn, 1952; Connelly & Field, 1944; Lane, 1959). The Survey Research Center 1956 election data showed Catholics more likely than Protestants to vote but not more likely to engage in gladiatorial activities; Jews were more likely to engage in both spectator and gladiatorial activities. More recently Verba and Nie (1972) found in the United States that Catholics were a bit more likely than Protestants to vote, as well as more likely to take part in campaigns, but that they were somewhat less likely to engage in "communal" activity. This more party-related participation among Catholics possibly springs from stronger partisan attachments (Verba & Nie, 1972). Catholics are more likely to be strong democratic partisans. No data were found relating religion to unconventional political activity.

One can guess that factors of group cohesion and group tradition are important in differentiating the political behavior of religious groupings. It seems reasonable to suppose that Jews are the most cohesive of the groupings, Catholics next, and Protestants least cohesive, since that category is itself made up of many groups. Another factor might be that groups which fear religious discrimination and persecution participate more heavily in politics to forestall use of the machinery of the state for oppression. Groups without these fears would have less motive for political activity. No data could be found relevant to either of these hypotheses.

A study in Waukegan, Illinois, found persons affiliated with a church more likely to vote than nonaffiliates (M. Miller, 1952). The Survey Research Center 1956 election data showed regular attenders at church more likely than average to vote but not more likely to engage in gladiatorial activities (it was reported in Chapter 3 that most people felt a duty to vote but few felt a duty to become a gladiator); nonattenders and nonaffiliates were less likely to participate in both spectator and gladiator activities. The reader is reminded of the relevance of this to the relationship between group participation and political participation previously discussed.

BLACKS, WHITES, AND POLITICAL PARTICIPATION Participation patterns among Negroes in the United States have undergone revolutionary change in the past two decades. Negroes have moved from being an inactive and disenfranchised minority, especially in the South, to a more self-assured and vocal group in the 1970s. This striking change has attracted considerable study, and a number of books and monographs have appeared on Negro politics.[3]

Physiological racial characteristics do not account for participation differences between races; rather, it is the relative social position of racial groupings that creates these differences. It seems clear that in the United States, Negro and other racial minorities have been located toward the periphery rather than toward the center of society. Generally, they have less education, fewer job opportunities, lower incomes, and fewer opportunities to interact with prominent people. It has repeatedly been found in nationwide studies in the United States that **Negroes participate in politics at a lower rate than whites** (Campbell, Gurin & Miller, 1954; Campbell, et al., 1960; Janowitz & Marvick, 1956: Verba, Ahmed & Bhatt, 1971; Verba & Nie, 1972; Matthews & Prothro, 1966). Voting rates for Negroes are about 12 percent lower than for whites; the respective white-black voting percentages in three presidential elections are: 70.7 percent against 57.6 percent in 1964, 69.1 percent against 57.6 percent in 1968, and 64.5 percent against 52.1 percent in 1972 (*Current Population Reports*, 1972). Voting turnout among Negroes in the South is lower than in other regions. In the 1968 presidential election, 52 percent of Negroes in the South reported having voted as compared to 64.8 percent in the North *(Current Population Reports,* 1972). **The lower the level of office,**

---

[3] See Hanes Walton, Jr., *Black Politics* (Philadelphia: Lippincott, 1972) for an extended bibliography.

the greater the black-white voting differential. In one study of the South, black voting rate as a proportion of white voting rate was 78 percent in the presidential election, but only 59 percent in local elections (Matthews and Prothro, 1966).

Distinguishing between types of political activities is important for understanding Negro political participation. Fewer Negroes enter politics, but of those who do, a greater percentage go on to participate in difficult acts. Thus, **once Negroes become engaged in politics, they are as likely as white (and sometimes more likely) to participate at high levels** (Verba & Nie, 1972; Matthews & Prothro, 1966). In the Matthews and Prothro study of the South (1966), Negroes voted less frequently than whites; they also lagged behind the whites in campaigning (although by a smaller percentage than for voting), but a higher proportion of Negroes belonged to political organizations and associations. Hunter found more than 350 organizations within the Negro subcommunity of Atlanta and he stated that the Negro associational groupings tend to "have a political content not found in the larger community" (Hunter, 1953). In the Buffalo Survey (1968), blacks were found to be somewhat more active in party work than whites, and a great deal more active in protests and demonstrations.

The distinctiveness of racial differences in political participation can be understood only if we simultaneously consider the impact of socioeconomic variables. We know that SES is positively related to conventional and unconventional political participation. We also know that blacks are more likely to be found in the lower strata of society. The question therefore arises, is it the low SES of Negroes that impedes their participation, or is it their blackness? This question has been investigated rather thoroughly and we can confidently state that the somewhat lower participation among blacks is a reflection of their lower SES, and not of any racial characteristics. **Class by class Negroes are as active as whites (and sometimes more)** (Verba & Nie, 1972; Verba, Ahmed & Bhatt, 1971; Orum, 1966; Olsen, 1970; Cataldo, Johnson & Kellstedt, 1968). In two different samples, when corrections were made for SES, blacks were found to exceed whites in all forms of participation (Olsen, 1970; Orum, 1966).

The real question, therefore, is not why the Negro under-participates, but given his deprived social position, what explains his activism? The answer to this question lies mainly in the ability of Negro organizations to mobilize black citizens. In several places in this book we have already discussed how class-based political parties help narrow the participation gap between lower- and upper-strata persons. In similar fashion, black organizations have had marked success in mobilizing politically passive blacks within a lower-SES environment which normally is associated with lower political participation. Black organizations strive to instill feelings of group consciousness and racial pride. It has been found that **blacks who manifest racial pride and a sense of group consciousness participate substantially more than the average black** (Olsen, 1970; Verba & Nie, 1972; Buffalo Survey, 1968).

It has been hypothesized that concentration of an ethnic minority tends to increase its political participation by increasing communication, group consciousness, and feelings of togetherness (Lipset, 1960). The opposite of this hypothesis has been found to hold for blacks in the South, however. **The larger the percentage of blacks in a southern community, the smaller the number who are politically active.** On the basis of county level data, a correlation of $-.46$ was found between Negro population as a proportion of total population and voter registration (Matthews & Prothro, 1966).

The areas where southern Negroes are concentrated tend to be rural, poor and remote, and it could be argued that these characteristics of the community, and not Negro concentration, are the real causes of lower participation rates. But this is not the case. **Regardless of controls for other factors, Negro voting registration in southern communities goes down, as their share of the population goes up** (Matthews & Prothro, 1966). The explanation for this finding is that as the potential Negro share of the vote increases, so do white fears and white pressures to prevent Negroes from voting. White pressures to restrict Negro participation can succeed rather easily if the bulk of Negroes are economically vulnerable. Counties where blacks are concentrated in economically subordinate occupations (farm tenancy, domestic service) have been found to have the lowest voting turnout (Salamon & Van Evera, 1973). With continuing militancy in the years to come, concentration of black population may prove to be an asset rather than a liability for blacks' participation. Indeed, a concentration of black population would seem to be necessary for increasing black representation in public offices. The effect of such concentration is already being felt as more and more blacks are elected to public office in the South.

Earlier we spoke of the powerful impact of Negro organizations. Some of these organizations have persuaded their followers to vote as a bloc. A study of Negroes in Florida politics found a significant amount of bloc voting (Price, 1955). In vigorously contested electoral contests between white candidates, a bloc of Negro votes can tip the balance toward candidates selected by Negro leaders. This gives important bargaining power to Negroes as they plead for policies helpful to their race. It is important in Negro bloc voting in the South that knowledge of the Negro-endorsed candidates be kept from the white community until the majority of the white ballots have been cast, otherwise the Negro endorsement may act as the "kiss of death" among white voters. The Negro bloc vote in Durham, North Carolina, managed in that fashion, has been a significant swing factor in many elections there.

If a minority is prevented from using normal political channels for the redress of grievances, does it turn to extraordinary means or even attempt to destroy the political system? Extreme alienation accompanied by feelings of futility and despair may lead to a withdrawal into isolation. Apparently, many American Negroes had this posture toward politics until very recently, and, conceivably, a majority do even today. Sometimes, however, a deprived minority begins to feel that its situation may be improved if some extraordinary means can be used to tap the latent political power of the group. In this situation, feelings of alienation combine with feelings of expectation and confidence to produce extremist behavior, as discussed in Chapter 3.

Currently, dark-skinned peoples all around the world seem to be caught up in a "revolution of rising expectations." As their expectations rise, they can no longer be content with the slow processes of social and political change. American Negroes in recent years have turned to sit-ins, boycotts, and street demonstrations as their choice of extraordinary means when ordinary means failed or were too slow. The bulk of recent research shows most whites rejecting protests and demonstrations as a viable means of political change, but Negroes tend to embrace the tactics as legitimate and viable.

It is important that most of the Negro community has chosen to accept rather than try to overthrow the existing political system. Some minority-group members, however, may believe that action within the system is futile; at the same time they may feel that they must try something drastic to dislodge the equilibrium of the system. Such persons may try to subvert the system or sweep it away. We need to know more about the conditions under which persons who feel politically deprived shift to extraordinary or destructive means in order to redress their grievances.

Chapter 5 Political Participation as a Function of Environmental Variables

So far we have discussed factors which are "internal to" individuals: level of education, sense of efficacy, alienation, sociability and so on. Here we will explore the impact on political participation of "external" or environmental variables. Environmental factors shape human behavior independent of the personal traits of an individual. For instance, the presence of white-collar Negroes in a southern community has a multiplier effect—it enhances the participation rate of the whole black community (Matthews & Prothro, 1966, p. 121).

There are a variety of contextual or environmental variables that could affect political participation: the non-human biological and physical aspects of the surrounding world; the cultural milieu; the social-structural character of the community, and the political setting. Most of the emphasis in the following pages will be on exploring the connection between certain socioeconomic development variables and political setting variables on the one hand and political participation on the other. Specifically, we will be concerned with the following: the level of modernization; rules of the game about the conduct of politics; political institutions, especially the nature of the party system; the characteristics of a given election; and regional differences. Most studies relating environmental factors to participation utilize voting turnout as the only indicator of political activity because turnout can be ascertained and measured rather easily. Research is thin on the impact of environmental factors on gladiatorial activities. Recent studies of recruitment to public office are an exception to this point (Seligman, et al., 1974).

Even when emphasis is placed on sociopolitical factors, the reader ought to remember that purely physical factors such as terrain, distance, and weather affect politics, too. The person who has to climb over a mountain, or travel a long distance, or go out in inclement weather has a greater energy and time cost for his participation than does a person without such barriers. A higher degree of positive attraction to participate must be present to overcome them. University of California researchers found physical proximity to protest sites to be a crucial factor. Both among the alienated and the nonalienated, proximity to central protest localities (Golden Gate Park, Berkeley campus) had the effect of increasing participation in demonstrations (Shanks, 1975; Citrin, 1975). In certain settings, the cost of overcoming physical barriers is approximately equal for each citizen and need not be considered in trying to explain individual differences in behavior. When the costs of surmounting these barriers are unequal from individual to individual, they should be taken into account in the explanation of behavior differences.

THE LEVEL OF MODERNIZATION   Modernization and social change became an exciting field of study in the post-World War II era. By modernization we mean the industrial penetration of traditional societies (nations) with concomitant changes in their sociopolitical structures and cultural values. The predominance of "primary" institutions (family, village, church) gives way to "secondary" institutions (voluntary organizations, unions, parties, state structures); face-to-face communications give way to mass communications; local autonomy to interdependence; tribal loyalties to national loyalties, and so on. It follows that one of the consequences of modernization is an increase in the levels of political awareness and political participation.

In the literature on political development and modernization it is commonplace to speak of changing participatory patterns in the new nations. Indeed some scholars suggest that these patterns are at the very core of the process of development (Lerner, 1958; Deutsch, 1961; Almond & Verba, 1963; Weiner, 1966). Myron Weiner states: "The process of modernization itself creates conditions for increased political participation; and if modernization continues to take place in the developing areas, we can expect both authoritarian regimes and representative governments to be challenged by new participants who want to share power" (1966, p. 212).

In a similar vein, Almond and Verba (1963) declare: "If there is a political revolution going on throughout the world, it is what might be called the participation explosion. In all the new nations of the world the belief that the ordinary man is politically relevant—that he ought to be an involved participant in the political system—is widespread. Large groups of people who have been outside of politics are demanding entrance into the political system. And the political elites are rare who do not profess commitment to this goal" (p. 4). Available empirical evidence tends to support the generalization that, with everything else being equal, **the more modernized societies have higher political participation levels than the less modernized ones.** In the five-nation study, for instance, the United States and the United Kingdom led other nations in rates of participation. These two nations were followed by Germany, Mexico and Italy (in that order) (Almond & Verba, 1963; secondary analysis of the same data by Nie, Powell & Prewitt, 1969). There also is modified support for this finding in the comparative study of the United States, Japan, Austria, Nigeria, and India (Kim, Nie & Verba, 1974). In that study the United States and Japan exhibited the highest political activity, and India lagged behind all others. Both studies suggest a rough correlation between socioeconomic development and level of political participation.

What components of modernization are responsible for heightened political involvement? This general question has been extensively treated in a secondary analysis of Almond and Verba's (1963) five-nation data by some of their students (Nie, Powell & Prewitt, 1969). Their overall conclusion is that with economic development comes an expansion in the size of the middle and upper classes, as well as in the number and pervasiveness of secondary organizations. "Social class and organizational life are the components of economic development which most strongly affect mass political participation" (p. 370). When both these factors are taken into account, some differences between the five nations remain, but these are of small magnitude.

MODERNIZATION AND POLITICAL VIOLENCE The relationship between modernization and potential for political violence differs from the relationship between modernization and conventional political participation. Huntington (1968) declares that whereas modernity breeds stability, modernization breeds instability. Most students of political change suspect that there is a *curvilinear* relationship between the level of modernization and the potential for political violence. Thus, the highly developed as well as the most traditional societies are perceived as more peaceful and stable, and those in the process of modernization are perceived as being more violence-prone.

Why are citizens in a "transitional" society more likely to participate in unconventional political activities? Why is the potential for political violence common? The most prevalent theories to account for this phenomenon are based on a "gap" hypothesis. Huntington argues that in emerging nations the development of political institutions (or political institutionalization) does not keep pace with social mobilization. Political institutionalization is seen as increasing the capability and adaptability of institutions to cope with new pressures that are placed on them during the transitional phase. Social mobilization is defined by increasing urbanization, literacy, and exposure to mass media—all of which gives rise to new awarenesses, demands, and aspirations. Social mobilization occurs at a more rapid rate than does political institutionalization, leading to anomic behavior (Huntington, 1968).

Another "gap" theory goes under the name of relative deprivation (RD), and is defined as the gap between "aspirations" and "achievements." When people believe that they are justifiably entitled to greater rewards than they are achieving, they experience relative deprivation. Leading theorists in the use of relative deprivation as a general explanatory model are Gurr (1970), Feierabend, Feierabend and Gurr (1972), and Davies (1962, 1971, 1973). It can be argued that conditions which produce RD are at their peak during the transitional phase. Less modernized societies are exposed to the modern ways of more advanced nations. This exposure gives rise to new aspirations that are not realized simultaneously by the economic and political systems of the less modernized nations. The hypothesis advanced to explain why RD leads to violence is derived from frustration-aggression theory. According to this theory, people who feel deprived often become frustrated and angry, and it is then that they are inclined to strike out at the sources of frustration. Therefore, the **more a society is exposed to modernity while it continues at a low level of development, the greater its potential for political violence** (Gurr, 1970; Feierabend, Feierabend & Gurr 1972; Lerner, 1958; Greene, 1974).

The most systematic test of this hypothesis has been undertaken with cross-national aggregate data. In one study, eighty-four nations were rank ordered on a modernity index, and this ranking was correlated with instability scores. The group of countries classified as "modern" experienced less civil commotion than those classified as "transitional." In that study the rate of change on key socioeconomic indices also was correlated with turmoil, disclosing that *the higher the rate of change on the indices, the greater the increase in violence* (Feierabend, Feierabend & Gurr, 1972).

The major shortcoming of the RD theory lies in the indirect measurement of the chief explanatory variable. An individual micro-level factor is operationalized by aggregate indicators at the macro level. Thus, unemployment rates become indicators of individual discontent, as do urban crowded conditions, the existence of colonial rule, and particular land tenure arrangements. The level of aspirations and expectations is inferred from educational rates, mobility patterns, or the extent of dissemination of the mass media. At best, these are weak indicators of the true psychological feelings of individuals. This is not to say that these theories are not suggestive; they are intuitively impressive. For example, Davies (1973) argues that a sudden and rapid decline in achievement levels after a period of increasing expectations is especially likely to precipitate dissent and lead to participation in unconventional political activities (the J-curve hypothesis).

In order to avoid the dangers of inferring from the aggregate level to the individual level we must eventually test these propositions with individual level data. However, the evidence which does exist by way of direct tests of the RD theory through individual level data is ambiguous and contradictory. In a study of 270 black residents in a riot area in Detroit, Harlan Hahn (1970) correlated an individual's level of deprivation with the extent the respondent's radicalness and propensity for violence, but found no significant association. It is impossible to determine if this lack of relationship is due to the inadequacy of the RD-civil strife hypothesis or to the weak operationalization of the concept.* When a different measurement device was used, Muller (1975) found in a study of 266 adults in Germany that RD and political violence did occur together under certain conditions. Gurr (1970) also cites several studies where the RD-civil strife hypothesis has been supported. Further careful research should help to clarify the dynamics at work here.

RULES OF THE GAME Eligibility rules are the primary consideration of this section. These have their strongest impact on the likelihood of voting, but they have some influence on participation in gladiatorial activities as well. Persons not eligible to vote in a society are not likely to engage in other political activities either. Mere eligibility, on the other hand, by no means guarantees participation.

Although "universal suffrage" is a common phrase, no society grants total universal suffrage. Children are excluded from voting in every society. Criminals and persons who are physically and mentally incapable usually are excluded. Some scholars estimate that 3 percent of American adults are excluded from the electorate because of capability rules (Campbell, et al., 1960). Even today, there are many societies where persons are not allowed to vote because they are propertyless, are illiterate, are of the female sex, and so forth.

The struggle for the extension of the suffrage is a fascinating chapter in history.[1] Most of this development occurred after the American and French revolutions and went on simultaneously, with variations in pace, in many Western countries. Although there may have been pressure from the disfranchised to be given the vote, in many cases a more important factor was the expectation by a ruling faction that extension of the suffrage would help insure the maintenance of its position in power

---

*Deprivation was measured on Cantril's Self-Anchoring Striving Scale, which is discussed in H. Cantril, *The Pattern of Human Concerns* (New Brunswick, N.J.: Rutgers University Press, 1965). It has been argued that the Cantril scale measures discrepancy between a person's actual achievement level and "the best possible" life he faintly hopes to achieve. Gurr, on the other hand, conceives RD as the gap between that achievement level to which a person believes he is *justifiably entitled* and his actual achievement level. See Grofman & Muller (1973), and Gurr (1970). For further explanation of the Self-Anchoring Striving Scale see the Appendix.

[1] See Lane (1959) and Rokkan (1962b) for a more detailed summary of that history.

(Rokkan, 1962b). The impact on the political system of an extension of the suffrage generally was gradual and delayed rather than immediate. The percentage of the newly enfranchised participating in politics tended to rise very gradually with succeeding elections because, in most cases, the new eligibles were mobilized after, rather than before, extension of the suffrage (Rokkan & Valen, 1962; Tingsten, 1937). Since the newly enfranchised generally were less politicized than those eligible at an earlier date, *as suffrage expanded, the total number of participants rose, but the percentage of eligibles participating declined* (Kyogoku & Ike, 1959).

The secret ballot was introduced in many nations in the nineteenth century. The campaign for ballot secrecy was partly justified on the ground that voters needed to be protected from pressure by their superiors. It was also justified by the belief that vote-buying would drop off because there would be no way to be certain of delivery of the vote. However, another, and largely unintended, consequence of the secret ballot was that it protected a voter from pressure by his peers. His work-mates, his friends, and perhaps even his family need not know how he voted, if indeed he voted at all, unless he chose to reveal it. The secret vote could be an irresponsible vote, in that the act is separated from the role; normal role sanctions, such as ostracism, rebuke, and so forth, are difficult to apply. Although one might suspect that the separation of the act from role constraints, by the secret ballot, could have important consequences for the functioning of the political system, there is insufficient research on this to be able to say what those consequences are.

Even though suffrage may be "universal," there often are other legal barriers to participation, the most significant being residence requirements. The United States compared to other Western democracies imposes stricter residence requirements as conditions for voting. Typically, the prospective voter must have lived in the state one year, in the county 90 days, and in the precinct 30 days (Andrews, 1966). According to a report published in 1963 by the President's Commission on Registration and Voting, only twelve states had residence requirements of less than one year, but fifteen states allowed new residents to vote for national candidates (president and vice-president) even if they did not meet the full-term requirements for state and local candidates. The extended residence requirements are on the way out, however. On May 25, 1972, the Supreme Court ruled that Tennessee's 90-day residence stipulation was unconstitutional. This ruling is likely to have important consequences in broadening the potential electorate.

Obviously, the more mobile the population, the greater the barrier of residence requirements. It was recently estimated that 40 million American adults change residence each year. The President's Commission (1963) estimated that 4 million persons were disfranchised by residence rules in 1950, 5 million in 1954, and 8 million in 1960. Sufficient research is not yet available on how this number is being reduced as the states bring their laws in conformity with the new Supreme Court ruling.

Registration rolls can be maintained either to facilitate or to hinder voting. Many democracies have what is called official or automatic registration. In such a system, no initiative by the potential voter is required to get his name on the list of eligibles; the responsibility for keeping the list up to date is with the registration officials. In Britain and Canada, for example, government officials canvass local areas to see that every eligible voter is placed on the electoral rolls. In direct contrast, voter registration laws in the United States, with only a few exceptions, place the responsibility for maintaining registration on the individual. Citizens often are required to take a trip to the county court house, usually during working hours. Some states (over half) facilitate this process by making provisions for precinct or mobile registration on designated days preceding elections. Some allow registration by mail, and a few states use a system akin to automatic registration. Idaho, for example, selects and pays a deputy registrar in each precinct to canvass from door to door and keep registration rolls up to date; Idaho is also the top-ranking state in voting turnout. California law also authorizes the appointment of deputy registrars and door-to-door canvassing. There is a great deal of variation among states on the restrictiveness of their legal structures. Several research analyses have shown that the **states with the least facilitative legal systems have the lowest turnout** (Campbell, et al., 1960; Kelley, Ayers & Bowen, 1967; Milbrath, 1971c).*

---

* The states with the least facilitative legal structures (mostly southern states) tend to be states with a disproportionate number of individuals of low socioeconomic status. For a multivariate analysis which sorts out the relative impact of socioeconomic, legal, and political factors for turnout variation among states, the reader should consult Kim, Petrocik & Enokson (1975). A description of the electoral systems in various Western nations is given in Rose (1974).

In some states, mainly in the South, requirements for voting registration until recently were not only inconvenient, but downright difficult. Registration forms deliberately were made complicated. Some jurisdictions required witnesses to testify to the identity and residence of the applicant. Literacy tests in many jurisdictions were extremely difficult and, if the applicant were black, letter-perfect accuracy often was required in order to be registered. Such a literacy test was administered to his class of white students by a political science professor at a good southern university; the results showed that a majority of the class would have failed to qualify to vote under the test.

In response to strong national pressure and to rectify the registration injustices of seven southern states (Alabama, Georgia, Louisiana, Mississippi, North Carolina, South Carolina, and Virginia) Congress passed the Voting Rights Act of 1965. It banned literacy and other discriminatory voter registration tests and requirements wherever less that 50 percent of the voting age residents were registered or where less than 50 percent had voted in the 1964 presidential election. Federal action also has provided federal registrars to register voters for federal elections where local registrars could not be counted on to facilitate registration. The act has had dramatic impact; in the seven states nearly one million black voters were added to the registration rolls. As expected, the states that had been most restrictive of registration (usually those with the highest black concentration) showed the greatest increase: in Mississippi, for example, the black registration rate jumped from 8.3 percent in 1965 to 67.6 percent in 1970, and the white rate from 57.9 percent to 92.2 percent (Kimball, 1972).

The Federal Voting Rights Act of 1965 can be regarded as a natural political experiment since it is possible to clearly trace the changes in registration rates that derive from it. They were so dramatic that we must view ease of registration as a major contributor to increasing turnout rates. This clear rise in registration also may contribute to the recent rise in general participation levels for the South.

Nearly all states permit some type of permanent voting registration so that citizens need not reregister before each election. Seventeen states also permit absentee registration, which shows a significant, positive relationship with turnout ranking. It also facilitates registration if the registration books can be kept open reasonably close to the election. Most states close registration about one month before the election. Of course, this objective must be balanced against the registrar's practical and time-consuming task of preparing lists of eligibles by election day.

Certain other legal arrangements also may facilitate voting. Voting procedures standardized from locality to locality and from election to election help remove the fear of "not knowing how." *Short ballots reduce the burden of attempting to become informed and thus facilitate turnout* (Gosnell, 1930; Rokkan, 1962b). Even a highly educated and informed citizen may feel poorly prepared when confronted by a ballot with fifty or more candidates. Certain localities have elections so frequently that voters find it difficult to maintain interest; less frequent elections probably would increase the percentage turning out for elections for more important offices (Lane, 1959). Compulsory voting has been tried at one time or another in several countries, including Belgium, Holland, Switzerland, and Austria, and it does seem to increase turnout. One study concluded that *compulsory voting tended to bring less qualified persons to the polls and increased the percentage of invalid ballots* (Tingsten, 1937). The practice has not spread widely, and some countries have abandoned it.

What social groups are most impacted by compulsory voting legislation? In a study of the Netherlands that analyzed turnout data just before and after the compulsory voting legislation was withdrawn (1970), the following pattern was found. Persons belonging to groups least likely to vote do not vote under either system—voluntary or compulsory. On the other hand, persons belonging to groups most likely to vote (the more informed, the more efficacious, and so on) vote under both systems. *Persons on the borderline of whether to vote or not are most encouraged to get to the polls by compulsory voting legislation* (Irwin, 1974).

THE PARTY SYSTEM Political parties were invented, among other reasons, to help citizens interpret political information and events and to organize and channel their political participation. The political party system inevitably affects patterns and rates of participation in politics. In some localities, there is vigorous party competition, but in other localities the majority party may win so consistently and easily that minor party supporters do not contest very vigorously. Although it is necessary to be cautious about application of the rule to specific situations, it is generally true that **the more competitive the parties, the greater the likelihood of high rates of participation** (n.a. to unconventional participation). A rank ordering of the states on party competition correlated .807 with a ranking of the states on turnout in gubernatorial and senatorial elections from 1952 through 1960 (Milbrath, 1965a). A study of four cities in the United States shows that competition between elites (party competition) stimulates mass participation, especially if the competition is ideological (Agger, Goldrich & Swanson, 1964). A study in the South (where the Democratic party dominates state and local elections) reports that bifactional rivalry within the Democratic party tends to be correlated with increased Negro registration when one or more of the candidates seems favorable to Negroes; contested primaries also tended to stimulate turnout (Matthews & Prothro, 1966). In Finland, a strong challenge from the Communist party in a constituency tends to increase turnout (Allardt & Bruun, 1956). Nonpartisan elections do not necessarily depress turnout if there is some competition for offices. Turnout in primaries generally is lower than in general elections, but primary turnout tends to be higher where party competition is greater (Lane, 1959).

Party competition probably affects participation by stimulating interest in a campaign and giving citizens the impression that their individual efforts affect the outcome. If party competition does not produce greater interest and a greater sense of efficacy, it probably has little impact on participation.

The theory of party competition seems to correctly predict turnout variation in India. Peter McDonough (1971) divided Indian constituencies into four categories: multi-party, two-party, one dominant party, and monopoly party. These categories were developed on the basis of closeness of vote among the winning party and the losing parties. Turnout was lowest in multi-party constituencies, and highest in two-party constituencies, with the other two types falling in between. Two party contests tend to be most competitive because each party stands to gain or lose at the cost of the other. In a dominant party system, the party is likely to have an effective organization capable of mobilizing voters. In a multi-party system, the parties may be little more than factions without adequate resources to mount mobilization campaigns and to generate competition.*

---

* On this point Huntington (1968) observes: "Party competition is obviously impossible in a single-party system, but it is also likely to be less in a multi-party system than in a dominant-party or two-party system" (p. 428). Only in a few modernized societies is multipartism associated with heightened competition. In such cases, the parties are likely to be solidly grounded in social forces, each party identifying with a particular group or class.

Beyond a certain number, *a multiplicity of political parties tends to depress voting because it confuses voters, especially those who are minimally involved or who are nonpartisan* (Huntington, 1968; McDonough, 1971). In similar fashion, *it is probable that beyond a certain number, a multiplicity of candidates tends to confuse voters.*

The competitiveness of parties also affects the activities and roles of political gladiators. A safe major party has no problem recruiting candidates because it is the major, or only, channel to political office; its minor party opponent may have to conscript candidates to run (Seligman, 1961: Standing & Robinson, 1958). Competitive party localities seem to be as likely to develop party factions as safe party localities (Seligman, 1961). Bifactional rather than multi-factional rivalry tends to occur in states with one major party, but where there is also some opposition from a minor party (Key, 1949). Factions in competitive parties tend to be vigorous in recruiting and supporting candidates. There seems to be little central control of candidate recruitment in competitive parties (Seligman, 1961). Improved theorizing and additional research are needed in order to know the applicability and limitations of these generalizations.

The presence or absence of party conflict can affect the relationship of other variables to political participation. We note several places in this book that persons of higher education are more likely to participate in politics. A study in Norway, however, found no relationship between amount of education and participation in politics. This led to the speculation that *the relationship between education and political participation is more marked where the politics of the area play down class differences* (Rokkan, 1962b). The explanation of this has been suggested on a previous occasion, but a brief description of the Norwegian party system would help. Norway has several political parties, and the party divisions follow socioeconomic cleavages more closely than in the United States. There is a labor party, a farmer's party, a party mainly supported by white-collar persons, and a conservative party supported by business. The Norwegian parties might be called "status-polarized parties," whereas those in the United States might be called "heterogeneous," since many persons from all statuses are found in each party. The leadership of a low-status party, such as the Norwegian labor party, must recruit and train less educated workers to participate in politics; it does not have a readymade educated elite to call on. Thus, the correlation of education with participation in a status-polarized party system tends to be low. Education becomes a more significant variable determining participation in a setting with heterogeneous parties which play down instead of accentuate class differences.

An unusual finding from the Norwegian election studies is that *turnout is higher where the socioeconomic status of an area is more homogeneous* (Rokkan, 1962b; Rokkan & Campbell, 1960). The proposition does not seem to hold for non-partisan local elections, only for elections where there is some competition between status-polarized parties in a proportional representation system. The interpretation is not so certain as the finding. One can surmise that persons living in homogeneous communities are subjected to fewer cross-pressures. Most of the people around them believe and vote the same way, and they are swept along with the crowd. We know from other studies that *indecision resulting from cross-pressures leads certain persons not to vote at all* (Berelson, Lazarsfeld & McPhee, 1954; Lazarsfeld, Berelson & Gaudet, 1944). Peripheral areas in Norway (those with low population density and difficult geographical access) have fewer party organizations and lower turnout than the more urban and central areas (Rokkan & Valen, 1962).

It has generally been found that turnout at elections in western Europe is higher than turnout in the United States. Some scholars have attempted to trace this to differences in the system of representation. Many western European countries have proportional representation, whereby each party receives seats in the national legislature according to its ratio of the popular vote. Most areas in the United States use a system of single-member districts in which the candidate who obtains a plurality of the vote wins the seat.

Does proportional representation tend to produce higher turnout than the plurality system? The evidence is inconclusive. A study of turnout figures from several countries disclosed that in some countries that switched from the plurality to the proportional representation system turnout increased; the electorate in these countries was maturing simultaneously, however (women were given the vote at about the same time) (Tingsten, 1937). Tingsten concluded that a single-member district system, where one party was dominant, would be likely to have lower turnout (p. 223). New York City tried the proportional representation system for ten years, but it made little difference in turnout (Zeller & Bone, 1948). Turnout was found to be higher for proportional representation than plurality elections in Norway, but the plurality elections also were nonpartisan and generally held in rural areas (both of the latter are correlated with lower turnout) (Rokkan & Valen, 1962). This pattern of evidence leads one to suspect that political interest is the major intervening variable. If the system of representation and election contesting stirs up interest in the populace, they will turn out to vote. If there is little difference between the parties, or if one party is sure to win, the people are likely to be bored and stay at home.

One of the most important stimulants to political participation is personal contact by a party worker; if that worker is also a friend, the contact is even more impressive. It has been found repeatedly that **persons contacted by party workers are more likely to vote and also to participate in gladiatorial activities** (Berelson, Lazarsfeld & McPhee, 1954; Campbell, et al., 1960; Janowitz & Marvick, 1956; Kitt & Gleicher, 1950; McPhee & Glaser, 1962; Milne & Mackenzie, 1954; Wolfinger, 1963).

Contacting citizens individually is one of the most expensive (in terms of time) of all campaign activities. A get-out-the-vote experiment conducted by a graduate seminar at the University of Michigan required an investment of 400 hours to induce 39 persons out of 203 probable nonvoters to vote, a cost of 10 man-hours per vote (Eldersveld, 1956). Precinct captains for the dominant party in an area were found to be much more active in daily contacts with citizens than captains for minor parties. The higher the number of contacts, the more effective the captains were in increasing their party's vote for president (Rossi & Cutright, 1961).

Get-out-the-vote experiments showed that any kind of contact had some discernible impact on increasing turnout, but personal contact was the most effective (Eldersveld, 1956; Eldersveld & Dodge, 1954). It didn't seem to matter whether the personal contact was by student or party worker, by telephone or at the door. Those personally contacted retained the most information about the election and had the most interest in it. This suggests that the variable relationship may read this way: *personal contact stimulates interest and provides information which, in turn, increases the likelihood of coming out to vote.*

CHARACTERISTICS OF SPECIFIC ELECTIONS   Individuals differ in their perceptions of the same events; therefore, a very important factor for the political behavior of a person in an election is the way he perceives that election. He may see it as important or unimportant; he may think his vote counts or doesn't count; he may see it as a choice between Tweed-ledum and Tweedledee. It is important to note that individuals do not perceive in a vacuum: some elections are more important than others, some are more exciting than others, some are easier to understand than others. This has an aggregative effect, stimulating masses of people to perceive an election in a similar way.

Campbell (1960) has defined several differences between high-stimulus and low-stimulus elections. In a high-stimulus election, persons generally perceive that the vote will be close and, therefore, that their vote will count; they feel that the office being decided is an important one; they tend to perceive a clear choice between alternative candidates or parties; the candidates tend to be attractive; there is a high flow of campaign propaganda. A high-stimulus election brings out a relatively high turnout at the polls. Many of the voters are peripheral to the political process and tend to stay home in low-stimulus elections, for which only core voters tend to turn out. Each of the characteristics of a high-stimulus election is examined in turn.

Closeness of the Vote This factor is highly relevant to the party-competition factor discussed above; competitive parties tend to produce close votes. The two factors are not identical, because close votes can occur in nonpartisan elections or in primary elections within a dominant party. We said above that party competition stimulates interest, and this, in turn, stimulates participation. Similarly, *a perception by people that the vote will be close piques their interest and strengthens their belief that their vote will count.* It is the individual's perception which is critical here; a widespread belief that the vote will be close is likely to bring out a high turnout, even if the vote should eventually be lopsided. Conversely, a widespread perception that one party or candidate will win depresses turnout, even if the vote turns out to be close. In the 1948 presidential election, when it was widely believed that Dewey would win, turnout dropped about 10 percent from the normal percentage before and after that election (Milbrath, 1965a, Fig. 2).

Perceptions of closeness of the vote may operate on two or more levels. Persons may perceive the local vote as very lopsided but the national vote as very close; the latter perception still tends to bring them to the polls, even though their local vote is not critical to the outcome. In

Finland, turnout tended to be higher in those districts where more than 50 percent of the vote was cast for a dominant party, but this tendency did not hold if citizens perceived that there was little chance to change the parties forming the national government (Allardt, 1956; Allardt & Bruun, 1956). In Britain in 1950, the highest turnout tended to be found in closely contested constituencies or in those that were heavily dominated by Labor (Nicholas, 1951). The closeness of vote seems not to be related to turnout in French local elections. A comparison of competition in national and local elections showed that competition was less acute in local elections than in national, and yet turnout at the local level was not depressed (Kesselman, 1966).

The potential relationship between closeness of the vote and turnout is weakened by two factors. Many people feel a duty to vote whether or not their vote is essential to the outcome of the election. Second, the activity of the local party organizations is very important in bringing out the vote, and the vigor of this activity is dependent on many factors in addition to the perceived closeness of the vote. In fact, a very strong and dominant party organization in an area can easily produce a whopping turnout without the added prodding of a close election. One naturally would expect party gladiators who know the vote will be close to lend every effort to help their side win, but sometimes they may work just as hard when they know they are sure winners.

These generalizations about the relationship between closeness of vote and turnout probably apply to gladiatorial activities as well (n.a. unconventional participation). There is relatively little research on this. The Norwegian election study shows that *when the marginal value of a vote is high* (a few votes may turn the tide) *party organizations work harder to mobilize the vote* (Rokkan & Valen, 1962). Another scholar has speculated that close contests increase financial participation (Lane, 1959). As additional research relating closeness of vote to gladiatorial activities is conducted, our hypothesis may be confirmed or denied.

Importance of Elections: Persons are more likely to turn out for elections they perceive to be important (Campbell, 1960; Campbell, 1962; Pesonen, 1968). Individuals vary in their perceptions of the importance of a given election, but certain elections are widely perceived as more important than others. **The more powerful the office being decided, the more important the election is likely to be perceived.**

National elections are nearly always perceived as more important than local elections, and turnout is nearly always higher for national elections (Campbell, 1962; Converse & Dupeux, 1961; Lane, 1959; Milbrath, 1965a; Robinson & Standing, 1960; Rokkan & Valen, 1962; Tingsten, 1937). The tendency for national elections to produce a higher turnout than local elections has been observed in several other Western nations in addition to the United States (Campbell, 1962; Converse & Dupeux, 1961; Lane, 1959; Milbrath, 1965a; Robinson & Standing, 1960; Rokkan & Valen, 1962; Tingsten, 1937; Pesonen, 1968; Rose, 1974). Japan seems to be an exception; turnout is routinely higher for local elections than for national elections (Richardson, 1973, 1974).

The trend for elections for higher office to produce higher turnout is so persistent that one scholar has suggested it might be wise to elect a chief executive (president, governor, mayor) at each election as one way to increase turnout for other offices (Lane, 1959). In Norway, the trend for national turnout to be greater than local was most pronounced in rural areas and in areas where the labor party was weakest (the Norwegian labor party is an effective agency for enlisting political participation from low SES persons) (Rokkan & Valen, 1962).

Crisis elections, which obviously are perceived as important, produce higher turnouts than noncrisis elections (Converse & Dupeux, 1961; Key, 1955; Lane, 1959; Lipset, 1960). A study in France found that crises increased interest and psychological involvement in the election (Converse & Dupeux, 1961). In certain areas of Finland where the Communist party is strong (and therefore the election may be perceived as vital by non-Communist voters), the turnout by both Communist and non-Communist voters is high (Allardt & Bruun, 1956). *If a certain segment of the population perceives an election as important or vital, that segment will turn out at a rate higher than normal* (Lane, 1959). A good example of this in the United States is the abnormally high turnout of labor union members in the 1958 congressional elections in those states where so-called right to work laws (perceived as threats to union labor) were to be voted on. In addition to perceiving an election as important, *the citizen must also perceive the government as responding to his efforts if he is to be highly motivated to act* (Campbell, 1962). The perception that an election is important seems most relevant to enlisting spectator activities such as voting (probably gladiators are more inclined to think every election is important), but the belief that the government responds to one's efforts may be more important for enlisting gladiatorial activity. (No data could be found relevant to these hypotheses.)

Clear Differences Between Alternatives: People are more likely to turn out for an election when clear differences are perceived between alternatives than when the alternatives are unclear (Campbell, 1960; Campbell, 1962; Rokkan & Valen, 1962). Clarity of alternatives seems especially important in mobilizing citizens who usually stand on the periphery of politics and do not participate (Campbell, 1960; Rokkan & Valen, 1962). When the alternatives are clear, the costs of collecting information and making a decision are reduced. This was suggested as one possible explanation of why turnout is usually higher for general elections than for primary elections (Matthews & Prothro, 1966). A study of Negroes in Florida politics reported that when the issues are blurred, or lack relevance to the problems of Negroes, the interest of the individual Negro drops, and the cohesion of Negroes as a voting bloc is reduced (Price, 1955). A study of a Swedish election showed that the stands on issues of party followers became much more polarized as the campaign progressed (Särlvik, 1961a).

If all the alternatives in an election are perceived as unattractive, turnout is likely to be lowered even further than normal (Campbell, 1962). Many people perceived both United States presidential candidates (Truman and Dewey) as unattractive in 1948, whereas both candidates (Eisenhower and Stevenson) were perceived as attractive by many persons in 1952; turnout was unusually low in 1948 and unusually high in 1952 (Campbell, Gurin & Miller, 1954; Campbell, et al., 1960). The reader should keep in mind that clarity and attractiveness of alternatives apply to issues and parties as well as to candidates; all three factors interact to produce the total image of an election. The presence of candidates does seem to lend a spark to an election. A study of election returns from several countries showed that **turnout generally was lower for referenda and other noncandidate elections than for elections with candidates** (Tingsten, 1937).

Clarity and attractiveness of alternatives mainly affect election-day turnout and other spectator activities. Gladiators, by virtue of being more involved in the political contest, generally perceive much clearer differences between sides than do spectators. Not only is their knowledge greater and perhaps more accurate, but also they have a need to justify their stand both to themselves and to persons whom they may try to convince that they are right. It was found in a study of national convention delegates that there are much wider differences in policy views between Democratic and Republican party leaders than between Democratic and Republican party followers (ordinary citizens) (McClosky, Hoffman & O'Hara, 1960).

Flow of Propaganda Some campaigns are characterized by a heavier exchange of propaganda between the contesting teams than other campaigns. Some scattered bits of evidence suggest that *the heavier the flow of propaganda, the higher the voting turnout* (Eldersveld, 1956; Eldersveld & Dodge, 1954; Pesonen, 1961). The evidence is not extensive enough to know whether this is a simple linear relationship or whether it is curvilinear. Certainly, if one starts from the bottom (no campaign propaganda at all), succeeding increments of propaganda will produce some increase in turnout. But is there a saturation point beyond which additional propaganda has little or no effect? It may even be possible that propaganda flow could become so heavy as to offend citizens, thus driving them away from the polls instead of attracting them. Much more adequate evidence is needed before we can specify the nature of the relationship between level of propaganda and turnout.

REGIONAL DIFFERENCES WITHIN A POLITICAL SYSTEM Little research attention has been given to region itself as a variable in political behavior research. Often regional differences coincide with differences in social and economic factors or with differences in political system, and these are treated as variables rather than region. Without evidence directly relevant to the point, it is difficult to say whether or not region by itself is a differentiating variable. The following should be taken only as suggestive.

Studies of the national electorate in the United States have repeatedly found that the South as a region acts differently from the rest of the country (Campbell, Gurin & Miller, 1954; Campbell, et al., 1960). These studies consistently show that *persons from the South are significantly less likely to vote and slightly less likely to participate in gladiatorial activities than persons living in other regions of the country* (n.a. unconventional participation). The endeavor in the South to keep Negroes from voting by no means accounts for all of the difference. The party system is less competitive in the South, especially for state and local elections. More persons are engaged in agriculture. Industrialization is less advanced there, and income and educational levels are lower. One study has attempted to weigh the relative impact of these several factors (Kim, Petrocik & Enokson, 1975). The South as a region had a 25.1 percent lower turnout than the national average in the 1960 presidential election. The lower socioeconomic standing of southern residents contributed 8.1 points to this deviation: the two political factors—less facilitative legal structures, and lower electoral competition—together contributed another 13.14 points, leaving 3.79 points as unexplained deviation from the national norm. The fact that southern states tend to have the least competitive elections, the most restrictive legal stipulations, and lower than average socioeconomic standards explains to a large extent their lower turnout. However, other factors need to be considered to account for all the variation. It is conceivable that differences in climate, in topography, and in political history and traditions also contribute to regional differences.

NONELECTORAL AND NONPARTY FACTORS IN POLITICAL SETTING Not all political activity is oriented toward elections and party competition. Much interelection activity is designed to communicate policy preferences to official decision-makers. The amount of this activity depends partly on the pain felt from the social ills persons want corrected and partly on the perceptions citizens have of the responsiveness of officials to their pleas. *Persons who perceive themselves or their group as having an impact on public policy are more likely to communicate their policy preferences to officials than are those perceiving little or no impact* (Lane, 1959). Certain political leaders tend to invite messages from citizens and generally receive an increased flow of communications as a result (Sussman, 1959). Members of Congress who do so are known as those who "court mail." A study in Finland shows that political leaders who take an interest in the people and their problems stimulate a higher level of communicative activity from citizens to officials (Allardt & Pesonen, 1960). Persons in certain environments may perceive that their messages are not being listened to and may choose extraordinary means, such as protest demonstrations, to help make sure that the messages are received.

In addition to using routine and extraordinary means to communicate their policy desires to public officials, citizens of most countries have set up institutions to aggregate their collective interests and to communicate their policy desires. These institutions are variously known as special-interest groups, pressure groups, or lobby groups. They provide a quality and intensity of policy representation that cannot be achieved by political parties or individuals acting separately. In the United States, these groups often take the extra step of hiring a special envoy, called a lobbyist, to spend full time at the seat of government acting as a communication link between his group and the government (Milbrath, 1963). Having organizations of this type available in the political environment provides an additional channel for participation in politics. More than a third of United States citizens belong to one or more of these intermediary political groups, but probably less than half of them are active in their group (only 4 or 5 percent of Americans are members of political parties). Many of the same factors that draw persons into electoral activity also draw persons into group activity.[2] It is difficult, however, to go beyond this kind of broad generalization about a propensity for being active in groups. Although there have been many studies of interest groups and interest-group activity,[3] there is very little research on the specific factors recruiting persons for membership and participation in interest groups.

In summary, the environment of citizens provides opportunities for and places boundaries on political participation. The impact of these environmental factors on participation can be changed or influenced by the design of the constitution and political system of a nation. In thinking about system design one must ask, "how much participation, in which ways, and by whom" is most likely to produce a stable society where people generally find a high quality of life. Some ideas on this topic are discussed in the next chapter.

---

[2] Agger & Goldrich (1958); Allardt (1962); Allardt, et al. (1958); Allardt & Pesonen (1960); Birch (1950); Buchanan (1956); Campbell (1962); Campbell & Kahn (1952); Coser (1951); Dahl (1961); Dogan (1961); Hastings (1954); Jensen (1960); Lane (1959); McClosky & Dahlgren (1959); Marvick & Nixon (1961); Milbrath & Klein (1962); Rokkan (1959); Rosenberg (1954–1955). Lipset (1960, p. 67) has cited nine studies in five countries supporting this proposition.

[3] See the bibliography to Milbrath (1963).

Chapter 6   Political Participation and Constitutional Democracy

The last decade, and in particular the late sixties, could be characterized as an era of the "participation revolution." Many minority groups, especially blacks, students, and women, campaigned vigorously for better and presumably equal opportunities to participate in societal decisions. When their clamorings for recognition seemed frustrated by a political system that responded slowly, if at all, to their urgings, many of these people turned to unconventional protests and demonstrations, even riots, in order to open up a larger place for themselves in the political system. Throughout the days of conflict democracy was upheld as a societal value; it was proclaimed that almost everything that was wrong with society could be improved if democracy were made purer and if everyone participated fully in making democratic decisions.

Now that the clamorings have died down, perhaps we can take stock to evaluate whether or not more participation improves the working of society. It should be apparent from the material in this book thus far that the political participation of ordinary citizens falls far short of their democratic ideals which say that citizens should be interested in and informed about politics, should participate actively in political parties and election campaigns, and should try in every way possible to make their voices heard as political decisions are being made. Political scientists recognized the existence of this gap a long time ago. Many have given considerable thought to the question: "How can democracy continue to function if the political participation of the citizens is so infrequent and so superficial?"(Almond & Verba, 1963, Ch. 15; Berelson, 1952; Berelson, Lazarsfeld & McPhee, 1954, Ch. 14; Campbell, et al., 1960, Ch. 20; Dahl, 1956, Dahl, 1961, Bk VI; Duncan & Lukes, 1963; Eckstein, 1961; Key, 1961, Ch. 21; Lane, 1959, Ch. 22; Lane, 1962; Lipset, 1960, Ch. 13; McClosky, 1964; Prothro & Grigg, 1960). Although these scholars are not in total agreement in their analyses, none expresses great concern about the future of democracy. One reason for this lack of intense concern is that these scholars are confronted by evidence from many societies, accumulated over a considerable period of time, that, despite the low level of political interest and activity, democratic governments continue to flourish and provide reasonably satisfactory governance for their citizens.

In reconciling the fact of low participation with the fact of adequately functioning democracies, political scientists have enlarged their understanding of the political process and of the role of the average citizen in that process. The role of the citizen has evolved into something different from that envisaged by classical democratic theorists. They had in mind a small homogeneous society where most persons were engaged in primary economic activities (agriculture, forestry, fishing, and the like) and where any average man was considered qualified to hold public office and to resolve public issues (which usually were much simpler than those confronting society today). Each man was expected to take an active role in public affairs.

Modern society, in contrast, has evolved a very high division of labor, not only in the economic sector but also in politics and government. Political roles have become highly differentiated and specialized. This enables some persons (elected and appointed officials) to devote their full attention to the complex public issues facing modern society. This division of labor allows others (most of the citizens) to pay relatively little attention to public affairs. Politics and government are a peripheral rather than a central concern in the lives of most citizens in modern Western societies. As long as public officials perform their tasks well, most citizens seem content not to become involved in politics.

The fact of indifference to politics by many citizens should not be taken to mean that government would function well if citizens ignored it completely. In order to keep public actions responsive to the wishes and desires of the people, citizens must at least participate in the choice of their public officials. The institutions of modern democracies have so evolved that policy leadership is left in the hands of elected officials who at periodic intervals go before the people at an election to see which of two or more competing elites will have policy leadership in the next ensuing period. Both the leaders and the public acknowledge the essentiality of this electoral link between the public and its governing elite.

The burden upon the citizen is much less if he is called upon only to select who his rulers will be than if he is asked to decide the pros and cons of an abstract policy. Furthermore, choices of public officials confront the citizen only at periodic elections, thus taking very little of his time. Society has evolved helpful mechanisms, called political parties, to simplify further the choice between alternative sets of public officials. Instead of having to become informed about a number of individual candidates, the citizen can manage simply by knowing the record and reputation of the political parties under whose labels the candidates run. Parties also are helpful in calling the voter's attention to the failures of the opposition party and to their own successes. The citizen does not need to dig for information, it is literally thrust at him.

Another device for keeping public officials responsive to the people is to require and insure open channels of communication, so that citizens who so wish can be heard or consulted when public officials are making policy decisions. In part, this is achieved by constitutional provisions for freedom of speech, press, assembly, and petition. Society also has evolved social institutions, such as interest groups and the mass media, which keep citizens informed of what public officials are doing and public officials informed of what citizens want. The fact that top officials are placed there by election is very significant in insuring that channels of communication stay open between the public and its leaders. If an official should refuse to listen (thus closing the channel), he would probably pay for his folly by losing his position at the next election.

As we think about the role of the average citizen, then, we should not expect him to give a lot of attention to, and be active in resolving, issues of public policy. Nor should we expect him to stand up and be counted on every issue that comes along. The most we can expect is that he will participate in the choice of decision-makers and that he will ask to be heard if an issue comes along that greatly concerns him or on which he can make some special contribution. Many citizens do not even vote or speak up on issues, yet their passive role has the consequence of accepting things as they are. Indeed, it is impossible to escape at least a passive role in the choice of decision-makers. The choice process can proceed and government can continue to function even if many citizens choose to be so inactive as to fail to vote.

Because democracy seems to function more or less adequately with moderate to low levels of political participation, this should not be taken to mean that moderate levels of participation automatically guarantee the maintenance of constitutional democracy. A special burden of responsibility for the maintenance of the system rests on the shoulders of the political elites. If these elites are to perform their roles adequately, it is important that they array themselves into two or more competing groups (usually called political parties). As these elites compete for the support of the voters, they perform functions of vigil and criticism *vis-à-vis* their opponents that moderately interested and active citizens might not perform for themselves. Partisan criticism functions best if it is tempered by the realization that after the next election the elite currently in the role of critic may be called upon to govern. This tempered criticism not only gives the party in power a chance to carry a program through to completion and stand responsible for it, but it also enables bridging of cleavages and helps maintain overall coherence of the society.

Several conditions are critical to the adequate functioning of a system of competitive elites in a constitutional democracy[1]. It is important that the elites be committed to democratic values and believe in the rules of the game. It must be taken for granted, for example, that the elites will compete for mass support and that expression of that support in an election will determine which elite will rule for the ensuing period. Several bits of research suggest that participation in politics builds a commitment to democratic values and that elites are much more likely to understand and adhere to specific applications of general democratic principles than are average citizens (Almond & Verba, 1963; McClosky, 1964; Prothro &

[1] This section is largely indebted to Key (1961, Ch. 21).

Grigg, 1960). An elite in power must have a live-and-let-live policy *vis-à-vis* its opponents out of power; elite political actors should be gladiators but not revolutionaries. Property rights may be important to insure that opponents out of power have some way to support themselves until they can regain power. From another perspective, no elite will readily relinquish power, should it be defeated in an election, if it has no alternative base of economic support. That base might be income-earning property, practice of a profession, jobs in industry not controlled by the government, and so forth. An elite also will be reluctant to relinquish power if it is convinced that its opponents will destroy the group, perhaps by imprisonment or other harassment, once the opponents have been given power.

In order that the interests of all sectors of society be adequately taken care of by the government, it is important that each elite recruit from many sectors of society. An elite from a single class or group would have difficulty gaining the confidence of the people, and competitive elites would be reluctant to entrust it with the reins of power. It is vital that the recruits be socialized to elite norms and customs, especially basic democratic principles and the rules of the political game.

The system demands much less from the political beliefs and behavior of the mass of the citizens than from the elites. To perform its role, the attentive public must believe in the right of the public to watch and to criticize the behavior of the elites. It also needs a minimal sense of involvement in public matters and a sense of loyalty to the whole community rather than to only a segment of the society. It must perform the minimal chore of selecting among the elites at election time. This low level of attention and control by the mass of the public leaves a wide latitude to the elected elite for creative leadership (and perhaps also for mischief).

Although we expect only this minimal surveillance by the public and their participation in the choice of elites, is even this effort too much to expect? What is to prevent a society from becoming widely apathetic and allowing an unscrupulous elite to destroy the chances for an opposing group to compete fairly? In the final analysis, there is no iron-clad guarantee that this will not happen; eternal vigilance is still the price of liberty. Careful training of elite members in the norms and rules of democratic politics is one insurance against such an eventuality. Another is the outcry from the opposing group against the tactics of the party in power.

This outcry has meaning, however, only if the public is listening, understands, and responds decisively.

The idea that moderate to low levels of political participation were acceptable and that elites could be entrusted as managers and protectors of the political system raised an outcry from many students of political philosophy in the late sixties. Some of them protested against the "undemocraticness" of such an argument. Some argued that political participation would become more meaningful and would be sustained at high levels if the political system were restructured so that citizen participation was more decisive for making societal political decisions. Some argued, additionally, that participation in politics and in public debate helps build a better and more noble character in the people. They advocated that public participation in democratic processes should be strongly encouraged as a societal norm because people would be better human beings if they so participated.

This debate revolves mainly around beliefs and values about how society ought to work and very little around research evidence.[2] Is democracy a condition of society which is an end in itself; something to be valued for its own sake, as is argued by normative democratic theorists? Or, as it is argued by some pluralists, is democracy a means to an ends; the end being, perhaps, a good or a happy society? If one takes the position of the pluralist that democracy is a means to an end rather than an end in itself, it is conceivable that some other form of government also could lead to a good or happy society. Democracy may not be the preferred system of government. The normative theorist, on the other hand, would argue that democracy is necessarily the best system.

Similarly, is participation in politics an end in itself? Is it to be valued for its own sake, whether or not it contributes to the smooth effective working of a society? The normative theorist would assert that participation is the essence of democracy and, as such, must be highly valued; it is an end in itself. If participation is a means to an end, it is conceivable that a good or a happy society could be developed which did not require active participation by the majority of citizens. One could then ask the question, "Does society work better if participation in politics is at a high or a low level?" It is even possible that society could work to provide a

---

[2] Prominent participants in this discussion are Mayo (1960); Bachrach (1967); Pateman (1970); Walker (1966); Pranger (1968).

good life for its citizens when participation is low as well as when it is high; in other words, the level of participation may not be critical for the felicitous working of society. The presumed link between political participation and the effective working of government to produce the good life has not been demonstrated to our satisfaction either theoretically or empirically.

Do we have nothing to say, then, about the relationship of participation to democracy and the good life? The recent research set forth in this book can make some modest contributions to this question which might be helpful to the student as he ponders eternal questions of politics such as this. Recent research shows that persons can take several meaningful roles *vis-à-vis* the polity. Some persons choose to be actively involved in several different ways, Verba and Nie call them the "complete activists." Others choose to be completely inactive. Many emphasize a style or mode of activity, be it protestor, party activist, community activist, or patriot. This list of possible modes covers most of the participant types found in recent research in five nations. There is good reason to believe that the basic modes of participation delineated from these studies will be found over time and in a variety of democratic political cultures.

We hope that future research will focus on trying to explain more adequately the factors or reasons *why* individuals select the modes or patterns they do for relating to the political system. Studies which only focus on the frequency or pattern of a single political behavior, such as voting or campaigning, are inherently inadequate for understanding fully the dynamics of participation. Specific acts are components of modes or postures toward the polity, and it is delineation and explanation of these postures which is most illuminating. Political roles, or modes, are shaped by the social milieu in which persons live, by their personality, and most particularly by their own conception of themselves and their responsibility to society. Most people relate to government in a purposeful fashion. Research, to date, has underemphasized the ideational aspect of self-conception; yet, this information readily can be revealed by respondents to researchers. The societal and personality correlates of these self-conceptions can then be used to help explain the origins of the conceptions.

Even though several modes of participation have been discovered, there does exist "a general activist syndrome" in political participation. A certain proportion of the people (usually from 10 to 30 percent) are clearly more active than the rest in community and political affairs. This phenomenon has been found in so many studies and so many countries that it surely is a characteristic of all political democracies. This book shows that the correlates of general activism also are thoroughly established. The most direct antecedent of activism is psychological involvement in politics. As discussed earlier, psychological involvement is more likely to be found among the more advantaged members of the society: those of higher socioeconomic status, those possessing greater verbal skills, those with less vulnerable—more self-sufficient personalities, those with strong feelings about political matters, and those who are generally active in community affairs.

If the more advantaged participate more, do they reap any special benefits as a result of their participation? This is a difficult question to answer. How is it possible to measure whether a particular group is receiving more advantages because of its participation than it would have received had it not participated? Verba and Nie (1972) tried to measure this by ascertaining the policy views of local leaders and comparing them with the policy views of persons active in politics. The researchers discovered a higher congruence in views between leaders and active participants than between leaders and those who are not active. However, this relationship is confounded by the fact that most active participants, and leaders, are drawn from higher socioeconomic levels. As a consequence, Verba and Nie (1972) also ran a statistical control for SES and discovered that it explained only part of the relationship, and that a substantial part was attributable to the greater attentiveness of political leaders to the views of those who were active in politics. While this finding seems perfectly understandable in that we would predict leaders to pay special attention to their supporters, it is, to some extent, a violation of our norm of equality. Do we believe that a political system ought to serve the needs of all of the people and not give special preference to those who are most active in the political arena? This finding from the Verba and Nie study is the first of this type to be supported empirically. Future studies undoubtedly will test and challenge it.

Verba and Nie's finding raises a profound value question about the relationship of participation to the good life: Is it bad for society if the system responds more to those who are politically active and gives them advantages over those who choose not to be active? Perhaps the moral question here is not so much equality in levels of participation, but rather equality in opportunities to participate. If a system presents barriers to participation for some people and eases the path to participation for others, these differences in opportunities to participate might be considered system defects which violate an important societal norm for justice and equality. It seems entirely appropriate to us that a system should strive to remove such barriers.

But even if all of the barriers were removed, there is ample research evidence in this book to suggest that many people still would choose not to become politically active. To put it another way, people choose a variety of roles or modes for relating themselves to the polity. If one reflects for a moment on the various kinds of political actors playing out their roles in a complex political society, one begins to marvel at the unconscious social invention that has occurred. Our traditional theories of democracy do not recognize the complex set of roles that empirical research has discovered. Our traditional democratic theories generally envisage "the people" on one hand and "public officials" on the other. The behavior of public officials is to be guided by the wishes of the people. We believe such a theory is too simplistic. It cannot account for the reality of the complex relationships between people and their rulers.

Another aspect of this role differentiation is that even though people emphasize one role or another, they also may be simultaneously playing other roles. For example, it is possible for a protestor also to be a party activist, a patriotic supporter, and an obedient subject. Undoubtedly, there is a tension between these roles as a person may try to uphold all of them simultaneously; yet, it is possible for a person to be all of these things at once. We need a society which is flexible enough and diverse enough to accommodate this diversity of roles. Coming from diverse social milieus, living in different classes, working in different jobs, having different sets of friends, people develop different personalities, with different personal needs. Some seek solitude while others seek excitement; some enjoy combat while others avoid it; some hunger for public approval while others seek approval only from themselves; some feel nourished by political interaction while others feel out of place.

In addition to this diversification of roles, the very nature of the political system demands role specialization. Only a few can lead while most others must follow. A few can be public office holders, but most spend their time in other occupations. A few devote considerable time to campaign activities, but it would be a tense and conflictual society if everyone were busy campaigning. It would be an even more unhappy society if everyone were busy protesting. Most of us communicate, of course, but if everyone were busy communicating all the time, and expecting others to listen, imagine the communication overload on us all. It is possible to have strong patriotism by everybody in a good society, but would it be good if this patriotism foreclosed other kinds of political inputs? It seems, then, that the diverse roles reflect not only diverse backgrounds, but diverse personal needs and the demands of the system for diverse actors.

Does a mixture of political roles lead to a democratic society which satisfies most of the people who live in it? It is our judgment that it is more likely to. Those who value a society which tries to make everyone equal might deplore a society with diverse roles. Similarly, those who fervently believe that public officials should be closely guided by citizen participation would deplore the fact that many people might choose to be inactive. But, in our judgment, equality and citizen guidance of officials are not ends in themselves; presumably, they are means to the end of a happy society. If they do not lead to happiness, they are not to be preferred. This discussion should not be trapped by the traditional exhortations of democratic theory. The only value that matters, in our judgment, for evaluating political systems is the quality of life of the people living in them.

While our knowledge at this time is too preliminary to prescribe the optimum mix of political roles which might lead to the most happy democracy, it is possible to venture some preliminary observations about conditions most likely to lead in that direction. First, it seems that *diversity is essential.* There is no single role that is best or most proper for everyone. It would not be a happy society if everyone were active, if everyone were protesting, if everyone were campaigning, if everyone were communicating at a high rate. While we can accommodate everyone who wishes to vote, there is no reason to believe a *priori* that society is less well off if many people choose not to vote. If one can free oneself from the bias of traditional democratic theory, one can recognize that every posture toward the polity is meaningful. This should not be taken to mean that everyone is acting wisely to achieve his preferred political ends as he plays his political role. Few of us understand ourselves or society well enough to do that; even very active people pursue strategies that defeat the very end that they seek. We are only saying that one cannot prescribe, by any absolute standard, a clearly defined role that everyone in a given society must follow in order to make democracy work best.

A recognition that diversity is essential leads to the second basic principle, *the system must be kept open* so that people can choose from a variety of roles. Should laws, or social customs, foreclose protesting, or campaigning, or communicating, or voting, it not only would constrict individual freedom but also would constrict the capacity of the political system to change so that it might serve more adequately the wishes of the people. The flexibility and responsiveness of public officials generally is enhanced if a variety of messages and pressures are directed their way by people playing different roles. People are likely to be happier if they are allowed to take an active role or to withdraw as they choose; furthermore, they are likely to select that active role that best suits their own talents and needs. We must recognize that emphases and role selection will shift over time. Strong waves of protesting are likely to occur in some periods of history. Partisan and campaign contesting may be very prominent in other periods. Still other eras may be very quiescent and most people will be content to be patriotic supporters (and public commentators will bemoan the terrible apathy of the people). A system that is kept open can adapt more readily to these changing needs.

A third basic condition derives from the first two: *an open society requires an open communication network.* People must have ways of becoming informed so that they can know when and if it is important to act. The communication system should not only be open but carry a high level of political content so that actors can, with minimum effort, find out what is going on in politics and government. Lack of an open communication network would make it easier for an unscrupulous elite to subvert democracy. Almost the first act of any group seizing power by *coup d'état* is to take control of the communications system.

Fourthly, the smooth meshing of political roles likely is enhanced if *politics play only a limited role* in the overall functioning of society. Limited constitutional democracies have evolved painfully over centuries of political learning; by consensus they place boundaries on politics and on rulers. In constitutional democracies it is deemed proper that political considerations should not determine a person's opportunities for an education, a job, advancement on the job, a place to live, goods to enjoy, the friends one makes, the thoughts ones utters, the religion one follows, one's chances for justice, and so forth. People have found that life is happier if politics are kept out of the above areas.

How can we be sure that society will be kept open and that politics will be confined to the proper sphere? We must recognize that tyranny is forever possible and that we must use eternal vigilance to protect liberty. But, if we must encourage people to be vigilant, how can we also allow them to be inactive if they so choose? Even though it seems paradoxical, we must do both. We cannot expect that the mass of citizens will be eternally vigilant, but we can hope realistically that a small cadre of politically interested and active people will hold a vigil. It is important to keep alive the norm that citizens should be interested and active in politics, even though we know that many will choose not to be so. Some will respond to that norm and keep the vigil. Should they sound an alarm, the norm to be active will encourage many who have been passive to become more active. An open political system which encourages people to be active, and where citizens can move freely in and out of a variety of active roles, can respond effectively to such dangers. It also should be highly adaptive to changing social conditions. We are probably asking too much of ourselves if we aspire to develop a blueprint for the perfect society made up of more or less perfect individuals. We will probably do better if we take people as they are and try to design a society and political system which allows for diversity, which is open, and adaptive to changing conditions.

Appendix on
Scales and Indexes

Two very useful handbooks have been published which provide an extensive listing of measuring instruments used by social scientists. In addition to providing multiple scales for each attitudinal area, these manuals assess the strengths and weaknesses of the instruments included. We recommend these books to both professionals as well as beginning students.

> Robinson, John P., J. G. Rusk, and K. B. Head, *Measures of Political Attitudes* (Ann Arbor, Mich.: Institute of Social Research, University of Michigan, 1968).

> Robinson, John P., and P. R. Shaver, *Measures of Social Psychological Attitudes*, rev. ed. (Ann Arbor, Mich.: Institute of Social Research, University of Michigan, 1973).

Below we discuss the measurement of several attitudes that are important for understanding political participation.

PSYCHOLOGICAL INVOLVEMENT The measure of psychological involvement used by the Michigan Survey Research Center is in form a measure of concern about the particular presidential campaign but probably also taps a more general psychological concern about politics. It rests on responses to two questions. Respondents were asked in the early warm-up phase of the pre-election interview: "Generally speaking, would you say that you personally care a great deal which party wins the presidential election this fall or that you don't care very much which party wins?" Replies to this question were coded on a five-point scale from least to most "care" about the election outcome. Another question was: "Some people don't pay much attention to the political campaigns. How about you, would you say that you have been very much interested, somewhat interested, or not much interested in following the political campaigns so far this year?" By combination of the responses to these two questions, individuals were ranked on an index of psychological involvement.

SENSE OF CITIZEN DUTY Respondents were asked to agree or disagree with the following four statements:

"It isn't so important to vote when you know your party doesn't have a chance to win."

"A good many local elections aren't important enough to bother with."

"So many other people vote in the national election that it doesn't matter much to me whether I vote or not."

"If a person doesn't care how an election comes out, he shouldn't vote in it."

Persons disagreeing with those statements were scored as having a sense of citizen duty. Respondents fell in one of five positions (0, 1, 2, 3, 4) on the scale. For a detailed discussion of the scale, see Campbell, Gurin and Miller (1954, pp. 194–199), and Robinson, Rusk & Head (1968).

SENSE OF POLITICAL EFFICACY A measure of variations in the strength of the sense of political efficacy among respondents was constructed from expressions of agreement or disagreement with the following statements:

1. "I don't think public officials care very much what people like me think."
2. "The way people vote is the main thing that decides how things are run in this country."
3. "Voting is the only way people like me can have any say about how the government runs things."
4. "People like me don't have any say about what the government does."
5. "Sometimes politics and government seems so complicated that a person like me can't really understand what's going on."

"Disagree" responses to items 1, 3, 4, and 5 and an "agree" response to item 2 were coded efficacious. The items were interspersed in the schedule with other statements included for other purposes. The responses were grouped into five types. Variations in the sense of political efficacy, so measured, had a positive relationship with variations in political participation. For a detailed discussion of the concept of the sense of political efficacy, see Campbell, Gurin and Miller (1954, pp. 187–194), and Robinson, Rusk & Head (1968).

SUBJECTIVE POLITICAL COMPETENCE The subjective political competence scale was first developed by Almond and Verba in their five-nation study,

The Civic Culture (1963). In many respects, this scale resembles the Political Efficacy Scale discussed above, but there are important differences. The Efficacy Scale taps the generalized notion that political institutions are responsive to citizen pressure; the Almond-Verba scale highlights the sense that the respondent himself has the capacity to exert influence. The following questions were asked in an interview situation:

"Suppose a regulation were being considered by (appropriate local government unit specified by the interviewer) that you considered very unjust or harmful. What do you think you could do?"

"If you made an effort to change this regulation, how likely is it that you would succeed?"

"If such a case arose, how likely is it that you would actually do something about it?"

"Have you ever done anything to try to influence a local regulation?"

The same set of questions was asked about an unjust law or policy being considered by a national government unit. Persons scoring high on subjective competence were more likely to expose themselves to political communications, to participate in political affairs, to take pride on their political system, and to have a sense of citizen duty. For further information on the effect of this attitude dimension, see Matthews and Prothro (1966).

POLITICAL CYNICISM/DISTRUST This scale was develped by the Michigan Survey Research Center and has been used in their biennial election studies since 1964. The following items were asked:

"Do you think that people in the government waste *a lot* of the money we pay in taxes, waste some of it, or don't waste very much of it?"

"How much of the time do you think you can trust the government in Washington to do what is right—just about always, most of the time, or *only some of the time?*"

"Would you say the government is pretty much run by a *few big interests* looking out for themselves or that it is run for the benefit of all the people?"

"Do you feel that almost all of the people running the government are smart people who usually know what they are doing, or do you think that quite a few of them *don't seem to know what they are doing?*"

"Do you think that *quite a few* of the people running the government are a little crooked, not very many are, or do you think hardly any of them are crooked at all?"

The five items form a Guttman scale with scores that range from 0 = most trusting to 5 = least trusting. The scale represents the number of items to which the individual gave distrusting responses (italicized in the above questions). Thus, a score of 5 indicates distrusting responses to all five questions, whereas a score of 0 indicates that trusting responses were given to all five items.

POLITICAL ANOMIE/ALIENATION In contrast to feelings of distrust, feelings of political anomie are more deep seated. They question the very basic principles and norms of the polity. A number of researchers have tried to measure this concept but the scholarly community has not yet arrived at any general consensus on which is best. The following list developed by a University of California research team uses several different question formats in the development of what the authors call "The Political Alienation Index" (Citrin, et al., 1975). (The italicized options were coded as alienated.)

Forced Choice Items   (Choose one statement of each pair.)
1. "The way our system of government operates, almost every group has a say in running things."

   or

   "This country is really run by a small number of men at the top who only speak for a few special groups."
2. "I am proud of many things about our system of government."

   or

   "I can't find much in our system of government to be proud of."
3. "Our government officials usually tell us the truth."

   or

   "Most of the things that government leaders say can't be believed."

Agree-Disagree Questions
"How much of the time do you think you can trust the government to do what is right? Just about always, most of the time, *only some* of the time, or *none* of the time?"

"Would you say that most of the political leaders in this country stand for the things you really believe in, that only some of them do, that *only a few* do, or that *none* of them do?"

Adjectives Used to Describe the National Government
Corrupt
Disgusting
Fair

There is an obvious content overlap between this scale and the Political Cynicism/Distrust Scale. It is, therefore, not fully established whether the scale measures alienation from the basic system, or merely opposition to incumbents at a particular time.

For numerous other indexes of alienation, consult Robinson & Shaver, *Measures of Social Psychological Attitudes,* 1973.

PARTY IDENTIFICATION   The two-part question to measure party identification reads as follows:
"Generally speaking, do you usually think of yourself as a Republican (R), a Democrat (D), an Independent, or what?"

"(If REPUBLICAN or DEMOCRAT) Would you call yourself a strong (R) (D) or a not very strong (R) (D)?"

"(If INDEPENDENT) Do you think of yourself as closer to the Republican or Democratic party?"

For further examination of this concept, the student should consult Campbell, et al., (1960), Campbell, et al., (1966).

THE SELF-ANCHORING STRIVING SCALE In this technique, the respondent is shown a picture of a ladder, symbolizing the "ladder of life," and asked to place himself on a step which best represents his present position, his past position, and his hopes for a future position. The steps on the ladder are numbered from 0 to 10, representing the worst possible life at the bottom to the best possible life at the top. In this system, respondents define their own scale of values from worst to best, and hence the designation the "self-anchoring" scale.

"Here is a ladder representing the 'ladder of life.' Let us suppose the top of the ladder represents the *best* possible life for you; and the bottom, the *worst* possible life for you. On which step of the ladder do you feel you personally stand at the present time?"

"On which step would you say you stood *five years ago?*"

"Just as your best guess, on which step do you think you will stand in the future, say about *five years from now?*"

For results of the application of this scale, see Cantril (1965).

Bibliography

Abcarian, Gilbert, and Sherman M. Stanage
1965   "Alienation and the Radical Right," *Journal of Politics*,
            27: 776-796.
Abcarian, Gilbert, and John W. Soule
1971   *Social Psychology and Political Behavior*. Columbus, Ohio:
            Charles Merrill Publ. Co.
Aberbach, Joel D.
1969   "Alienation and Political Behavior," *American Political
            Science Review*, 63: 86-99.
Aberbach, Joel D., and Jack L. Walker
1970   "Political Trust and Racial Ideology." *American Political
            Science Review*, 64: 1199-1219.
Abrams, Mark
1957-1958   "Press, Poll and Votes in Britain since the 1955 General
            Elections," *Public Opinion Quarterly*, 21: 543-547.

Abramson, Paul R., and Ronald Inglehart
1970 "The Development of Systematic Support in Four Western Democracies." *Comparative Political Studies*, 2: 419-442.

Adorno, Theodore W., Else Frenkel-Brunswik, Daniel J. Levinson, and R. N. Sanford
1950 *The Authoritarian Personality*. New York: Harper.

Agger, Robert E.
1956a "Lawyers in Politics." *Temple Law Quarterly,* 29: 434-452.
1956b "Power Attributions in the Local Community: Theoretical and Research Considerations." *Social Forces,* 34: 322-331.

Agger, Robert E., and Daniel Goldrich
1958 "Community Power Structures and Partisanship." *American Sociological Review*, 23: 383-392.

Agger, Robert E., Daniel Goldrich, and Bert E. Swanson
1964 *The Rulers and the Ruled: Political Power and Impotence in American Communities*. New York: Wiley.

Agger, Robert E., Marshall N. Goldstein, and Stanley A. Pearl
1961 "Political Cynicism: Measurement and Meaning." *Journal of Politics*, 23: 477-506.

Agger, Robert E., and Vincent Ostro
1956 "Political Participation in a Small Community," in Heinz Eulau, Samuel J. Eldersveld, and Morris Janowitz, eds., *Political Behavior: A Reader in Theory and Research*. Glencoe, Ill.: The Free Press. Pp. 138-148.

Ahmed, Bashiruddin
1975 "Political Stratification of the Electorate," in D. L. Sheth, ed., *Citizens and Parties*. New Delhi: Allied. Pp. 21-37.

Alexander, Franz
1959 "Emotional Factors in Voting Behavior," in Eugene Burdick and Arthur J. Brodbeck, eds., *American Voting Behavior*. Glencoe, Ill.: The Free Press. Pp. 300-307.

Alford, Robert R., and Roger Friedland
1974 "Nations, Parties, and Participation: A Critique of Political Sociology." *Theory and Society* 1: 307-328.
_____ "Political Participation and Public Policy." *Annual Review*
1975 *of Sociology* 1: 429-479.

Alford, Robert R., and Eugene C. Lee
1968 "Voting Turnout in American Cities." *American Political Science Review* 62: 796-813.

Alford, Robert R., and Harry M. Scoble
1968   "Sources of Local Political Involvement." *American Political Science Review* 62: 1192-1206.

_____.   *Bureaucracy and Participation: Political Cultures in Four*
1969   *Wisconsin Cities.* Chicago: Rand McNally.

Allardt, Erik
1956   *Social Struktur och Politisk Activitet.* Helsinki: Soderstroms.

_____.   "Community Activity, Leisure Use and Social Structure."
1962   *Acta Sociologica* 6: (fasc. 1-2): 67-82.

_____.   "Types of Protests and Alienation," in Erik Allardt and
1970   Stein Rokkan, eds., *Mass Politics.* New York: The Free Press. Pp. 45-63.

Allardt, Erik, and Kettil Bruun
1956   "Characteristics of the Finnish Non-voter." *Transactions of the Westermarck Society* 3: 55-76.

Allardt, Erik, Pentti Jartti, Faina Jyrkila, and Vrjo Littunen
1958   "On the Cumulative Nature of Leisure Activities." *Acta Sociologica* 3: (fasc. 4): 165-172.

Allardt, Erik, and Pertti Pesonen
1960   "Citizen Participation in Political Life in Finland." *International Social Science Journal* 12: 27-39.

Allport, Gordon W.
1945   "The Psychology of Participation." *Psychological Review* 52: 117-132.

Almond, Gabriel Abraham
1954   *The Appeals of Communism.* Princeton, N. J.: Princeton University Press.

Almond, Gabriel Abraham, and Sidney Verba
1963   *The Civic Culture.* Princeton, N. J.: Princeton University Press.

Ambler, John
1975   "Trust in Political and Non-political Authorities in France." *Comparative Politics* 8: 31-58.

Anderson, H. Dewey
1935   "The Educational and Occupational Attainments of Our National Rulers." *Scientific Monthly* 40: 511-518.

Ando, Hirofumi
1969   "A Study of Voting Patterns in the Philippine Presidential

and Senatorial Elections, 1946-1965." *Midwest Journal of Political Science* 13: 567-586.

Andrews, William G.
1966 "American Voting Participation." *Western Political Quarterly* 19: 639-652.

Arora, Satish
1976 "Participation and Nation Building: Considerations on Facts, Forms and Consequences," in Rajni Kothari, ed., *State and Nation Building*. New Delhi: Allied. (In press.)

Asher, Herbert
1974 "The Reliability of Political Efficacy Items." *Political Methodology* 1, no. 2: 45-72.

Ashford, Douglas Elliot
1972 *Ideology and Participation*. Beverly Hills, Calif.: Sage Publications.

Babchuk, Nicholas, and Ralph V. Thompson
1962 "Voluntary Associations of Negroes." *American Sociological Review* 27: 647-655.

Bachrach, Peter
1967 *The Theory of Democratic Elitism: A Critique*. Boston: Little, Brown.

Bachrach, Peter, and M. S. Baratz
1970 *Power and Poverty: Theory and Practice*. New York: Oxford University Press.

Baer, Michael A., and Dean Jaros
1974 "Participation as Instrument and Expression: Some Evidence From the States." *American Journal of Political Science* 18: 365-383.

Baker, Kendall L.
1973 "Political Participation, Political Efficacy, and Socialization in Germany." *Comparative Politics* 6: 73-98.

Banfield, Edward Christie
1970 *The Unheavenly City: The Nature and Future of Our Urban Crisis*. Boston: Little, Brown.

Barber, James David
1969 *Citizen Politics*. Chicago: Markham.

Barnes, Samuel H.
1966 "Participation, Education and Political Competence:

Evidence from a Sample of Italian Socialists." *American Political Science Review* 60: 348-353.

———.   "Leadership Style and Political Competence," in Lewis
1967   J. Edinger, ed., *Political Leadership in Industrialized Societies*. New York: Wiley. Pp. 59-83.

———.   "Left, Right, and the İtalian Vote." *Comparative Political*
1971   *Studies* 4: 157-175.

Bay, Christian
1968   "Needs, Wants, and Political Legitimacy." *Canadian Journal of Political Science* 1: 241-260.

Bell, Roderick
1969   "The Determinants of Psychological Involvement in Politics: A Causal Analysis." *Midwest Journal of Political Science* 13: 237-253.

Bell, Wendell, Richard J. Hill, and Charles R. Wright
1961   *Public Leadership*. San Francisco: Chandler.

Benjamin, Roger W., Richard N. Blue, and Stephen Coleman
1971   "Modernization and Political Change: A Comparative Aggregate Data Analysis of Indian Political Behavior." *Midwest Journal of Political Science* 15: 219-261.

Bennett, Stephen E., and William R. Klecka
1970   "Social Status and Political Participation: A Multivariate Analysis of Predictive Power." *Midwest Journal of Political Science* 14: 355-382.

Benney, Mark, and Phyllis Geiss
1950   "Social Class and Politics in Greenwich." *British Journal of Sociology* 1: 310-327.

Berelson, Bernard R.
1960   "Communications and Public Opinion," in Wilbur Schramm, ed., *Mass Communication*. 2nd ed. Urbana: University of Illinois Press. Pp. 527-543.

———.   "Democratic Theory and Public Opinion." *Public Opinion*
1952   *Quarterly* 16: 313-330.
1966   Reprinted in Berelson and Janowitz, eds., *Reader in Public Opinion and Communication*. 2nd ed. New York: The Free Press. Pp. 489-504.

Berelson, Bernard R., Paul F. Lazarsfeld, and William N. McPhee
1954   *Voting: A Study of Opinion Formation in a Presidential*

Campaign. Chicago: University of Chicago Press.

Berelson, Bernard R., and Gary A. Steiner
1964   *Human Behavior: An Inventory of Scientific Findings*. New York: Harcourt, Brace and World.

Birch, Anthony Harold
1950   "The Habit of Voting." *Journal of the Manchester School of Economics and Social Studies* 18: 75-82.

_____   *Small-Town Politics: A Study of Political Life in Glossop*.
1959   London: Oxford University Press.

_____   "England and Wales," in *Citizen Participation in Political*
1960   *Life,* issue of *International Social Science Journal* 12: 15-26.

Birch, Anthony Harold, and Peter Campbell
1950   "Voting Behavior in a Lancashire Constituency." *British Journal of Sociology* 1: 197-208.

Blumenthal, Monica D., R. L. Kahn, F. M. Andrews, and K. B. Head
1972   *Justifying Violence: Attitudes of American Men*. Ann Arbor: University of Michigan. Institute for Social Research.

Boesel, David
1970   "The Liberal Society, Black Youths, and the Ghetto Riots." *Psychiatry* 33: 265-281.

Bone, Hugh Alvin, and Austin Ranney
1963   *Politics and Voters*. New York: McGraw-Hill.

Bonham, John
1952   "The Middle Class Elector." *British Journal of Sociology* 3: 222-230.

_____   *The Middle Class Vote*. London:Faber and Faber.
1954

Booth, Alan
1972   "Sex and Social Participation." *American Sociological Review* 37: 183-193.

Boskoff, Alvin, and Harmon Zeigler
1964   *Voting Patterns in a Local Election*. Philadelphia: Lippincott.

Bowman, Lewis, and George Robert Boynton
1966   "Recruitment Patterns Among Local Party Officials: A Model and Some Preliminary Findings in Selected Locales." *American Political Science Review* 60: 667-676.

Bowman, Lewis, and George Robert Boynton, eds.
1974 *Political Behavior and Public Opinion*. Englewood Cliffs, N. J.: Prentice-Hall.

Brink, William J., and Louis Harris
1967 *Black and White*. New York: Simon & Schuster.

Bronfenbrenner, Urie
1960 "Personality and Participation: The Case of the Vanishing Variables." *Journal of Social Issues* 16, no. 4: 54-63.

Browning, Rufus P., and Herbert Jacob
1964 "Power Motivation and the Political Personality." *Public Opinion Quarterly* 28: 75-90.

Bruhns, F. C., F. Cazzola, and J. Wiatr, eds.
1974 *Local Politics, Development and Participation: A Cross-National Study of Interrelationships*. Pittsburgh: University of Pittsburgh Center for International Studies.

Buchanan, William
1956 "An Inquiry into Purposive Voting." *Journal of Politics* 18: 281-296. Also in Bobbs-Merrill Reprint Series, No. PS-34.

Buck, Philip Wallenstein
1963 *Amateurs and Professionals in British Politics, 1918-1959*. Chicago: University of Chicago Press.

Buffalo Survey
1968 Conducted by Everett Cataldo, Richard M. Johnson, Lyman Kellstedt, Lester Milbrath, Albert Somit. Sponsored by the Office of Economic Opportunity, 1966-1969.

Bullock, Charles S. and Harrell R. Rodgers, Jr., eds.
1972 *Black Political Attitudes: Implications for Political Support*. Chicago, Markham.

Burdick, Eugene and Arthur J. Brodbeck, eds.
1959 *American Voting Behavior*. Glencoe, Ill.: The Free Press.

Burnham, Walter Dean
1965 "The Changing Shape of the American Political Universe." *American Political Science Review* 59: 7-28.

Butler, David E.
1952 *The British General Election of 1951*. London: Macmillan.
——— *The British General Election of 1955*. London: Macmillan.
1955

_____. *Elections Abroad*. London: Macmillan.
1959
Butler, David E., and Richard Rose
1960   *The British General Election of 1959*. London: F. Cass.
Butler, David E., and Donald Stokes
1969   *Political Change in Britain: Forces Shaping Electoral Choice*. New York: St. Martin's Press.
Cameron, David R., J. Stephen Hendricks, and Richard I. Hofferbert
1972   "Urbanization, Social Structure, and Mass Politics: A Comparison Within Five Nations." *Comparative Political Studies* 5: 259-290.
Campbell, Angus
1960   "Surge and Decline: A Study of Electoral Change." *Public Opinion Quarterly* 24: 397-418.
_____. "The Passive Citizen." *Acta Sociologica* 6 (fasc. 1-2): 9-21.
1962
_____. *White Attitudes Toward Black People*. Ann Arbor: Institute for Social Research. University of Michigan.
1971
Campbell, Angus, and Philip E. Converse, eds.
1972   *The Human Meaning of Social Change*. New York: Russell Sage Foundation.
Campbell, Angus, Philip E. Converse, Warren Miller, and Donald Stokes
1960   *The American Voter*. New York: Wiley.
Campbell, Angus, Philip E. Converse, and Willard Rogers
1976   *The Quality of American Life*. New York: Russell Sage Foundation.
Campbell, Angus, and Homer C. Cooper
1956   *Group Differences in Attitudes and Votes*. Ann Arbor: Survey Research Center. Institute for Social Research, University of Michigan.
Campbell, Angus, Gerald Gurin, and Warren E. Miller
1954   *The Voter Decides*. Evanston, Ill.: Row, Peterson.
Campbell, Angus, and Robert L. Kahn
1952   *The People Elect a President*. Survey Research Center. Institute for Social Research. University of Michigan.
Campbell, Angus, and Howard Schuman
1968   "Racial Attitudes in Fifteen American Cities," in *National*

Advisory Commission on Civil Disorders, Supplemental Studies. Washington, D.C.: Government Printing Office. Pp. 1-67.

Campbell, Angus, and Henry Valen
1961   "Party Identification in Norway and the United States." *Public Opinion Quarterly* 25: 505-525.
1974   Also reprinted in Lewis Bowman and G. R. Boynton, eds., *Political Behavior and Public Opinion*. Englewood Cliffs, N. J.: Prentice-Hall. Pp. 478-499.

Campbell, Donald T., and Donald W. Fiske
1959   "Convergent and Discriminant Validation by the Multi-trait-Multimethod Matrix." *Psychological Bulletin* 56: 81-105.

Cantril, Hadley
1965   *The Pattern of Human Concerns*. New Brunswick, N. J.: Rutgers University Press.

Caplan, Nathan
1970   "The New Ghetto Man: A Review of Recent Empirical Studies." *Journal of Social Issues* 26: 59-73.
1974   Also reprinted in Lewis Bowman and G. R. Boynton, eds., *Political Behavior and Public Opinion*. Englewood Cliffs, N. J.: Prentice-Hall. Pp. 325-339.

Caplan, Nathan S., and Jeffery M. Paige
1968   "A Study of Ghetto Rioters." *Scientific American* 219, no. 2: 15-21.

Cataldo, Everett F., and Richard M. Johnson, and Lyman Kellstedt
1968   "Social Strain and Urban Violence," in Louis H. Masotti, and Don R. Bowen, eds., *Riots and Rebellion*. Beverly Hills, Calif.: Sage Publications. Pp. 285-298.

Cataldo, Everett F., and Lyman Kellstedt
1968   "Conceptualizing and Measuring Political Involvement Over Time: A Study of Buffalo's Urban Poor," paper delivered at the 1968 Joint Statistical Meetings, Pittsburgh.

Chandidas, R.
1968   *India Votes: A Source Book on Indian Elections*. New York: Humanities Press.

Christie, Richard, and Peggy Cook
1958   "A Guide to Published Literature Relating to the Authori-

tarian Personality Through 1956." *Journal of Psychology* 45: 171-199.

Christie, Richard, Joan Havel, and Bernard Seidenberg
1958   "Is the F Scale Irreversible?" *Journal of Abnormal and Social Psychology* 56: 143-159.

Citrin, Jack
1974   "Comment: The Political Relevance of Trust in Government." *American Political Science Review* 68: 973-988.
_____.   "Political Alienation as a Social Indicator: Attitudes and
1975   Action." Berkeley: University of California. (Xeroxed.)

Citrin, Jack, Herbert McClosky, J. Merrill Shanks, and Paul M. Sniderman
1975   "Personal and Political Sources of Political Alienation." *British Journal of Political Science* 5: 1-31.

Clapp, Charles L.
1963   *The Congressman: His Work as He Sees It.* Washington, D. C.: The Brookings Institution.

Clarke, James W., and Joseph Egan
1972   "Social and Political Dimensions of Campus Protest Activity." *Journal of Politics* 34: 500-523.

Clarke, James W., and Lester E. Levine
1971   "Marijuana Use, Social Discontent and Political Alienation: A Study of High School Youth." *American Political Science Review* 65: 120-130.

Cobb, Roger W., and Charles D. Elder
1972   *Participation in American Politics: The Dynamics of Agenda Building.* Boston: Allyn and Bacon.

Cohen, Nathan Edward, ed.
1970   *The Los Angeles Riots: A Socio-Psychological Study.* New York: Praeger.

Cohen, Paul M.
1974   "Men, Women and the Latin American Political System: Paths to Political Participation in Uruguay," paper delivered at the American Political Science Association Meeting, Chicago.

Cole, Richard L.
1974   *Citizen Participation and the Urban Policy Process.* Lexington, Mass.: Lexington Books.

Connelly, Gordon M., and Harry H. Field
1944   "The Non-voter: Who He Is, What He Thinks." *Public Opinion Quarterly* 8: 175-187.

Constantini, Edmond
1963   "Intraparty Attitude Conflict: Democratic Party Leader-
            ship in California."*Western Political Quarterly* 16: 956-972.
Converse, Philip E.
1958   "The Shifting Role of Class in Political Attitudes and
            Behavior," in Eleanor E. Maccoby, et al., eds., *Readings
            in Social Psychology*. New York: Henry Holt & Co.
            Pp. 388-399.

_____.   "The Nature of Belief Systems in Mass Publics," in David
1964   E. Apter, ed., *Ideology and Discontent*. New York: The
            Free Press. Pp. 206-261.

_____.   "Of Time and Partisan Stability." *Comparative Political
1969   Studies* 2: 139-171.

_____.   "Change in the American Electorate," in Angus Campbell
1972   and Philip E. Converse, eds., *The Human Meaning of
            Social Change*. New York: Russell Sage Foundation.
            Pp. 263-337.
Converse, Philip E., and Georges Dupeux
1961   "Some Comparative Notes on French and American
            Political Behavior." UNESCO Seminar, Bergen, Norway,
            June, 1961. (Mimeographed.)

_____.   "Politicization of the Electorate in France and the United
1962   States." *Public Opinion Quarterly* 26: 1-23.
1974   Also reprinted in Lewis Bowman and G. R. Boynton, eds.,
            Political Behavior and Public Opinion. Englewood Cliffs,
            N. J.: Prentice-Hall. Pp. 248-269.
Converse, Philip E., and Roy Pierce
forthcoming "Basic Changes in French Politics and the Disorders of
            May and June, 1968," In R. Rose, ed., *Political Behavior
            in Western Societies*. New York: Interscience Wiley.
Coser, Rose Laub
1951   "Political Involvement and Interpersonal Relations."
            Psychiatry 14: 213-222.
Crain, Robert L., Elihu Katz, and Donald B. Rosenthal
1969   *The Politics of Community Conflict: The Fluoridation
            Decision.* Indianapolis: Bobbs-Merrill.
Crawford, Thomas J., and Murray Naditch
1970   "Relative Deprivation, Powerlessness and Militancy: The
            Psychology of Social Protest." *Psychiatry* 33: 208-223.

Crenson, Matthew
1974 "Organizational Factors in Citizen Participation." *Journal of Politics* 36: 356-378.

Crittenden, John
1963 "Aging and Political Participation." *Western Political Quarterly* 16: 323-331.

Cutright, Phillips
1963 "Measuring the Impact of Local Party Activity on the General Election Vote." *Public Opinion Quarterly* 27: 372-386.

Cutright, Phillips, and Peter H. Rossi
1958 "Grass Roots Politicians and the Vote." *American Sociological Review* 23: 171-179.

Dahl, Robert Alan
1956 *A Preface to Democratic Theory*. Chicago: University of Chicago Press.

_____ *Who Governs? Democracy and Power in an American City*.
1961 New Haven: Yale University Press.

_____ *Modern Political Analysis*. Englewood Cliffs, N.J.: Prentice-
1963 Hall.

Davies, James Chowning
1954 "Charisma in the 1952 Campaign." *American Political Science Review* 48: 1083-1102.

_____ "Toward a Theory of Revolution." *American Sociological*
1962 *Review* 27: 5-19.

_____ *Human Nature in Politics*. New York: Wiley.
1963

_____ *When Men Revolt and Why*. New York: The Free Press.
1971

_____ Aggression, Violence, Revolution, and War," in Jeanne N. Knutson, ed., *Handbook of Political Psychology*.
1973 San Francisco: Jossey-Bass. Pp. 234-260.

Dawidowicz, Lucy S., and Leon J. Goldstein
1963 *Politics in a Pluralist Democracy*. New York: Institute of Human Relations Press.

Dean, Dwight G.
1960 "Alienation and Political Apathy." *Social Forces* 38: 185-189.

—————. "Alienation: Its Meaning and Measurement." *American*
1961   *Sociological Review* 26: 753-758.

Degras, Henry Ernest, [Mark Benney, pseud.], A. P. Gray, and R. H. Pear.
1956   *How People Vote: A Study of Electoral Behavior in Green-*
            wich. London: Routledge & Kegan Paul.

Dennis, Jack
1966   "Support for the Party System by the Mass Public."
            American Political Science Review 60: 600-615.

—————.   "Support for the Institution of Elections by the Mass
1970   Public." *American Political Science Review* 64: 819-835.

Dennis, Jack, Leon Lindberg, and Donald McCrone
1971   "Support for Nation and Government among English
            Children." *British Journal of Political Science* 1: 25-48.

Dennis, Wayne
1930   "Registration and Voting in a Patriotic Organization."
            Journal of Social Psychology 1: 317-318.

Deutsch, Karl
1961   "Social Mobilization and Political Development." *Ameri-*
            can Political Science Review 55: 493-514.

DiPalma, Giuseppe
1970   *Apathy and Participation*. New York: The Free Press.

DiPalma, Giuseppe, and Herbert McClosky
1970   "Personality and Conformity: The Learning of Political
            Attitudes." *American Political Science Review* 64: 1054-
            1073.

DiRenzo, Gordon J.
1967   *Personality, Power and Politics. A Social Psychological*
            Analysis of the Italian Deputy and his Parliamentary
            System. Notre Dame, Ind.: University of Notre Dame
            Press.

Dizard, Jan E.
1970   "Black Ideology, Social Class and Black Power." *Psychia-*
            try 33: 195-207.

Dobson, Douglas, and Douglas St. Angelo
1975   "Party Identification and the Floating Vote: Some Dy-
            namics." *American Political Science Review* 69: 481-490.

Dogan, Mattei
1961   "Political Ascent in a Class Society: French Deputies

1870-1958," in Dwaine Marvick, ed., *Political Decision-Makers*. Glencoe, Ill.: The Free Press. Pp. 57-90.

Dogan, Mattei, and J. Narbonne
1955 *Les Francaises face a la politique*. Paris: Armand Colin.

Douvan, Elizabeth, and Alan M. Walker
1956 "The Sense of Effectiveness in Public Affairs." *Psychological Monographs* 70, no. 22, (no. 429).

Downes, Bryan T.
1970 "A Critical Reexamination of the Social and Political Characteristics of Riot Cities." *Social Science Quarterly* 51: 349-360.

Downton, James V., Jr.
1973 *Rebel Leadership: Commitment and Charisma in the Revolutionary Process*. New York: The Free Press.

Duncan, Graeme, and Steven Lukes
1963 "The New Democracy." *Political Studies* 11: 156-177.

Duverger, Maurice
1954 *Political Parties: Their Organization and Activity in the Modern State*. New York: Wiley.

Duverger, Maurice, ed.
1955 *The Political Role of Women*. Paris: UNESCO.

Easton, David, and Jack Dennis
1967 "The Child's Acquisition of Regime Norms: Political Efficacy." *American Political Science Review* 61: 25-38.

Eckstein, Harry
1961 *A Theory of Stable Democracy*. Princeton: Princeton University. Woodrow Wilson School of Public and International Affairs, Center of International Studies.

Edinger, Lewis Joachim
1965 *Kurt Schumacher: A Study in Personality and Political Behavior*. Stanford: Stanford University Press.

Eisinger, Peter K.
1973 "The Conditions of Protest Behavior in American Cities." *American Political Science Review* 67: 11-28.
———. "Racial Differences in Protest Participation." *American*
1974 *Political Science Review* 68: 592-606.

Eldersveld, Samuel James
1956 "Experimental Propaganda Techniques and Voting Behavior." *American Political Science Review* 50: 154-165.

1956   Reprinted in Eulau Heinz, et. al., eds., *Political Behavior: A Reader in Theory and Research*. Glencoe, Ill.: The Free Press. Pp. 210-217.

_____.   *Political Parties: A Behavioral Analysis*. Chicago: Rand
1964   McNally.

Eldersveld, Samuel James, and Bashir Ahmed
forthcoming *Parties and Political Behavior in India: A Comparative Analysis*.

Eldersveld, Samuel James, and Richard W. Dodge
1954   "Personal Contact or Mail Propaganda? An Experiment in Voting Turnout and Attitude Change," in Daniel Katz, ed., *Public Opinion and Propaganda*. New York: Holt, Rinehart and Winston. Pp. 532-542.

Eldersveld, Samuel James, V. Jagannadham, and A. P. Barnabas
1968   *The Citizen and the Administrator in a Developing Democracy*. Glenview, Ill.: Scott, Foresman.

Eldersveld, Samuel James, and Akira Kubota
1973   "Party Identification in India and Japan—In the context of Western Theory and Research," paper delivered at the 1973 Canadian Political Science Association Meeting, Montreal.

Elkins, David J.
1972   "Regional Contexts of Political Participation: Some Illustration from India." *Canadian Journal of Political Science* 5: 167-189.

Epstein, Leon D.
1956   "British Mass Parties in Comparison with American Parties." *Political Science Quarterly* 71: 97-125.

Erbe, William
1964   "Social Involvement and Political Activity: A Replication and Elaboration." *American Sociolgical Review* 29: 198-215.

Etzioni, Amitai
1970   *Demonstration Democracy*. New York: Gordon and Breach.

Eulau, Heinz
1962   *Class and Party in the Eisenhower Years*. New York: The Free Press of Glencoe.

Eulau, Heinz, William Buchanan, LeRoy Ferguson, and John C. Wahlke
1959   "The Political Socialization of American State Legislators."
          Midwest Journal of Political Science 3: 188-206.

Eulau, Heinz, and Peter Schneider
1956   "Dimensions of Political Involvement." *Public Opinion
          Quarterly* 20: 128-142.

Feagin, Joe R., and Harlan Hahn
1973   *Ghetto Revolts: The Politics of Violence in American
          Cities.* New York: Macmillan.

Feierabend, Ivo K., Rosalind L. Feierabend, and Ted Robert Gurr
1972   *Anger, Violence and Politics.* Englewood Cliffs, N. J.:
          Prentice-Hall.

Fensterwald, Bernard, Jr.
1958   "The Anatomy of American 'Isolationism' and Expansion-
          ism; I and II. *Journal of Conflict Resolution* 2: 111-139,
          280-309.

Fenton, John H., and Kenneth N. Vines
1957   "Negro Registration in Louisiana." *American Political
          Science Review* 51: 704-713.

Festinger, Leon, Stanley Schachter, and Kurt Back
1950   *Social Pressures in Informal Groups: A Study of Human
          Factors in Housing.* New York: Harper.

Field, John O.
1974   *Politicization and System Support in India: The Role of
          Partisianship.* Cambride, Mass.: MIT Center for Inter-
          national Studies.

Finifter, Ada W.
1970   "Dimensions of Political Alienation." *American Political
          Science Review* 64: 389-410.

_____   "The Friendship Group as a Protective Environment for
1974   Political Deviants." *American Political Science Review* 68:
          607-625.

Fischer, Claude S.
1975   "The City and Political Psychology." *American Political
          Science Review* 69: 559-571.

Flacks, Richard
1970   "Who Protests: The Social Bases of the Student Movement,"
          in Julian Foster and Durward Long, eds., *Protest:*

Student Activism in America. New York: Morrow. Pp. 134-157.

Flora, Cornelia B.
1974 "Working Class Women's Political Participation: Its Potential in Developed Countries," paper delivered at the American Political Science Association Meeting, Chicago.

Fogelson, Robert M.
1971 *Violence as Protest: A Study of Riots and Ghettos.* New York: Doubleday.

Fogelson, Robert M., and Robert B. Hill
1968 "Who Riots? A Study of Participation in the 1967 Riots," in *National Advisory Commission on Civil Disorders, Supplemental Studies.* Washington, D.C.: Government Printing Office. Pp. 217-248.

Ford, William F., and John H. Moore
1970 "Additional Evidence on the Social Characteristics of Riot Cities." *Social Science Quarterly* 51: 339-348.

Forthal, Sonya
1946 *Cogwheels of Democracy: A Study of a Precinct Captain.* New York: William-Frederick Press.

Forward, John R., and Jay R. Williams
1970 "Internal-External Control and Black Militancy." *Journal of Social Issues* 26: 75-92.

Foskett, John M.
1955 "Social Structure and Social Participation." *American Sociological Review* 20: 431-438.

Franklin, Joan
1975 "Political Participation, Voluntary Organization Membership and Sex Differences: An Examination of Relationships," paper delivered at the American Political Science Association Meeting, San Francisco.

Fraser, John
1970 "The Impact of Community and Regime Orientations on Choice of Political System." *Midwest Journal of Political Science* 14: 413-433.

———. "The Mistrustful-Efficacious Hypothesis and Political
1970 Participation." *Journal of Politics* 32: 444-449.

Freeman, J. Leiper
1958 "Local Party Systems: Theoretical Considerations and a

Case Analysis." *American Journal of Sociology* 64: 282-289.

Frenkel-Brunswik, Else
1952   "The Interaction of Psychological and Sociological Factors in Political Behavior." *American Political Science Review* 46: 44-65.

Fromm, Erich
1955   *The Sane Society*. New York: Rinehart.

Fuchs, Lawrence H.
1955   "American Jews and the Presidential Vote." *American Political Science Review* 49: 385-401.
_____.   *The Political Behavior of American Jews*. Glencoe, Ill.:
1956   The Free Press.

Galli, Giorgio, and Alfonso Prandi
1970   *Patterns of Political Participation in Italy*. New Haven: Yale University Press.

Gamson, William A.
1968   *Power and Discontent*. Homewood, Ill.: Dorsey Press.
_____.   *The Strategy of Social Protest*. Homewood, Ill.: Dorsey
1975   Press.

George, Alexander L.
1968   "Power as a Compensatory Value for Political Leaders." *Journal of Social Issues* 24: 29-49.

George, Alexander L., and Juliette L. George .
1964   *Woodrow Wilson and Colonel House: A Personality Study*. New York: Dover.

Geschwender, James A.
1964   "Social Structure and the Negro Revolt: An Examination of Some Hypotheses." *Social Forces* 43: 248-256.

Glantz, Oscar
1959   "Protestant and Catholic Voting Behavior in a Metropolitan Area." *Public Opinion Quarterly* 23: 73-82.
_____.   "The Negro Voter in Northern Industrial Cities." *Western
1960   Political Quarterly* 13: 999-1010.

Glaser, William A.
1958   "Intention and Voting Turnout." *American Political Science Review* 52: 1030-1040.
_____.   "The Family and Voting Turnout." *Public Opinion Quar-*

1959-1960   *terly* 23: 563-570.

_____.   "Television and Voting Turnout." *Public Opinion Quar-*
1965   *terly* 29: 71-86.

Glenn, Norval D.
1969   "Aging, Disengagement and Opinionation." *Public Opinion
            Quarterly* 33: 17-33.

Glenn, Norval D., and Michael Grimes
1968   "Aging, Voting and Political Interest." *American Socio-
            logical Review* 33: 563-575.

Goel, M. Lal.
1970a   "The Relevance of Education for Political Participation in
            a Developing Society." *Comparative Political Studies* 3:
            333-346.

_____.   "Distribution of Civic Competence Feelings in India."
1970b   *Social Science Quarterly* 51: 755-768.

_____.   "Urban-Rural Correlates of Political Participation in India."
1971   *Political Science Review* 10: 51-64.

_____.   "Social Bases of Party Support and Political Participation
1974   in India." *Political Science Review* 13: 59-88.

_____.   *Political Participation in a Developing Nation: India.* New
1975   York: Asia Publishing House.

_____.   "The Determinants of Conventional Political Partici-
forthcoming pation," in David Horton Smith and J. Macauley, eds.,
            Handbook of Informal Social Participation. (Tentative
            Title). San Francisco: Jossey-Bass.

Goldhamer, Herbert
1950   "Public Opinion and Personality." *American Journal of
            Sociology* 55: 346-354.

Goldman, Ralph
1956   "Move—Lose Your Vote." *National Municipal Review*
            45: 6-10.

Gordon, Daniel N.
1970   "Immigrants and Municipal Voting Turnout: Implications
            for the Changing Ethnic Impact on Urban Politics."
            American Sociological Review 35: 665-681.

Gordon, Leonard
1972   "A Comment on Political Orientation and Riot Partici-
            pation." *American Sociological Review* 37: 379.

Gore, Pearl Mayo, and Julian B. Rotter
1963   "A Personality Correlate of Social Action." *Journal of Personality* 31: 58-64.

Gosnell, Harold Foote
1927   *Getting Out the Vote*. Chicago: University of Chicago Press.

_____.   *Why Europe Votes*. Chicago, University of Chicago Press.
1930

_____.   *Machine Politics*. Chicago: University of Chicago Press.
1937

_____.   *Democracy, the Threshold of Freedom*. New York: Ronald.
1948

Gough, Harrison G.
1952   "Predicting Social Participation." *Journal of Social Psychology* 35: 227-233.

Greeley, Andrew M.
1974   "Political Participation among Ethnic Groups in the United States: A Preliminary Reconnaissance." *American Journal of Sociology* 80: 170-204.

Green, Thomas H.
1974   *Comparative Revolutionary Movements*. Englewood Cliffs, N. J.: Prentice-Hall.

Greenstein, Fred I.
1969   *Personality and Politics: Problems of Evidence, Inference, and Conceptualization*. Chicago: Markham.

_____.   Review of *Personality, Power and Politics*, by Gordon J.
1970   DiRenzo, in *Political Science Quarterly* 85: 365-368.

Greenstein, Fred I., and Michael Lerner, eds.
1971   *A Source Book for the Study of Personality and Politics*. Chicago: Markham.

Grofman, Bernard N., and Edward N. Muller
1973   "The Strange Case of Relative Gratification and Potential for Political Violence: The V-Curve Hypothesis." *American Political Science Review* 67: 514-539.

Gronseth, Erik
1953   *The Political Role of Women in Norway*. Oslo: Institute for Social Research (Mimeographed.) Excerpts from a contribution to the Norwegian report to the UNESCO

study of the political role of women. Oslo: Oslo University, Institute of Sociology.

1955   First published in Maurice Duverger, ed., *The Political Role of Women*. Paris: UNESCO. Pp. 194-221.

Gruberg, Martin

1968   *Women in American Politics: An Assessment and Sourcebook*. Oshkosh, Wis.: Academia Press.

Grundy, J.

1950   "Non-Voting in an Urban District." *Journal of the Manchester School of Economic and Social Studies* 18: 83-99.

Gurr, Ted Robert

1970   *Why Men Rebel*. Princeton, N. J.: Princeton Unversity Press.

_____   "A Causal Model of Civil Strife: A Comparative Analysis
1968   Using New Indices." *American Political Science Review* 62: 1104-24.

1972   Reprinted in Ivo K. Feierabend, et al., *Anger, Violence and Politics*. Englewood Cliffs, N. J..: Prentice-Hall. Pp. 184-222.

Guttman, Louis

1950   "The Basis for Scalogram Analysis," in Samuel Stouffer, et al., eds., *Studies in Social Psychology in World War II*. Vol. 4. *Measurement and Prediction*. Princeton, N. J.: Princeton University Press. Pp. 60-90. Also in Bobbs-Merrill Reprint Series No. S-413.

Guttsman, W. L.

1951   "The Changing Social Structure of the British Political Elite, 1886-1935." *British Journal of Sociology* 2: 122 134.

_____   "Social Stratification and Political Elite." *British Journal
1960   of Sociology* 11: 137-150.

Hacker, Andrew, and Joel D. Aberbach

1962   "Businessmen in Politics." *Law and Contemporary Problems* 27: 266-279.

Hahn, Harlan

1970   "Black Separatists: Attitudes and Objectives in a Riot-torn Ghetto." *Journal of Black Studies* 1: 35-53.

Hamilton, Howard D.
1971   "The Municipal Voter: Voting and Non-Voting in City Elections." *American Political Science Review* 65: 1135-1140.

Hansen, Susan B.
1975   "Participation, Political Structure and Concurrence." *American Political Science Review* 69: 1181-1199.

Harned, Louise
1975   "Participation in Political Parties: A Study of Party Committeemen." Unpublished doctoral dissertation, Yale University.

———   "Authoritarian Attitudes and Party Activity." *Public*
1961   *Opinion Quarterly* 25: 393-399.

Hastings, Philip K.
1954   "The Non-Voter in 1952: A Study of Pittsfield, Massachusetts." *Journal of Psychology* 38: 301-312.

Hawkins, Brett W., Vincent L. Marando, and George A. Taylor
1971   "Efficacy, Mistrust and Political Participation: Findings from Additional Data and Indicators." *Journal of Politics* 33: 1130-1136.

Heard, Alexander
1960   *The Costs of Democracy*. Chapel Hill: University of North Carolina Press.

Hennessy, Bernard
1959   "Politicals and Apoliticals: Some Measurements of Personality Traits." *Midwest Journal of Political Science* 3: 336-355.

Hibbs, Douglas A., Jr.
1973   *Mass Political Violence: A Cross-National Causal Analysis.* New York: Wiley.

Himmelstrand, Ulf
1960a   *Social Pressures, Attitudes, and Democratic Processes.* Stockholm: Almqvist and Wiksell.

———   "Verbal Attitudes and Behavior: A Paradigm for the Study
1960b   of Message Transmission and Transformation." *Public Opinion Quarterly* 24: 224-250.

———   "Depoliticization and Political Involvement: A Theoretical
1970   and Empirical Approach," in Erik Allardt and Stein Rok-

kan, eds., *Mass Politics*. New York: The Free Press. Pp. 64-
92.

Hirsch, Herbert, and David C. Perry, eds.
1973   *Violence as Politics: A Series of Original Essays*. New York:
Harper & Row.

Horowitz, Irving Louis
1967   "Electoral Politics, Urbanization, and Social Development
in Latin America," in Glenn H. Beyer, ed., *The Urban
Explosion in Latin America*. Ithaca, N. Y.: Cornell University Press. Pp. 215-273.

Hughes, Colin A.
1968   "Compulsory Voting," in Colin A. Hughes, ed., *Readings
in Australian Government*. St. Lucia, Queensland, Bris-
bane: University of Queensland Press. Pp. 225-239.

Hunt, Robert W., and M. Lal Goel
forthcoming "Explaining Individual Participation in Political Violence,"
in David Horton Smith and J. Macauley, eds., *Handbook
of Informal Social Participation*. (Tentative title). San
Francisco: Jossey-Bass.

Hunter, Floyd
1953   *Community Power Structure; A Study of Decision Makers*.
Chapel Hill: University of North Carolina Press.
1968   Reprinted by Doubleday.

Huntington, Samuel P.
1968   *Political Order in Changing Societies*. New Haven: Yale
University Press.

Hyman, Herbert H.
1972   "Dimensions of Social-Psychological Change in the Negro
Population," in Angus Campbell and Philip E. Converse,
eds., *The Human Meaning of Social Change*. New York:
Russell Sage Foundation. Pp. 339-390.

Inglehart, Ronald, and Avram Hochstein
1972   "Alignment and Dealignment of the Electorate in France
and the United States." *Comparative Political Studies*
5: 343-372.

Inkeles, Alex
1969   "Participant Citizenship in Six Developing Countries."
American Political Science Review 63: 1120-1141.

1974   Also reprinted in Lewis Bowman and G. R. Boynton, eds., *Political Behavior and Public Opinion*. Englewood Cliffs, N. J.: Prentice-Hall. Pp. 213-247.

Irwin, Galen A.
1974   "Compulsory Voting Legislation: Impact on Voter Turnout in the Netherlands." *Comparative Political Studies* 7: 292-315.

Irwin, Galen A., and Henk A. A. Moleman
no date "Political Participation in the Netherlands: A Preliminary Report." A xeroxed paper. Department of Political Science, Leiden University.

Jacob, Herbert
1962   "Initial Recruitment of Elected Officials in the United States: A Model." *The Journal of Politics* 24: 703-716.
_____.   "Contact with Government Agencies: A Preliminary
1972   Analysis of the Distribution of Government Services." *Midwest Journal of Political Science* 16: 123-146.

Janda, Kenneth
1965   "A Comparative Study of Political Alienation and Voting Behavior in Three Suburban Communities," in *Studies in History and the Social Sciences: Studies in Honor of John A. Kinneman*. Normal, Ill.: Illinois State University Press.

Janosik, Edward G.
about 1960 Business Executives' Research Committee, Philadelphia. *Report on Political Activity of Philadelphia Businessmen.* Sponsored by the Committee for Economic Development and the Wharton School of the University of Pennsylvania.

Janowitz, Morris, and Dwaine Marvick
1953   "Authoritarianism and Political Behavior." *Public Opinion Quarterly* 17: 185-201.
_____.   *Competitive Pressure and Democratic Consent: An Inter-
1956   pretation of the 1952 Presidential Election.* Ann Arbor: Bureau of Government, Inst. of Public Administration, University of Michigan.

1956   A summarization of this report appears in Heinz Eulau, et. al., eds., *Legislative Behavior; A Reader in Theory and Research*. Glencoe, Ill.: The Free Press. Pp. 275-286.

Jaquette, Jane S., comp.
1974   *Women in Politics*. New York: Wiley.

Jennings, M. Kent
1964   *Community Influentials: The Elites of Atlanta.* New York: The Free Press of Glencoe.

_____   "Partisan Commitment and Electoral Behavior in the
1972   Netherlands." *Acta Politica* 7: 445-470.

Jensen, Jack
1960   "Political Participation: A Survey in Evanston, Illinois."
            Unpublished master's thesis, Northwestern University.

Johnson, Gerald W.
1971   "Research Note on Political Correlates of Voter Partici-
            pation: A Deviant Case Analysis." *American Political
            Science Review* 65: 768-776.

Kaase, Max
1975   "Dynamics of Dissatisfaction and Protest Potential in
            Germany," paper delivered at the American Political
            Science Association Meeting, San Francisco.

Kabaker, Harvey M.
1969   "Estimating the Normal Vote in Congressional Elections."
            Midwest Journal of Political Science 13: 58-83.

Kahane, Reuven
1973   *The Problem of Political Legitimacy in an Antagonistic
            Society: The Indonesian Case.* Beverly Hills, Calif.: Sage
            Publications.

Karlsson, Georg
1958a   "Voting Participation among Male Swedish Youth." *Acta
            Sociologica* 3 (fasc. 2-3): 98-111.

_____   "Political Attitudes among Male Swedish Youth." *Acta
1958b   Sociologica* 3 (fasc. 4): 220-241.

Karnig, Albert K., and Oliver B. Walter
1974   "Electoral Turnout in Municipal Elections: A Multivariate
            Analysis." *Rocky Mountain Social Science Journal* 11,
            no. 2: 55-71.

_____   "Registration and Voting: Putting First Things Second."
1974   *Social Science Quarterly* 55: 159-166.

Katz, Daniel, and Samuel J. Eldersveld
1961   "The Impact of Local Party Activity Upon the Electorate."
            Public Opinion Quarterly 25: 1-24.

Katz, Elihu
1957   "The Two-Step Flow of Communication: An Up-to-Date

Report on an Hypothesis." *Public Opinion Quarterly* 21: 61-78.

Katz, Elihu and Paul F. Lazarsfeld
1955   *Personal Influence*. Glencoe, III.: The Free Press.

Kelley, Stanley, Jr., Richard E. Ayres, and William G. Bowen
1967   "Registration and Voting: Putting First Things First." *American Political Science Review* 61: 359-379.

Kelley, Stanley Jr., and Thad W. Mirer
1974   "The Simple Act of Voting." *American Political Science Review* 68: 572-591.

Kelman, Herbert C.
1970   "A Social-Psychological Model of Political Legitimacy and Its Relevance to Black and White Student Protest Movements." *Psychiatry* 33: 224-246.

Keniston, Kenneth
1965   *The Uncommitted: Alienated Youth in American Society*. New York: Harcourt, Brace & World.

_____.
1968   *Young Radicals: Notes on Committed Youth*. New York: Harcourt, Brace & World.

Kerpelman, Larry C.
1969   "Student Political Activism and Ideology: Comparative Characteristics of Activists and Non-Activists." *Journal of Counseling Psychology* 16: 8-13.

Kerr, C., and A. Siegel
1954   "The Interindustry Propensity to Strike—An International Comparison," in Arthur Kornhauser, Robert Dubin, and Arthur M. Ross, eds., *Industrial Conflict*. New York: McGraw-Hill. Pp. 189-212.

Kessell, John H.
1965   "Cognitive Dimensions and Political Activity." *Public Opinion Quarterly* 29: 377-389.

Kesselman, Mark
1966   "French Local Politics: A Statistical Examination of Grass Roots Consensus." *American Political Science Review* 60: 963-973.

Key, V. O., Jr.
1949   *Southern Politics in State and Nation*. New York: Alfred A. Knopf.

_____.
1955 .   "A Theory of Critical Elections." *Journal of Politics* 17: 3-18.

————. "Secular Realignment and the Party System." *Journal of*
1959   *Politics* 21: 198-210.

————. *Public Opinion and American Democracy.* New York:
1961   Alfred A. Knopf.

Key, V. O., Jr., and Frank Munger
1959   "Social Determinism and Electoral Decision: The Case of
            Indiana," in Eugene Burdick and Arthur J. Brodbeck, eds.,
            American Voting Behavior. Glencoe, Ill.: The Free Press.
            Pp. 281-299.

Kilpatrick, Franklin P., Milton C. Cummings, Jr., and M. Kent Jennings
1964   *The Image of the Federal Service.* Washington, D. C.: The
            Brookings Institution.

Kim, Chong Lim
1971   "Socio-Economic Development and Political Democracy
            in Japanese Prefectures." *American Political Science Re-
            view* 65: 184-186.

Kim, Jae-on, Norman Nie, and Sidney Verba
1974   "The Amount and Concentration of Political Participa-
            tion." *Political Methodology* 1: 105-132.

Kim, Jae-on, John R. Petrocik, and Stephen N. Enokson
1975   "Voter Turnout Among the American States: Systematic
            and Individual Components." *American Political Science
            Review* 69: 107-131.

Kimball, Penn
1972   *The Disconnected.* New York: Columbia University Press.

Kirby, Douglas
1971   "A Counter-Culture Explanation of Student Activism."
            Social Problems 19: 203-216.

Kirkpatrick, Samuel A.
1974   *Quantitative Analysis of Political Data.* Columbus, Ohio:
            Charles E. Merrill.

Kitt, Alice S., and David B. Gleicher
1950   "Determinants of Voting Behavior." *Public Opinion
            Quarterly* 14: 393-412.

Knupfer ,Genevieve
1947   "Portrait of the Underdog." *Public Opinion Quarterly*
            11: 103-114.

Knutson, Jeanne Nickel
1972   *The Human Basis of the Polity: A Psychological Study
            of Political Men.* Chicago: Aldine-Atherton.

Knutson, Jeanne Nickel, ed.
1973   *Handbook of Political Psychology*. San Francisco: Jossey-
            Bass.
Kobayashi, Bertrand Y.
1974   "Political Alienation and Political Participation: A Problem
            of Conceptualization and Theory as Applied to College
            Students," paper delivered at the American Political Sci-
            ence Association Meeting, Chicago.
Kornhauser, Arthur, William Harold Sheppard, and Albert J. Mayer
1956   *When Labor Votes: A Study of Auto Workers*. New York:
            University Books.
Kornhauser, William
1959   *The Politics of Mass Society*. Glencoe, Ill.: The Free Press.
Kothari, Rajni
1970   *Politics in India*. Boston: Little, Brown.
Kothari, Rajni, ed.
1976   *State and Nation Building: A Third World Perspective*.
            New Delhi: Allied.
Krause, Merton S., Kevin Houlihan, Mark I. Oberlander, and Lawrence
Carson
1970   "Some Motivational Correlates of Attitudes Toward Polit-
            ical Participation." *Midwest Journal of Political Science*
            14: 383-391.
Krauss, Ellis S.
1974   *Japanese Radicals Revisited: Student Protest in Postwar
            Japan*. Berkeley: University of California Press.
Kubota, Akira
1975   "Protest and the Japanese Political System." *Journal of
            Asian and African Studies* 10: 165-175.
Kuroda, Alice, and Yasumasa Kuroda
1968   "Aspects of Community Political Participation in Japan."
            Journal of Asian Studies 27: 229-251.
Kuroda, Yasumasa
1965a   "Sociability and Political Involvement." *Midwest Journal
            of Political Science* 9: 133-147.
_____.   "Measurement, Correlates, and Significance of Political
1967   Participation in a Japanese Community." *Western Political
            Quarterly* 20: 660-668.
_____.   "Political Role Attribution and Dynamics in a Japanese
1965b   Community." *Public Opinion Quarterly* 29: 602-613.

1974   Also reprinted in Lewis Bowman and G. R. Boynton, eds., *Political Behavior and Public Opinion*. Englewood Cliffs, N. J.: Prentice-Hall. Pp. 270-281.

Kyogoku, Jun-ichi

1961   "Political Behavior Studies in Contemporary Japan," paper prepared for the Fifth World Congress of the International Political Science Association, Paris, September, 1961.

Kyogoku, Jun-ichi and Nobutaka Ike

1959   *Urban-Rural Differences in Voting Behavior in Postwar Japan*. Stanford University, Dept. of Political Science. Stanford University Political Science Series, Reprint No. 66. Reprinted from the Proceedings of the Dept. of Social Sciences, College of General Education, University of Tokyo.

Lacey, Virginia P.

1971   "Political Knowledge of College Activist Groups: SDS, YAF, and YD." *Journal of Politics* 33: 840-845.

Lane, Robert Edwards

1955   "Political Personality and Electoral Choice." *American Political Science Review* 49: 173-190.

————. *Political Life: Why People Get Involved in Politics*. Glencoe, Ill.: The Free Press.
1959

————. *Political Ideology: Why the American Common Man Believes What He Does*. New York: The Free Press of Glencoe.
1962

————. *Political Thinking and Consciousness: The Private Life of the Political Mind*. Chicago: Markham.
1969

————. *Political Man*. New York: The Free Press.
1972

Lang, Kurt, and Gladys Engel Lang

1956   "The Television Personality in Politics: Some Considerations." *Public Opinion Quarterly* 20: 103-112.

Lapidus, Gail Warshofsky

1975   "Political Mobilization, Participation and Leadership: Women in Soviet Politics." *Comparative Politics* 8: 90-118.

Lasswell, Harold Dwight

1930   *Psychopathology and Politics*. Chicago: University of Chicago Press.

1951   Reprinted in *The Political Writings of Harold D. Lasswell*. Glencoe, Ill.: The Free Press. Pp. 1-282.

_____   "The Selective Effect of Personality on Political Participation," in Richard Christie and Marie Jahoda, eds., *Studies in the Scope and Method of the Authoritarian Personality*. Glencoe, Ill.: The Free Press. Pp. 197-225.
1954

Lazarsfeld, Paul Felix, Bernard Berelson, and Hazel Gaudet
1944   *The People's Choice: How the Voter Makes Up His Mind in a Presidential Campaign*. New York: Duell, Sloan, and Pearce.

Lazarsfeld, Paul Felix, and Robert K. Merton
1948   "Mass Communication, Popular Taste, and Organized Social Action," in Lyman Bryson, ed., *The Communication of Ideas*. New York: Harper. Pp. 95-118.

Lee, Eugene C.
1963   "City Elections: A Statistical Profile." *Municipal Year Book, 1963*. Chicago: International City Managers Association. Pp. 74-84.

Lenski, Gerhard E.
1956   "Social Participation and Status Crystallization." *American Sociological Review* 21: 458-464.

Lerner, Daniel
1958   *The Passing of Traditional Society: Modernizing the Middle East*. Glencoe, Ill.: The Free Press.

Levin, Murray Burton
1960   *The Alienated Voter: Politics in Boston*. New York: Holt, Rinehart and Winston.

Levinson, Daniel J.
1957   "Authoritarian Personality and Foreign Policy." *Journal of Conflict and Resolution* 1: 37-47.

_____   "The Relevance of Personality for Political Participation."
1958   *Public Opinion Quarterly* 22: 3-10.

Levy, Sheldon G.
1969   "A 150-Year Study of Political Violence in the U. S.," in Hugh Davis Graham and Ted Robert Gurr, eds., *Violence in America*. New York: Bantam Books. Pp. 84-100.

_____   "The Psychology of Political Activity." *Annals* of the
1970   American Academy of Political Science 391: 83-96.
1972   Reprinted in James F. Short and Marvin E. Wolfgang, eds., *Collective Violence*. Aldine-Atherton. Pp. 210-223.

Lewis, Paul H.
1971   "The Female Vote in Argentina, (1958-1965)." *Comparative Political Studies* 3: 425-441.
Lieberson, Stanley, and Arnold R. Silverman
1965   "The Participants and Underlying Conditions of Race Riots." *American Sociological Review* 30: 887-898.
Lippit, Gordon L., and Drexed A. Sprecher
1960   "Factors Motivating Citizens to Become Active in Politics as Seen by Practical Politicians." *Journal of Social Issues* 16: 11-17.
Lipset, Seymour Martin
1960   *Political Man: The Social Bases of Politics*. Garden City, N. Y.: Doubleday.
————.   *Student Politics*. New York: Basic Books.
1967a
————.   *Party Systems and Voter Alignments: Cross-National Perspectives*. New York: The Free Press.
1967b
————.   "The Activists: A Profile," in Daniel Bell and Irving Kristol,
1969   eds., *Confrontation: The Student Rebellion and the Universities*. New York: Basic Books. Pp. 45-57.
1968   First published in *The Public Interest*, No. 13. Pp. 39-51.
Lipset, Seymour Martin, Paul F. Lazarsfeld, Allen H. Barton, and Juan Linz
1954   "The Psychology of Voting: An Analysis of Political Behavior," in Gardner Lindzey, ed., *Handbook of Social Psychology*. Vol. 2 Cambridge, Mass.: Addison-Wesley. Pp. 1124-1175.
Lipsky, Michael
1970   *Protest in City Politics: Rent Strikes, Housing and the Power of the Poor*. Chicago: Rand McNally.
Litt, Edgar
1963   "Political Cynicism and Political Futility." *Journal of Politics* 25: 312-323.
Lynn, Naomi B., and Cornelia B. Flora
1973   "Motherhood and Political Participation: The Changing Sense of Self." *Journal of Political and Military Sociology* 1: 91-103.
McCallum, Ronald Buchanan, and Alison Readman
1947   *The British General Election of 1945*. London: Oxford University Press.

McCleskey, Clifton, and Bruce Merrill
1973   "Mexican American Political Behavior in Texas." *Social Science Quarterly* 53: 785-798.
McClosky, Herbert
1958   "Conservatism and Personality." *American Political Science Review* 52: 27-45.
1961   Reprinted in S. Sidney Ulmer, ed., *Introductory Readings in Political Behavior*. Chicago: Rand McNally. Pp. 33-44.
_____   "Consensus and Ideology in American Politics." *American*
1964   *Political Science Review* 58: 361-382.
_____.   "Political Participation." *International Encyclopedia of the*
1968   *Social Sciences* 12: 252-265. New York: Collier & Mc-Millan.
McClosky, Herbert, and Harold E. Dahlgren
1959   "Primary Group Influence on Party Loyalty." *American Political Science Review* 53: 757-776.
1961   Also reprinted in S. Sidney Ulmer, ed., *Introductory Readings in Political Behavior*. Chicago: Rand McNally. Pp. 221-237.
McClosky, Herbert, Paul J. Hoffman, and Rosemary O'Hara
1960   "Issue Conflict and Consensus among Party Leaders and Followers." *American Political Science Review* 54: 406-427.
McClosky, Herbert, and John H. Schaar
1965   "Psychological Dimensions of Anomy." *American Sociological Review* 30: 14-40.
Maccoby, Eleanor E., ed.
1966   *The Development of Sex Differences*. Stanford: Stanford University Press.
Maccoby, Herbert
1958   "The Differential Political Activity of Participants in a Voluntary Association." *American Sociological Review* 23: 524-532.
McConaughy, John B.
1950   "Certain Personality Factors of State Legislators in South Carolina." *American Political Science Review* 44: 897-903.
McCord, William, and John Howard
1968   "Negro Opinions in Three Riot Cities." *American Behavioral Scientist* 11: 24-27.

McCrone, Donald J., and Charles F. Cnudde
1967   "Toward a Communications Theory of Democratic Polit-
          ical Development: A Causal Model." *American Political
          Science Review* 61: 72-79.
McDill, Edward L., and Jeanne C. Ridley
1962   "Status, Anomia, Political Alienation and Political Parti-
          cipation." *American Journal of Sociology* 68: 205-213.
McDonough, Peter
1971   "Electoral Competition and Participation in India: A Test
          of Huntington's Hypothesis." *Comparative Politics* 4: 77-
          87. Taken from his doctoral dissertation, "Party Competi-
          tion and Electoral Participation in India," University of
          Michigan, 1969.
MacKenzie, William, James Millar, and K. Robinson, eds.
1960   *Five Elections in Africa*. London: Oxford University Press.
McPhail, Clark
1971   "Civil Disorder Participation: A Critical Examination of
          Recent Research." *American Sociological Review* 36:
          1058-1073.
McPhee, William N., and William A. Glaser, eds.
1962   *Public Opinion and Congressional Elections*. New York:
          The Free Press of Glencoe.
Mann, Dean E.
1965   *Federal Political Executives: Selection and Recruitment;
          Highlights of the Assistant Secretaries*. Washington, D. C.:
          The Brookings Institution.
Marquette, Jesse F.
1971   "Social Mobilization and the Philippine Political System."
          Comparative Political Studies 4: 339-347.
Martin, H. T., and L. Siegel
1953   "Background Factors Related to Effective Group Partici-
          pation." *Journal of Abnormal and Social Psychology* 48:
          599-600.
Marvick, Dwaine
1962   "The Middlemen of Politics," paper prepared for the
          American Political Science Association Annual Meeting.
          Washington.
Marvick, Dwaine, and Charles Nixon
1961   "Recruitment Contrasts in Rival Campaign Groups," in
          Dwaine Marvick, ed., *Political Decision-Makers*. New York:

The Free Press of Glencoe. Pp. 193-217.

Marx, Gary T.
1967 *Protest and Prejudice: A Study of Belief in the Black Community*. New York: Harper & Row.

Maslow, Abraham Harold
1943 "A Theory of Human Motivation." *Psychological Review* 50: 370-396.

————. *Motivation and Personality*. New York: Harper.
1954

Masotti, Louis H., ed.
1968 "Urban Violence and Disorder," a special issue of *American Behavioral Scientist* 11: No. 4.

Masotti, Louis H., and Don R. Bowen
1968 *Riots and Rebellion*. Beverly Hills, Calif.: Sage Publications.

Massey, Joseph A.
1975 "The Missing Leader: Japanese Youth's View of Political Authority." *American Political Science Review* 69: 31-48.

Masumi, Junnosuke
1961 "Japanese Voting Behavior: A Changing Nation and the Vote," paper prepared for the Fifth World Congress of the International Political Science Association, Paris, September, 1961.

Matthews, Donald R., and James W. Prothro
1962 "Southern Racial Attitudes: Conflict Awareness, and Political Change." *Annals of the American Academy of Political and Social Science* 344: 108-121.

————. "Social and Economic Factors and Negro Voter Registra-
1963a tion in the South." *American Political Science Review* 57: 24-44.

————. "Political Factors and Negro Voter Registration in the
1963b South." *American Political Science Review* 57: 355-367.

————. "Negro Voter Registration in the South," in Allan P. Sind-
1963c ler, ed., *Change in the Contemporary South*. Durham, N.C.: Duke University Press. Pp. 119-149.

————. "Southern Images of Political Parties: An Analysis of White
1964 and Negro Attitudes." *Journal of Politics* 26: 82-111.

————. *Negroes and The New Southern Politics*. New York: Har-
1966 court, Brace & World.

Mayntz, Renate
1961   "Citizen Participation in Germany: Nature and Extent,"
            paper prepared for the Fifth World Congress of the Inter-
            national Political Science Association, Paris, September,
            1961.
Mayo, Henry Bertram
1960   *An Introduction to Democratic Theory.* New York: Ox-
            ford University Press.
Meier, Dorothy L.
1963   "Anomia, Life Chances, Perceived Achievement, and
            Modes of Adaption," paper prepared for the American
            Sociological Association Annual Meeting, Los Angeles,

Meier, Dorothy L., and Wendell Bell
1959   "Anomia and Differential Access to the Achievement of
            Life Goals." *American Sociological Review* 24: 189-202.
Merriam, Charles Edward, and Harold Foote Gosnell
1924   *Non-Voting: Causes and Methods of Control.* Chicago:
            University of Chicago Press.
Merton, Robert King
1957   *Social Theory and Social Structure.* Glencoe, III.: The Free
            Press.
Michels, Robert
1949   *Political Parties: A Sociological Study of the Oligarchical
            Tendencies of Modern Democracy.* Glencoe, III.: The Free
            Press.

Milbrath, Lester W.
1960a   *Measuring the Personalities of Lobbyists.* (Mimeographed.)
_____.   "Predispositions toward Political Contention." *Western
1960b   Political Quarterly* 13: 5-18.
_____.   "Latent Origins of Liberalism: Conservatism and Party
1962   Identification: A Research Note." *The Journal of Politics*
            24: 679-688.
_____.   *The Washington Lobbyists.* Chicago: Rand McNally.
1963
_____.   "Political Participation in the States," in Herbert Jacob
1965a   and Kenneth Vines, eds., *Comparative State Politics.* Bos-
            ton: Little, Brown. Ch. 2.

————.   *Political Participation.* Chicago: Rand McNally.
1965b

————.   "The Nature of Political Beliefs and the Relationship of
1968   the Individual to the Government." *American Behavioral
             Scientist* 12 No. 2: 28-36.

————.   "A Paradigm for the Comparative Study of Local Politics."
1971a   *Il Politico* 36: 5-35.

————.   *People and Government.* (Mimeographed.) State University
1971b   of New York at Buffalo.

————.   "Individuals and the Government," in Herbert Jacob and
1971c   and Kenneth N. Vines, eds., *Politics in the American States:
             A Comparative Analysis.* 2nd ed. Boston: Little, Brown.
             Pp. 27-81.

————.   "Individuals and the Polity," in Kurt Back, ed., social
1972   psychology text to be published by Wiley.

Milbrath, Lester W., and Walter Klein
1962   "Personality Correlates of Political Participation." *Acta
             Sociologica* 6(fasc. 1-2): 53-66.

Miller, Arthur H.
1974a   "Political Issues and Trust in Government: 1964-1970."
             American Political Science Review 68: 951-972, 989-
             1001.

————.   "Change in Political Trust: Discontent with Authorities
1974b   and Economic Policies, 1972-1973," paper presented at the
             American Political Science Association Meeting, Chicago.

Miller, Mungo
1952   "The Waukegan Study of Voter Turnout Prediction."
             Public Opinion Quarterly 16: 381-398.

Miller, Norman N.
1970   "The Rural African Party: Political Participation in Tan-
             zania." *American Political Science Review* 64: 548-571.

Miller, Warren E.
1955-1956   "Presidential Coat-Tails: A Study in Political Myth and
             Methodology." *Public Opinion Quarterly* 19: 353-368.

————.   "One-Party Politics and the Voter." *American Political
1956   Science Review* 50: 707-725.

————.   "The Socio-Economic Analysis of Political Behavior."
1958   *Midwest Journal of Political Science* 2: 239-255.

Mills, Charles Wright

1951 *White Collar: The American Middle Classes.* New York: Oxford University Press.

Milne, Robert Stephen, and H. C. Mackenzie

1954 *Straight Fight: A Study of Voting Behavior in the Constituency of Bristol North-East at the General Election of 1951.* London: Hansard Society.

————. *Marginal Seat: A Study of Voting Behavior in the Constituency of Bristol North-East at the General Election of 1955.* London: Hansard Society.
1958

Milnor, Andrew J.

1969 *Elections and Political Stability.* Boston: Little, Brown.

Mitchell, William Clarence

1958 "Occupational Role Strains: The American Elective Public Official." *Administrative Science Quarterly* 3: 210-228. Also in Bobbs-Merrill Reprint Series No. PS-210.

————. "The Ambivalent Social Status of the American Politician."
1959 *Western Political Quarterly* 12: 683-698. Also in Bobbs-Merrill Reprint Series No. PS-209.

Morrison, Denton E.

1971 "Some Notes Toward a Theory on Relative Deprivation, Social Movements and Social Change." *American Behavioral Scientist* 14: 675-690.

Morse, Stanley J., and Stanton Peele

1971 "A Study of Participants in an Anti-Vietnam War Demonstration." *Journal of Social Issues* 27: 113-136.

Muller, Edward N.

1970a "Cross-National Dimensions of Political Competence." *American Political Science Review* 64: 792-809.

————. "Correlates and Consequences of Beliefs in the Legitimacy of Regime Structures." *Midwest Journal of Political*
1970b *Science* 14: 392-412.

————. "A Test of a Partial Theory of Potential for Political Violence." *American Political Science Review* 66: 928-959.
1972

————. "Relative Deprivation and Aggressive Political Behavior,"
1975 paper delivered at the American Political Science Association Meeting, San Francisco.

Mussen, Paul H., and Anne B. Wyszynski

1952 "Personality and Political Participation." *Human Relations* 5: 65-82.

Nandy, Ashish
1974   "Engagement and Alienation in Indian Politics." *Comparative Political Studies* 7: 334-356.

Nardin, Terry
1971   *Violence and the State: A Critique of Empirical Political Theory.* Beverly Hills, Calif.: Sage Publications.

Neal, Arthur G., and Salomon Rettig
1967   "On the Multidimensionality of Alienation." *American Sociological Review* 32: 54-64.

Needler, Martin Cyril
1968   "Political Development and Socioeconomic Development: The Case of Latin America." *American Political Science Review* 62: 889-897.

Nelson, Joel I.
1968   "Anomie: Comparisons Between the Old and New Middle Class." *American Journal of Sociology* 74: 184-192.

Nicholas, Herbert George
1951   *The British General Election of 1950.* London: Macmillan.

Nie, Norman H., G. Bingham Powell, Jr., and Kenneth Prewitt
1969   "Social Structure and Political Participation: Developmental Relationships, Part I and II." *American Political Science Review* 63: 361-378, 808-832.

Nie, Norman H., and Sidney Verba
1975   "Political Participation," in Fred I. Greenstein and Nelson W. Polsby, eds., *The Handbook of Political Science.* Vol. 4. *Non-governmental Politics.* Reading, Mass.: Addison-Wesley. Pp. 1-74.

Nie, Norman H., Sidney Verba, and Jae-on Kim
1974   "Political Participation and the Life Cycle." *Comparative Politics* 6: 319-340.

Nimmo, Dan, and Clifton McCleskey
1969   "Impact of the Poll Tax on Voter Participation: The Houston Metropolitan Area in 1966." *Journal of Politics* 31: 682-699.

Olsen, Marvin E.
1968   "Perceived Legitimacy of Social Protest Actions." *Social Problems* 15: 297-310.

_____. "Two Categories of Political Alienation." *Social Forces*
1969   47: 288-299.

_____. "Social and Political Participation of Blacks." *American*
1970   *Sociological Review* 35: 682-697.

_____. "Social Participation and Voting Turnout: A Multivariate
1972   Analysis." *American Sociological Review* 37: 317-33.

_____. "A Model of Political Participation Stratification." *Journal*
1973   *of Political and Military Sociology* 1: 183-200.

Orbell, John M.
1967   "Protest Participation among Southern Negro College
             Students." *American Political Science Review* 61: 446-
             456.

1974   Also reprinted in Lewis Bowman and G. R. Boynton, eds.,
             Political Behavior and Public Opinion. Englewood Cliffs,
             N. J.: Prentice-Hall. Pp. 282-300.

Orum, Anthony M.
1966   "A Reappraisal of the Social and Political Participation of
             Negroes." *American Journal of Sociology* 72: 32-46.

Orum, Anthony M., and Robert S. Cohen, Sherri Grasmuck, and Amy
W. Orum
1974   "Sex Socialization and Politics." *American Sociological*
             Review 39: 197-209.

Orum, Anthony M., and Amy W. Orum
1968   "The Class and Status Bases of Negro Student Protest."
             Social Science Quarterly 49: 521-533.

Paige, Jeffery M.
1971   "Political Orientation and Riot Participation." *American*
             Sociological Review 36: 810-820.

Parenti, Michael
1974   *Democracy for the Few.* New York: St. Martin's Press.

Parker, Glenn R.
1974   *Political Beliefs about the Structure of Government:*
             Congress and Presidency. Sage Professional Paper in Ameri-
             can Politics Series 2. Beverly Hills, Calif.: Sage Publications.
             Pp. 1-42.

Parsons, Talcott
1957   "Voting and the Equilibrium of the American Political

System," in Burdick and Arthur J. Brodbeck, eds., *American Voting Behavior.* Glencoe, Ill.: The Free Press. Pp. 80-120.

Pateman, Carole
1970   *Participation and Democratic Theory.* Cambridge: Cambridge University Press.
Pederson, Johannes
1974   "Age and Political Change in the Electorate," paper delivered at the American Political Science Association Meeting, Chicago, 1974.
Pesonen, Pertti
1960   "The Voting Behavior of Finnish Students," in *Democracy in Finland.* Helsinki: Finnish Political Science Association. Pp. 93-104.
_____.   "Citizen Participation in Finnish Politics," paper prepared
1961   for the Fifth World Congress of the International Political Science Association, Paris, September, 1961.
_____.   *An Election in Finland: Party Activities and Voter Re-*
1968   *actions.* New Haven: Yale University Press.
Pettigrew, Thomas F.
1964   *A Profile of the Negro American.* New York: Van Nostrand.
Pfeiffer, David G.
1967   "The Measurement of Inter-Party Competition and Systematic Stability." *American Political Science Review* 61: 457-467.
Pinard, Maurice
1968   "Mass Society and Political Movements: A New Formulation." *American Journal of Sociology* 73: 682-690.
Pizzorno, Alessandro
1966   "Introduzione allo Studio de la Partecipaione Politica." *Quaderni di Sociologia* 15: 235-287.
Pomper, Gerald
1966   "Ethnic and Group Voting in Nonpartisan Municipal Elections." *Public Opinion Quarterly* 30: 79-97.
Powell, G. Bingham, Jr.
1970   *Social Fragmentation and Political Hostility: An Austrian Case Study.* Stanford: Stanford University Press.
Pranger, Robert J.
1968   *The Eclipse of Citizenship: Power and Participation in*

Contemporary Politics. New York: Holt, Rinehart and Winston.

President's Commission

1963   *Report of Registration and Voting Participation.* Washington, D. C.: Government Printing Office.

Prewitt, Kenneth

1968   "Political Efficacy." *International Encyclopedia of the Social Sciences* 12: 225-227.

Prewitt, Kenneth, and Norman Nie

1971   "Review Article: Election Studies of the Survey Research Center." *British Journal of Political Science* 1: 479-502.

Price, Hugh Douglas

1955   "The Negro and Florida Politics, 1944-1954." *Journal of Politics* 17: 198-220. Also in Bobbs-Merrill Reprint Series No. PS 233.

Prothro, James W., and Charles M. Grigg

1960   "Fundamental Principles of Democracy: Bases of Agreement and Disagreement." *Journal of Politics* 22: 276-294.

Rabushka, Alvin

1970   "A Note on Overseas Chinese Political Participation in Urban Malaya." *American Political Science Review* 64: 177-178.

Rae, Douglas

1967   *The Political Consequences of Electoral Laws.* New Haven: Yale University Press.

Ranney, Austin

1972   "Turnout and Representation in Presidential Primary Elections." *American Political Science Review* 66: 21-37.

Ranney, Austin, and Leon D. Epstein

1966   "The Two Electorates: Voters and Non-Voters in a Wisconsin Primary." *Journal of Politics* 28: 598-616.

Ransford, H. Edward

1968   "Isolation, Powerlessness and Violence: A Study of Attitudes and Participation in the Watts Riot." *American Journal of Sociology* 73: 581-591.

1974   Also reprinted in Lewis Bowman and G. R. Boynton, eds., *Political Behavior and Public Opinion.* Englewood Cliffs, N. J.: Prentice-Hall. Pp. 310-324.

Reddy, Richard D., and David Horton Smith
1972   "Personality and Capacity Determinants of Individual Participation in Organized Voluntary Action," in David Horton Smith, Richard D. Reddy, and Burt R. Baldwin, eds., *Voluntary Action Research: 1972.* Lexington, Mass.: D. C. Heath. Pp. 277-298.

Renshon, Stanley Allen
1974   *Psychological Needs and Political Behavior: A Theory of Personality and Political Efficacy.* New York: The Free Press. Pp. 259-61.

Rhyne, Edward Hoffman
1958   "Political Parties and Decision Making in Three Southern Counties." *American Political Science Review* 52: 1091-1107.

Richardson, Bradley M.
1966   "Political Attitudes and Voting Behavior in Contemporary Japan: Rural and Urban Differences." Unpublished doctoral dissertation, University of California, Berkeley.

_____.   "Urbanization and Political Participation: The Case of
1973   Japan." *American Political Science Review* 67: 433-452.

_____.   *The Political Culture of Japan.* Berkeley, Calif.: University
1974   of California Press.

Riesman, David
1950   *The Lonely Crowd: A Study of the Changing American Character.* New Haven: Yale University Press.

_____.   *Faces in the Crowd.* New Haven: Yale University Press.
1952

Riesman, David, and Nathan Glazer
1950   "Criteria for Political Apathy," in Alvin Ward Gouldner, ed., *Studies in Leadership.* New York: Harper. Pp. 505-559. Also in Bobbs-Merrill Reprint Series No. S-236.

Riker, William Harrison, and P. C. Ordeshook
1968   "A Theory of the Calculus of Voting." *American Political Science Review* 62: 25-42.

Riley, Matilda White, Anne Foner, and Associates
1968   *Aging and Society.* New York: Russell Sage Foundation.

Robinson, James A., and William H. Standing
1960   "Some Correlates of Voter Participation: The Case of Indiana." *Journal of Politics* 22: 96-111.

Robinson, John P., and Jerrold G. Rusk, and Kendra B. Head
1968   *Measures of Political Attitudes.* Ann Arbor, Mich.: University of Michigan. Survey Research Center, Institute for Social Research.

Robinson, W. S.
1952   "The Motivational Structure of Political Participation." *American Sociological Review* 17: 151-156.

Rokeach, Milton
1960   *The Open and Closed Mind.* New York: Basic Books.

Rokkan, Stein
1955   "Party Preferences and Opinion Patterns in Western Europe: A Comparative Analysis." *International Social Science Bulletin* 7: 575-596.

_____.   "Electoral Activity, Party Membership, and Organizational
1959   Influence: An Initial Analysis of Data from the Norwegian Election Studies 1957." *Acta Sociologica* 4: (fasc. 1): 25-37.

_____.   "Mass Suffrage, Secret Voting and Political Participation."
1961   *(Archives Europeenes de Sociologie, European Journal of Sociology)* 2: 132-152.

_____.   "Approaches to the Study of Political Participation."
1962a   Introduction to special issue, edited by Rokkan, of *Acta Sociologica* 6 (fasc. 1-2): 1-8.

_____.   "The Comparative Study of Political Participation: Notes
1962b   Toward a Perspective on Current Research," in Austin Ranney, ed., *Essays on the Behavioral Study of Politics.* Urbana: University of Illinois Press. Pp. 47-90.

_____.   *Citizens, Elections, Parties.* New York: David McKay. (This
1970   book is a collection of many of Rokkan's previous essays.)

Rokkan, Stein, and Angus Campbell
1960   "Norway and the United States of America," in *Citizen Participation in Political Life, International Social Science Journal* 12: 69-99.

Rokkan, Stein, and Henry Valen
1960   "Parties, Elections, and Political Behavior in the Northern Countries," a review of recent research in O. Stammer, ed., *Politische Forschung.* Koln-Opladen:Westdeutscher Verlag Pp. 120-125, bibliography at 237-249.

_____.   "The Mobilization of the Periphery: Data on Turnout,

1962   Party Membership and Candidate Recruitment in Norway."
              Acta Sociologica 6 (fasc. 1-2): 111-158.

Rose, Arnold M.

1962   "Alienation and Participation: A Comparison of Group
              Leaders and the 'Mass.' " *American Sociological Review*
              27: 834-838.

Rose, Richard, ed.

1974   *Electoral Behavior: A Comparative Handbook*. New York:
              The Free Press.

Rose, Richard, and Harve Mossawir

1967   "Voting and Elections: A Functional Analysis." *Political
              Studies* 15: 173-201.

1974   Also reprinted in Lewis Bowman and G. R. Boynton, eds.,
              Political Behavior and Public Opinion. Englewood Cliffs,
              N. J.: Prentice-Hall. Pp. 159-187.

Rosen, Barney, and Robin Salling

1971   "Political Participation as a Function of Internal-External
              Locus of Control." *Psycholgical Reports* 29: 880-882.

Rosenau, James N.

1974   *Citizenship Between Elections: An Inquiry into the Mobili-
              zable American*. New York: The Free Press.

Rosenbaum, H. Jon, and Peter C. Sederberg

1974   "Vigilantism: An Analysis of Establishment Violence."
              Comparative Politics 6: 541-570.

Rosenberg, Morris

1951   "The Meaning of Politics in Mass Society." *Public Opinion
              Quarterly* 15: 5-15.

_____   "Some Determinants of Political Apathy." *Public Opinion
1954-1955   Quarterly* 18: 349-366.

1956   Also reprinted in Heinz Eulau,et al.,eds.,*Political Behavior:
              A Reader in Theory and Research*. Glencoe, Ill.: The Free
              Press. Pp. 160-169.

_____   "Misanthropy and Political Ideology." *American Socio-
1956   logical Review* 21: 690-695.

_____   "Self-Esteem and Concern with Public Affairs." *Public
1962   Opinion Quarterly* 26: 201-211.

Rosenzweig, Robert M.

1957   "The Politician and the Career in Politics." *Midwest
              Journal of Political Science* 1: 163-172.

Rossi, Peter H., and Phillips Cutright

1961   "The Impact of Party Organization in an Industrial Setting,"
            in Morris Janowitz, ed., *Community Political Systems.*
            Glencoe, Ill.: The Free Press. Pp. 81-116.
Rotter, Julian B., and Donald K. Stein
1971   "Public Attitudes toward the Trustworthiness, Competence
            and Altruism of Twenty Selected Occupations." *Journal
            of Applied Social Psychology.* 1: 334-343.
Roy, Ramashray
1972   *The Uncertain Verdict: A Study of the 1969 Elections in
            Four Indian States.* New Delhi: Orient Longman.
Rummel, Rudolph J.
1963   "Dimensions of Conflict Behavior Within and Between
            Nations." *General Systems* 8: 1-50.
Rushing, William A.
1972   *Class, Culture and Alienation: A Study of Farmers and
            Farm Workers.* Lexington, Mass.: Lexington Books.
Rusk, Jerrold G.
1976   "Political Participation in America: A Review Essay."
            American Political Science Review. 70: 583-591.
Russett, Bruce M.
1964   "Inequality and Instability: The Relation of Land Tenure
            to Politics." *World Politics* 16: 442-454.
Russett, Bruce M., Hayward M. Alker, Jr., Karl W. Deutsch, and Harold
D. Lasswell
1964   *World Handbook of Political and Social Indicators.* New
            Haven: Yale University Press.
Rutherford, Brent M.
1966   "Psychopathology, Decision-Making and Political Involve-
            ment." *Journal of Conflict Resolution* 10: 387-407.
Saenger, Gerhart H.
1945   "Social Status and Political Behavior." *American Journal
            of Sociology* 51: 103-113. Also in Bobbs-Merrill Reprint
            Series No. 245.
Salamon, Lester M., and Stephen Van Evera
1973   "Fear, Apathy, and Discrimination: A Test of Three
            Explanations of Political Participation." *American Political
            Science Review* 67: 1288-1306.
Sallach, David L., Nicholas Babchuk, and Alan Booth
1972   "Social Involvement and Political Activity: Another View."
            Social Science Quarterly 52: 879-892.

Sanford, Fillmore H.
1950   *Authoritarianism and Leadership: A Study of the Follow-
            er's Orientation to Authority.* Philadelphia: Stephenson
            Brothers.

Sanford, Nevitt
1973   "Authoritarian Personality in Contemporary Perspective,"
            in Jeanne N. Knutson, ed., *Handbook of Political Psycho-
            logy.* San Francisco: Jossey-Bass. Pp. 139-170.

Sarlvik, Bo
1961a   "The Role of Party Identification in Voter's Perception
            of Political Issues," paper prepared for the Fifth World
            Congress of the International Political Science Association,
            Paris, September.

_____   "The Swedish General Election of 1960," UNESCO Semi-
1961b   nar, Bergen, Norway, June. (Mimeographed.)

Scheuch, Erwin K.
1961   "Leisure Patterns and Social Integration," paper prepared
            for UNESCO Seminar, Bergen, Norway, June. (Mimeo-
            graphed.)

Schlesinger, Joseph A.
1957   "Lawyers and American Politics: A Clarified View." *Mid-
            west Journal of Political Science* 1: 26-39.

Schwartz, David C.
1973   *Political Alienation and Political Behavior.* Chicago: Aldine.

Scott, William Abbott
1960   "International Ideology and Interpersonal Ideology."
            Public Opinion Quarterly 24: 419-435.

Searing, Donald D., and Joel J. Schwartz, and Alden E. Lind
1973   "The Structuring Principle: Political Socialization and
            Belief Systems." *American Political Science Review* 67:
            415-432.

Sears, David O., and John B. McConahay
1973   *The Politics of Violence: The New Urban Blacks and the
            Watts Riot.* Boston: Houghton Mifflin.

Seeman, Melvin
1959   "On the Meaning of Alienation." *American Sociological
            Review* 24: 783-791.

_____   "Alienation and Engagement," in Angus Campbell and
1972   Philip E. Converse, eds., *The Human Meaning of Social*

Change. New York: Russell Sage Foundation. Pp. 467-527.

Seligman, Lester George
1961 "Political Recruitment and Party Structure: A Case Study." *American Political Science Review* 55: 77-86.

Seligman, Lester George, Michael R. King, Chong Lim Kim, and Roland E. Smith
1974 *Patterns of Recruitment: A State Chooses Its Law Makers.* Chicago: Rand McNally.

Shanks, Merrill
1975 "Survey Based Political Indicators: The Case of Political Alienation," paper delivered at the American Political Science Association Annual Meeting, San Francisco.

Sheth, D. L., ed.
1975 *Citizens and Parties: Aspects of Competitive Politics in India.* New Delhi: Allied, Chs. 1 and 6.

Shils, Edward
1961 "Influence and Withdrawl: The Intellectuals in Indian Political Development," in Dwaine Marvick, ed., *Political Decision-Makers.* Glencoe, Ill.: The Free Press. Pp. 29-56.

Shinn, Allen M., Jr.
1971 "A Note on Voter Registration and Turnout in Texas, 1960-1970." *Journal of Politics* 33: 1120-1129.

Shively, W. Phillips
1972 "Party Identification, Party Choice and Voting Stability: The Weimar Case." *American Political Science Review* 66: 1203-1225.

Sigel, Roberta S.
1962 "Presidential Leadership Images, With Some Reflections on the Political Outlook of Negro Voters," paper prepared for the American Political Science Association Annual Meeting, Washington.

Silberman, Charles E.
1964 *Crisis in Black and White.* New York: Vintage.

Sindler, Allan P.
1955 "Bifactional Rivalry as an Alternative to Two-Party Competition in Louisiana." *American Political Science Review* 49: 641-662.

Smelser, Neil J.
1968   "Personality and the Explanation of Political Phenomena at the Social-System Level: A Methodological Statement." *Journal of Social Issues* 24: 111-126.

Smith, David Horton
1966   "A Psychological Model of Individual Participation in Formal Voluntary Organizations: Applications to Some Chilean Data." *American Journal of Sociology* 72: 249-266.

Smith, David Horton, and Richard D. Reddy
1972   "Contextual and Organizational Determinants of Individual Participation in Organized Voluntary Action," in David Horton Smith, Richard D. Reddy and Burt R. Baldwin, eds., *Voluntary Action Research 1972.* Lexington, Mass.: D. C. Heath. Pp. 299-319.

Smith, David Horton, Richard D. Reddy, and Burt R. Baldwin, eds.
1972   *Voluntary Action Research: 1972.* Lexington, Mass.: D. C. Heath.

Smith, Mortimer Brewster, Jerome S. Bruner, and Robert W. White
1956   *Opinions and Personality.* New York: Wiley.

Smith, Robert B.
1972   "Rebellion and Repression and the Vietnam War," in James F. Short, Jr., and Marvin E. Wolfgang, eds., *Collective Violence.* Chicago: Aldine-Atherton. Pp. 224-235.

Smith, T. E.
1960   *Elections in Developing Countries: A Study of Electoral Procedures Used in Tropical Africa, South-east Asia and the British Caribbean.* New York: St. Martin's Press.

Sniderman, Paul M.
1975   *Personality and Democratic Politics.* Berkeley: University of California Press.

Sniderman, Paul M., and Jack Citrin
1971   "Psychological Sources of Political Belief: Self-Esteem and Isolationist Attitudes." *American Political Science Review* 65: 401-417.

Spilerman, Seymour
1971   "The Causes of Racial Disturbances: Tests of an Explanation." *American Sociological Review* 36: 427-442.

Srole, Leo
1951   "Social Dysfunction, Personality and Social Distance Atti-

tudes," paper prepared for the American Sociological Society Annual Meeting, Chicago.

————. "Social Integration and Certain Corollaries: An Explora-
1956 tory Study." *American Sociological Review* 21: 709-716.

Standing, William H., and James A. Robinson
1958 "Inter-party Competition and Primary Contesting: The Case of Indiana." *American Political Science Review* 52: 1066-1077.

St. Angelo, Douglas, and James W. Dyson
1968 "Personality and Political Orientation." *Midwest Journal of Political Science* 12: 202-223.

Steiner, Kurt
1968 "Popular Political Participation and Political Development in Japan: The Rural Level," in Robert Edward Ward, ed., *Political Development in Modern Japan.* Princeton, N. J.: Princeton University Press. Pp. 213-247.

Stern, Larry N., and Monte Palmer
1971 "Political Socialization, Student Attitudes and Political Participation: A Sample of Columbian University Students." *Journal of Developing Areas* 6: 63-76.

Stiehm, J., and Ruth Scott
1974 "Female and Male: Voluntary and Chosen Participation: Sex, SES, and Participation," paper delivered at the American Political Science Association Meeting, Chicago.

Stokes, Donald
1962 "Popular Evaluations of Government: An Empirical Assessment," in Harlan Cleveland and Harold Lasswell, eds., *Ethics and Bigness.* New York: Harper.

Stokes, Donald E., Angus Campbell, and Warren E. Miller
1958 "Components of Electoral Decision." *American Political Science Review* 52: 367-387.

Strong, Donald S.
1948 "The Rise of Negro Voting in Texas." *American Political Science Review* 42: 510-522.

Struening, Elmer L., and Arthur H. Richardson
1965 "A Factor Analytic Exploration of the Alienation, Anomia and Authoritarianism Domain." *American Sociological Review* 30: 768-776.

Suchman, Edward A., and Herbert Menzel
1955 "The Interplay of Demographic and Psychological Vari-

ables in the Analysis of Voting Surveys," in Paul F. Lazarsfeld and Morris Rosenberg, eds., *The Language of Social Research.* Glencoe, Ill.: The Free Press. Pp. 148-155.

Sussman, Leila
1959 "Mass Political Letter Writing in America: The Growth of an Institution." *Public Opinion Quarterly* 23: 203-212.

Tanter, Raymond
1966 "Dimensions of Conflict Behavior Within and Between Nations, 1958-1960." *Journal of Conflict Resolution* 10: 41-64.

Tarrow, Sidney
1971 "The Urban-Rural Cleavage in Political Involvement: The Case of France." *American Political Science Review* 65: 341-357.

Templeton, Frederic
1966 "Alienation and Political Participation: Some Research Findings." *Public Opinion Quarterly* 30: 249-261.

Tessler, Mark A.
1972 "The Application of Western Theories and Measures of Political Participation to a Single-Party North African State." *Comparative Political Studies* 5: 175-191.

Thomas, L. Eugene
1970 "The I-E Scale, Ideological Bias and Political Participation." *Journal of Personality* 38: 273-286.

Thompson, Wayne E., and John E. Horton
1960 "Political Alienation as a Force in Political Action." *Social Forces* 38: 190-195.

Tilly, Charles
1969 "Collective Violence in European Perspective," in Hugh Davis Graham and Ted R. Gurr, eds., *Violence in America.* New York: Bantam Books. Pp. 4-42.

Tingsten, Herbert Lars Gustaf
1937 *Political Behavior: Studies in Election Statistics.* London: P. S. King.

———— "Stability and Vitality in Swedish Democracy." *Political*
1955 *Quarterly* 26: 140-151.

Tomlinson, T. M.
1970a "Ideological Foundations for Negro Action: A Compara-

tive Analysis of Militant and Non-Militant Views of the Los Angeles Riot." *Journal of Social Issues* 26: 93-119.

——. "Determinants of Black Politics: Riots and the Growth
1970b   of Militancy." *Psychiatry* 33: 247-264.

Townsend, James Roger
1967   *Political Participation in Communist China.* Berkeley: University of California Press.

Turner, Ralph H.
1969   "The Public Perception of Protest." *American Sociological Review* 34: 815-831.

Uchida, Mitsuru
1972   "The Present Condition and Problems of Voting Behavior in Japan." *Waseda Political Studies* (Tokyo), 35-48.

U. S. Bureau of the Census
1975   *Current Population Reports.* Series P-20. Population Characteristics. Washington, D. C.: Government Printing Office.

U. S. Commission on Civil Rights
1968   *Political Participation; A Study of the Participation by Negroes in the Electoral and Political Processes in 10 Southern States Since the Passage of the Voting Rights Act of 1965.* Washington, D. C.: Government Printing Office.

Valen, Henry
1961   "The Motivation and Recruitment of Political Personnel," paper prepared for UNESCO Seminar, Bergen, Norway, June. (Mimeographed.)

Valen, Henry, and Daniel Katz
1964   *Political Parties in Norway.* Oslo: Universitetsforlaget.

Verba, Sidney, Bashir Ahmed, and Anil Bhatt
1971   *Caste, Race and Politics: A Comparative Study of India and the United States.* Beverly Hills, Calif.: Sage Publications.

Verba, Sidney, and Gabriel A. Almond
1964   "National Revolutions and Political Commitment," in Harry Eckstein, ed., *Internal War.* New York: The Free Press of Glencoe. Pp. 205-232.

Verba, Sidney, and Norman H. Nie
1972   *Participation in America: Political Democracy and Social Equality.* New York: Harper & Row.

Verba, Sidney, Norman Nie, Ana Barbic, Galen Irwin, Henk Molleman, and Goldie Shabad
1973   "The Modes of Participation: Continuities in Research." *Comparative Political Studies* 6: 235-250.

Verba, Sidney, Norman Nie, and Jae-on Kim
1971   *Modes of Democratic Participation: A Cross-National Comparison.* Beverly Hills, Calif.: Sage Publications.

_____.   Social Stratification and Political Stratification: A Seven
1975   Nation Comparison. (Manuscript.)

Von der Mehden, Fred R.
1973   *Comparative Political Violence.* Englewood Cliffs, N. J.: Prentice-Hall.

Wahlke, John C., Heinz Eulau, William Buchanan, and LeRoy C. Ferguson
1962   *The Legislative System: Explorations in Legislative Behavior.* New York: Wiley.

Walker, Jack
1966   "A Critique of the Elitist Theory of Democracy." *American Political Science Review* 60: 285-295.

Walton, Hanes
1972   *Black Politics: A Theoretical and Structural Analysis.* Philadelphia: Lippincott.

Warner, William Lloyd, Paul P. Van Riper, Norman H. Martin, and Orvic F. Collins
1963   *The American Federal Executive: A Study of the Social and Personal Characteristics of the Civilian and Military Leaders of the United States Federal Government.* New Haven: Yale University Press.

Watanuki, Joji
1972   "Social Structure and Political Participation in Japan." Tokyo: Sophia University, Institute of International Relations. (Mimeographed.)

Weiner, Myron
1971   "Political Participation: Crisis of the Political Process," in Leonard Binder, et al., *Crisis and Sequences in Political Development.* Princeton, N. J.: Princeton University Press. Pp. 159-204.

Weiner, Myron, ed.
1966   *Modernization: The Dynamics of Growth.* New York: Basic Books.

Weiner, Myron, and John Osgood Field

1976   "India's Urban Constituencies." *Comparative Politics* 8: 183-222.

Welch, Susan, and Alan Booth

1975   "Crowding and Civil Disorder: An Examination of Comparative National and City Data." *Comparative Political Studies* 8: 58-74.

Welch, Susan, John Comer, and Michael Steinman

1973   "Political Participation Among Mexican Americans: An Exploratory Examination." *Social Science Quarterly* 53: 799-813.

Westby, David L., and Richard G. Braungart

1966   "Class and Politics in the Family Backgrounds of Student Political Activists." *American Sociological Review* 31: 690-692.

_____   "The Alienation of Generations and Status Politics: Al-

1970   ternative Explanations of Student Political Activism," in Roberta S. Sigel, ed., *Learning about Politics*. New York: Random House. Pp. 476-489.

Williams, Oliver Perry, and Charles R. Adrian

1959   "The Insulation of Local Politics under the Non-Partisan Ballot." *American Political Science Review* 53: 1052-1063.

Wilson, James Q.

1961   "The Strategy of Protest: Problems of Negro Civic Action." *Journal of Conflict Resolution* 5: 291-303.

Wolfenstein, E. Victor

1967   *The Revolutionary Personality: Lenin, Trotsky, Gandhi*. Princeton, N. J.: Princeton University Press.

Wolfinger, Raymond E.

1963   "The Influence of Precinct Work on Voting Behavior." *Public Opinion Quarterly* 27: 387-398.

Wood, James L.

1974   *The Sources of American Student Activism*. Lexington, Mass.: Lexington Books.

Woodward, Julian L., and Elmo Roper

1950   "Research on Political Parties and Leadership." *American Political Science Review* 44: 872-885.

1956   Reprinted under the title "Political Activity of American Citizens" in Eulau, et al., eds., *Political Behavior: A Reader*

in Theory and Research. New York: The Free Press Pp. 133-137.

Wright, Charles R., and Herbert H. Hyman
1958   "Voluntary Association Memberships of American Adults: Evidence from National Sample Surveys." *American Sociological Review* 22: 284-294.

Yates, Willard Ross
1962a   "The Functions of Residence Requirements for Voting." *Western Political Quarterly* 15: 469-488.

————.   "Residence Requirements for Voting: Ten Years of
1962b   Change." paper presented at the American Political Science Association Annual Meeting, Washington.

Yinger, J. Milton
1973   "Anomie, Alienation and Political Behavior," in Jeanne N. Knutson, ed., *Handbook of Political Psychology*. San Francisco: Jossey-Bass. Pp. 171-202.

Zeller, Belle, and Hugh A. Bone
1948   "The Repeal of P. R. in New York City—Ten Years in Retrospect." *American Political Science Review* 42: 1127-1148.

Zikmund, Joseph
1967   "A Comparison of Political Attitudes and Activity Patterns in Central Cities and Suburbs." *Public Opinion Quarterly* 31: 69-75.

Ziller, Robert Charles, J. Cunningham, L. H. Golding, and M. King
1969   *The Political Personality*. University of Oregon. Unpublished Manuscript.

Index